Accession no.
01047468

KT-509-727

Teaching Popular Culture

Teaching Popular Culture:
Beyond Radical Pedagogy

edited by

David Buckingham

LIBRARY
ACC. NO.
01047468
CLASS NO.
375.30223 BUC
UNIVERSITY
COLLEGE CHESTER
WITHDRAWN

UCL
PRESS

Selection and editorial material © David Buckingham 1998

This book is copyright under the Berne Convention.
No reproduction without permission.
All rights reserved.

First published in 1998 by UCL Press

UCL Press Limited
1 Gunpowder Square
London EC4A 3DE
UK

and

1900 Frost Road, Suite 101
Bristol
Pennsylvania 19007-1598
USA

The name of University College London (UCL) is a registered
trade mark used by UCL Press with the consent of the owner.

British Library Cataloguing-in-Publication Data
A Catalogue Record for this book is available from the British Library.

Library of Congress Cataloging-in-Publication Data are available

ISBNs: 1-85728-792-4 HB
         1-85728-793-2 PB

Typeset in 10/12pt Times by Best-set Typesetter Ltd, Hong Kong
Printed by Arrowhead Books, Reading, UK

Contents

List of Illustrations

Chapter 1

Introduction: Fantasies of Empowerment?
Radical Pedagogy and Popular Culture

David Buckingham

What does it mean to talk about radical pedagogy today? Twenty-five years ago, in the wake of 1968, it all seemed crystal clear. Armed with their copies of *Teaching as a Subversive Activity*, *Deschooling Society* and *The Pedagogy of the Oppressed*, a whole generation of young teachers went out into the blackboard jungle, determined to 'conscientize' their students, to arm them with the skills of 'crap detecting' and to liberate them from the shackles of ideology. Now, amid the enormous social upheavals which have characterized the closing years of the century, everything seems much more confused and contradictory. While there are some for whom the libertarian rhetoric of the 1960s and 1970s still has a place, the mission of radical pedagogy now seems much harder to sustain.

Of course, this may be partly a matter of exhaustion in the face of some concerted opposition. In many of the countries from which the contributors to this book are drawn, the dramatic rightward drift of educational policy over the past 10 years has created a striking contrast with the expansiveness of earlier decades. In the UK, for example, the public debate about education has been dominated by the shrill caricature of Margaret Thatcher's attacks on 'anti-racist mathematics' and the prehistoric bluster of John Patten's condemnation of 'the radical whores of sociology'. Meanwhile, on US college campuses, multiculturalism, feminism and other radical innovations have been attacked and ridiculed as mere 'political correctness'. Even in more hospitable regimes, radical educational initiatives have been compromised by the growth of instrumentalism and 'free market' models, and by the attempt to reduce teaching to a matter of 'curriculum delivery'.

The target of much of this invective has been the fashionable but misguided teaching methods which are seen to emanate from the liberal educational establishment, and from the privileged echelons of higher education. In the UK, this has led to the government's attempt to sever the connection between higher education and schools, and to replace teacher education with a form of instrumental on the job training; to the penalizing (and in the case of London, the abolition) of those local authorities which were most assiduous in promoting educational innovation; and to the implementation of a traditional, subject-centred curriculum, backed up by a centralized and highly reductive form of testing. These are policies which have been steadily resisted by the teaching profession, yet they have gained widespread popular support; and many of them have since been adopted wholesale by the Labour left (see CCCS Education Group II, 1991; Chitty, 1992; Jones, 1989, 1994).

This backlash against educational innovation can be interpreted in several ways. On the one hand, it clearly attests to the continuing ability of the political Right to mobilize deep-seated anxieties about social change – an ability which has been amply demonstrated in many other areas of social policy. In this respect, it could be understood as a form of 'authoritarian populism', to use Stuart Hall's (1983) characterization of Thatcherism. It mobilizes a popular resentment against experts, intellectuals and middle-class do-gooders – a resentment which is clearly fuelled by the continuing authoritarianism of many on the Left. Yet it may also speak to a sense of disappointment at the failure of the great educational experiments of the post-war period to live up to the claims that were made on their behalf. For the promise that progressive education would bring about social equality – let alone that it would bring about a form of liberation – has proven transparently false.

Of course, the reasons for that resentment and sense of disappointment cannot be explained simply in terms of the failures of the progressive project; indeed, in some respects it is fair to say that progressive education has never been fully implemented. Equality of access and opportunity in education has remained largely a matter of official rhetoric: the accidents of birth – and particularly of social class – still overwhelmingly determine the outcomes of schooling. And, as the contributors to this book make clear, the notion of the teacher as liberator and the classroom as an egalitarian community are still (perhaps unavoidably) a long way from realization.

On the other hand, however, this backlash against educational innovation could also be seen to reflect the power and influence of a certain (albeit institutionalized) form of radicalism. For some, the virulence of recent attacks on 'political correctness' and on progressive teaching methods has been inter-preted as an indication of the *success* of such initiatives, and the continuing threat they pose to those who would wish to return to more traditional meth-ods. Such attacks are, it is argued, merely the responses of those whose old-fashioned, elitist values and ideals are passing away before their eyes. And, so it is said, we must be doing something right if these people are trying to stop us. While the backlash may have forced us onto the defensive, it may also have induced a paradoxical sense of self-righteousness and even a degree of complacency.

Part of the intention of this book is to question who 'we' might be, and to challenge the notion that we have necessarily got it right. In doing so, it will be necessary to disrupt some of the stories 'we' tell ourselves; to question some of the certainties of radical pedagogy, and to acknowledge some of its limitations and failures; but also, crucially, to point *beyond* them. While none of the contributors here would support the arguments of the political Right, and while our own perspectives are (we hope productively) diverse, we share an acknowledgement of the considerable contradictions and tensions which characterize so much radical educational practice. Yet our concern here is not only to identify or explore these; it is also, however tentatively, to suggest some practical and theoretical ways of moving *beyond* the dilemmas they appear to pose.

What is This Thing Called Pedagogy?

As David Lusted (1986) once remarked, the word *pedagogy* is an ugly term, and one which is rarely used by teachers. It derives from an academic discourse about education which is largely sustained within the walls of elite universities and in the pages of obscure scholarly journals. To discuss pedagogy is to focus on the theories of teaching and learning which inform classroom practice – and, more specifically, on the *social relationships* between teachers and students to which they give rise. Yet it is often, unfortunately, to do so at a distance from the difficulties and contradictions of that practice itself. The notion of pedagogy is, in this respect, always an abstraction.

Needless to say perhaps, there is no such thing as a single 'radical pedagogy'. Indeed, the alert reader will already have noticed a tendency in this introduction to slide between terms like 'radical' and 'progressive', and to resort to related terms such as 'innovative' and 'left-wing', as though these were somehow synonymous. Some brief discussion of these terms is necessary here, if only in order to indicate some of the confusions that surround them.

Popular debates about pedagogy are often conducted in terms of a stand-off between 'progressive' and 'traditional' perspectives. Thus, in one corner, we have progressive pedagogy – the 'child-centred' approach, based on notions of 'readiness' and 'discovery learning'; while in the other, we have traditional pedagogy – based on the 'rote learning' of a given body of skills and information. This opposition is one that is routinely defined and reinforced through a process of mutual caricature, from which academics and teachers themselves have been far from immune. Thus, the progressive approach is condemned for its liberal sloppiness, its lazy celebration of children's experience, and ultimately for its rejection of *teaching*. Meanwhile, the traditional approach is depicted as a form of educational terrorism, in which children are drilled and intimidated into acquiring arbitrary, disembodied fragments of information. If progressive pedagogy is accused of abandoning the authority of the teacher, traditional pedagogy is accused of abusing it. If traditional pedagogy is condemned for ignoring children's own perspectives, progressive pedagogy is condemned for simply celebrating them. And so the debate goes on.

The problems here are not simply to do with the degree of polarization between these positions, or with the insistence on either/or choices. I would argue that these rhetorical constructions of 'progressive' and 'traditional' pedagogy – whether positive or negative – are in fact a very inadequate representation of the nature of classroom practice. Of course, this is not to suggest that such characterizations are simply false; on the contrary, they are extremely influential, not least in terms of how teachers themselves account for what they do. Nevertheless, it is very doubtful whether 'progressive' or 'traditional' pedagogy actually *exist* in the terms in which they are typically described. There are numerous empirical studies which suggest that the realities of both approaches are much more contradictory and much less uniform than the debate itself might lead one to suppose (see, for example, Edwards and Mercer, 1987; Galton, Simon and Croll, 1980; Sharp and Green, 1975; Willis, 1977). It is not simply that, in practice, teachers will consciously combine a variety of approaches – or that their attempts to meet the needs of their students will actively require them to do this. It is also that neither position would seem to offer a theory that helps us to understand the ways in which students *learn* – and indeed, the ways in which teachers might enable this to happen.

Despite the rhetoric which often characterizes these debates, it is also important to emphasize that 'progressive' pedagogy cannot necessarily be aligned with socialist politics. There are certainly those who have argued that the child-centred classroom represents a working model of democracy in action – a kind of prefiguring of the egalitarian socialist society. Yet the history of the implementation of this approach has been a complex one, in which the ideals of its pioneers have been steadily compromised and incorporated into an official version. Indeed, there are those on the Left who have argued that progressivism is little more than a disciplinary strategy which has been designed to ensure the more effective surveillance of working-class children (Walkerdine, 1984) – although, as Brehony (1992) points out, this does not quite explain why it seems to have attracted so much hostility from the political Right.

Nevertheless, it is possible to identify variants of both positions on the Left. Thus, one can point to a radical version of traditional pedagogy, which has remained highly influential. From this perspective, the teacher's task is essentially to transmit a body of 'radical information' and analytical techniques which will alert the students to the operations of the 'dominant ideology'. Such an approach is neatly summed up in Entwistle's (1979) phrase 'conservative schooling for radical politics'. On the other hand, there is a form of progressivism – albeit one which is often more a matter of rhetoric than reality. This approach stresses the validity and authenticity of students' out-of-school cultures and experiences, and prioritizes creativity and self-expression. The teacher here becomes little more than a 'senior colleague' who engages students in an 'equal dialogue', rather than an authority whose perspective is necessarily privileged (Masterman, 1980). Despite their differences, however, advocates of both positions seem to share a faith in the ease with which teachers can politicize their students – whether this is seen as a matter of rigorous training in the skills of objective analysis, or of enabling students to 'find a voice' in which they can express themselves in truly authentic ways.

In practice, however, these perspectives are often combined in ways which give rise to some significant confusions and contradictions – and in this respect, the boundary between 'progressive' and 'radical' approaches is often far from clear. Perhaps the central anxiety here is that which surrounds the exercise of authority in the classroom. For radicals and progressives alike, the central aim of education is one of emancipation; pedagogy is seen as the means whereby oppression, injustice and inequality will be overcome. Yet if the logic of this position is carried through, one might expect that the classroom itself should be structured in an egalitarian way. If teachers are seeking to 'empower' their students, surely they must do so without at the same time imposing their authority or oppressing them? As Simons (1994) indicates, there is a fundamental ideological dilemma here. On the one hand, we want our teaching to serve left-oriented liberatory goals; yet on the other, it would seem to be a betrayal of these goals to exercise power in the classroom.

The crucial problem, of course, is what happens when students resist or reject the 'emancipation' that is provided. What if they do not want to be 'liberated' or 'empowered' in the way that the teacher has envisaged for them? One familiar way of resolving this dilemma is through recourse to a notion of false consciousness; because they are seen to be mystified or deluded in some way, the students are unable to realize their own true interests, and the teacher must therefore act on their behalf. This approach has the advantage of being a self-confirming argument: the more students resist, the more they are seen to be in need of ideological remediation, and the more the teacher's intervention and authority are justified. Yet this approach can also be seen to lead to a form of educational vanguardism, in which the teacher (like the Party) is uniquely able to define the true path to liberation.

As I shall indicate below, this radical approach has held a particular attraction for media educators, where it has been strongly supported by arguments about the ideological power of the media. And while its contradictions are clearly apparent in the university seminar rooms described by Simons (1994), they are bound to be much more apparent in situations where there is a vast social gulf between teacher and student, as in the inner-city classrooms where I have taught. There are clearly problems in store for middle-class teachers who attempt to 'empower' working-class students through class analysis, for male teachers who seek to enlighten female students about sexism, or for white teachers who set out to inform their black students about the evils of racism.

On the other hand, such problems cannot easily be resolved by the 'progressive' strategy of 'giving students a voice'. For what happens if students use the voice they have been offered to say things which directly sustain oppression and inequality – which are, for example, racist or sexist? Clearly, there can be no guarantee that students will use their many voices to say things which the radical teacher will support, or even permit within the classroom. One option, of course, is to set constraints to the kind of language that can be employed; yet this is simply domination at another remove. Ultimately, as Orner (1992) suggests, the notion that students can be 'given' a voice by the teacher and that they will then use this to express some kind of authentic self is an illusion. Indeed, she argues that the pedagogy of voice can represent another form of paternalism, in which the teacher functions as a kind of father confessor. Despite the appearance of open dialogue, the voice – and hence the authority – of the teacher is rarely challenged or questioned.

Whichever strategy is favoured here, the position of the radical teacher is unlikely to be a comfortable one. On the one hand, there is a substantial risk of contradiction between the preaching and the practice – a kind of 'do what I say, not what I do' position. On the other, there is the danger of abdicating power, and hence any responsibility for what others (students within the class) may do when they attempt to assume it. Yet the authority of the teacher is not simply a personal quality, which can be assumed or dropped at will within the confines of a single classroom. On the contrary, it is institutionally sanctioned and defined, and it is sustained through apparatuses of management, assessment and discipline, over which individual teachers and students generally have little control. For the self-professed radical teacher, these are dilemmas which are incapable of easy resolutions.

The Limits of Critical Pedagogy

At least in the UK, these debates about radical pedagogy have largely been conducted in the context of local struggles, for example, over particular curriculum subjects (notably English), over issues such as modes of assessment or mixed ability teaching, and in the context of other battles such as the resistance to national testing. While there have certainly been moments of grand theory – most obviously in the wake of the new sociology of education in the 1970s – discussions of pedagogy have generally been grounded in concrete analyses of classroom practice.

Internationally, however, the most dominant radical voice in such debates has been the highly theoretical perspective of the 'critical pedagogy' movement. While there are different variants of this approach (see Gore, 1993), the work of Henry Giroux, Peter McLaren and their associates in the US has been the most widely quoted (for recent instances, see Giroux, 1992, 1994; McLaren, 1995; McLaren *et al.*, 1995). Originating in a neo-marxist analysis, this work has increasingly taken on the identity politics of gender and ethnicity, and has sought to incorporate the insights of a wide range of new theoretical perspectives, including postmodernism, poststructuralism and postcolonial theory. At the same time, the work of the critical pedagogues has increasingly been challenged, not so much by the conservative Right as by feminists and others on the Left who might be expected to share its broad political aims (see Anyon, 1994; Ellsworth, 1989; Gore, 1993; Luke and Gore, 1992). It is here that many of the fundamental contradictions of radical pedagogy – and indeed the limitations of academic debates in the field – have been writ large.[1]

Thus, many critics have challenged the way in which 'critical pedagogy' seeks to incorporate quite distinct political and theoretical projects into a single overarching synthesis – or what feminists have termed its 'master discourse' (Luke, 1992). The potential contradictions between political movements – for example, between feminism, class politics and anti-racist struggles – are simply effaced in the grand narrative of liberation. Likewise, the texts of the critical pedagogues typically merge such diverse perspectives as neo-marxism, poststructuralism, postmodernism, feminism and postcolonial theory into one apparently seamless collage, in which repeated permutations of the same theoretical terms seem to serve as a form of self-validation. In addition to their own distinctive jargon, the critical pedagogues tend to appropriate 'establishment' terms such as *citizenship*, *democracy* and *literacy*; yet these terms are constantly recycled and combined without ever suffering the indignity of definition or concrete exemplification. In this respect, critical pedagogy seems to represent a curiously academic account of political action, in which heterogeneous struggles can be lined up against the oppressors, and united by means of a language which remains at the disposal of the leaders.

Ultimately, the central problem with critical pedagogy lies in its attempt to resolve complex pedagogical problems purely by means of theoretical rhetoric. Despite their apparent address to teachers, the critical pedagogues have consistently refused to consider the ways in which their theoretical perspectives might be implemented, or to clarify their notoriously opaque style of writing: such criticisms have been aggressively dismissed as mere anti-intellectualism – or indeed as an insult to the oppressed groups on whose behalf the discourse claims to speak. As Sue Turnbull points out in her contribution here, much of what motivates the feminist critique of critical pedagogy is a familiar resentment at encountering a situation in which men theorize, while women act – and in the process, have to deal with the contradictions and limitations of the theory. Indeed, it could be argued that the critical pedagogues simply reproduce a familiar division of power and labour between academics and teachers, which is not a million miles from the instrumentalism of conservative educational policy. Their texts are replete with injunctions about what teachers should do, but entirely devoid of suggestions about *how* they should do it. As Gore (1993) remarks, this approach places the burden for change on teachers, while simultaneously refusing to suggest the means by which it might be brought about.

The question of who is being 'empowered' by this discourse, and with what consequences, is certainly relevant here. Ultimately, as Hunter (1994) suggests, the display of abstract critical virtuosity that characterizes the critical pedagogy movement may represent little more than a claim to a prestigious social persona, rather than a universally rational reflection on the political situation. Educational critics, he suggests, would be better advised to concentrate on the contingent realities and technologies of schooling rather than pursuing illusory theoretical principles. To neglect such issues in favour of a hypothetical embrace of 'alternative democratic communities' (Giroux, 1994) might conceivably be construed as a form of morale-boosting, at least in the short term. Yet in the long term it could well prove actively *dis*empowering for teachers, by merely confirming the disparity between the 'grand mission' of education and the real constraints of their work.

Teaching Popular Culture

The media and popular culture have often had a particular significance for radical educators – and indeed, they would appear to have become a growing preoccupation for the critical pedagogy movement also (see Buckingham, 1996a). Of course, it would be false to pretend that media education (or *media literacy* as it is often termed in North America) is inevitably or necessarily a 'radical' intervention; teaching about rap music or soap operas, for example, does not in itself prescribe a particular set of classroom strategies or a particular set of relationships between teachers and students. Nevertheless, the reasons for this emphasis on popular culture, and hence the rationales for pedagogy in this field, do reflect many of the tensions and contradictions I have been discussing.

Thus, on the one hand, there is a familiar critical view of the media, which emphasizes their role in sustaining relations of oppression and domination. The media are seen here as purveyors of the 'dominant ideology', while children in particular are regarded as passive victims of their influence. From this perspective, teaching about the media is seen as a means of arming students against the false values they are seen to contain; and the central strategy here is that of critical analysis. Masterman (1980), for example, proposes that students and teachers should put their 'personal feelings and tastes' to one side. Rather than seeking to arrive at value judgments, they should analyse the media systematically and objectively, using broadly semiotic methods; only in this way will it be possible to identify how media texts are constructed and selected, and hence to reveal their 'suppressed ideological function'. Teaching about the media thus becomes a process of 'demystification', of revealing underlying truths which are normally hidden from view.

On the other hand, it is possible to regard teaching about popular culture as an extension of progressivism. From this perspective, popular culture is seen as an authentic part of students' experience, and hence as something which teachers should seek to validate and even to celebrate. This must, it is argued, necessarily entail a change in the dominant power relations of the classroom; the students are now the 'experts', and the teacher's knowledge is no longer privileged. This perspective finds some support in the recent tendency towards populism within academic Media and Cultural Studies: far from viewing the media as agents of the dominant ideology, advocates of this approach regard them as means of 'resistance' and potentially of 'liberation'. In terms of classroom strategies, this approach would place a much more central emphasis on students' explorations of their own cultural investments and concerns, not least through creative media production.

Historically, the evolution of media education in the UK could be seen as a process of negotiation between these two impulses.[2] On the one hand, there is the attempt to *defend* young people against what is seen as the harmful influence of the media – and in this respect, the political defensiveness I have identified has a great deal in common with the forms of cultural defensiveness which motivated earlier initiatives in this field (see Leavis and Thompson, 1933). On the other hand, there is the drive to *democratize* the curriculum, by making it responsive and relevant to students' out-of-school experiences – an approach which arose partly in response to the (limited) demise of selective schooling in the post-war period. Yet while media educators in the UK and elsewhere have gradually moved away from the defensive approach, it is fair to say that this motivation remains a prominent one. Particularly for those who are new to the field, the primary aim of media education is not to validate students' cultures – whatever that might ultimately mean – but on the contrary to rescue them from the negative influences of the media.

Here again, these two versions of media education are ideal types, which do not straightforwardly correspond to the realities of classroom practice. Indeed, advocates of media education often appear to combine these two perspectives in highly contradictory ways (see Buckingham, 1986). The emphasis on 'objective' analysis often sits uneasily alongside arguments for 'equal dialogue' between teacher and student, and for a process of open investigation. In practice, this often results in considerable tension, and even a degree of hypocrisy: much of what students are expected to 'discover' in such teaching is pre-determined, and much of what passes for 'analysis' is simply a sophisticated exercise in guessing what's in the teacher's mind (Buckingham, Fraser and Mayman, 1990). Likewise, the genuine opportunities for exploration which are provided by practical media production are frequently foreclosed by an insistence on written self-evaluation, in which the students are required to display evidence of their mastery of the teacher's academic discourse (Buckingham, Grahame and Sefton-Green, 1995).

These contradictions reflect a series of complex questions which have begun to be addressed by media educators in recent years, and which are pursued further in this collection. These are partly to do with students' existing relationships with popular culture. To what extent can popular culture adequately be seen as 'belonging' to the students, or as an 'authentic' expression of their own investments and identities? To what extent can young people be seen as 'active' or 'passive' in their relationships with the media – and indeed, what might these terms actually mean? To what extent are they able to reflect upon those relationships, and in what ways does that ability develop with age? How are different social groups positioned here, in terms of gender, ethnicity and social class? This leads on to further questions about *pedagogy* – that is, about the nature of teaching and learning about popular culture. What is the relationship between what teachers know about popular culture and what students know? Are these the same kinds of knowledge, and how might connections be made between them? What is the relationship between students' subjective investments and pleasures and the academic discourses and procedures of critical analysis? Again, how are different social groups positioned in these relationships? Finally, in both cases, there are significant questions about *methodology*. How can we know what students know? How can we identify what they have learnt? And how can we be sure that we have made a difference?

The attempt to address these questions has involved a range of different forms of investigation. First, media educators have begun to pay much closer attention to what students already know about the media – an issue which was largely neglected by earlier approaches. In line with recent developments in audience research, the view of children as passive victims of media effects has steadily been challenged and surpassed. Within some areas of psychology and social psychology, and particularly within Cultural Studies, researchers have begun to develop a much more complex view of the ways in which children make judgments about the media, and how they use the media to form their own personal and social identities (e.g. Buckingham, 1993a, 1993b; Hodge and Tripp, 1986; Willis, 1990). Broadly speaking, what has emerged here is a view that children are a much more sophisticated and critical audience than they are conventionally assumed to be – not least by many media educators themselves.

This is not, of course, to say that the media have *no* 'effects' on children, or that there are not areas which they need to know more about. There are bound to be gaps in children's knowledge – although those gaps may not necessarily be where they are often assumed to be. Likewise, children's knowledge of the media obviously develops as they grow older; and this clearly depends on the critical perspectives that are available to them, both within and beyond the media. It is not ultimately very profitable to reduce such questions about the power of the media – and the power of audiences – to an either/or debate. Nevertheless, this emphasis on the complexity and diversity of audiences has significant implications for media educators: it means that we need to begin by paying close attention to what children already know – rather than assuming that they know nothing, or that what they know is somehow invalid or 'ideological'.

Second, there has been a thorough discussion about the nature of teaching and learning in media education, much of which has developed from classroom-based research conducted by teachers themselves (see Alvarado and Boyd-Barrett, 1992; Buckingham, 1990; Buckingham, Grahame and Sefton-Green, 1995; Buckingham and Sefton-Green, 1994; Dewdney and Lister, 1988). As such research has shown, one of the central problems with 'demystification' is what it assumes about teachers and students: just as students are assumed to be 'mystified', so the teacher is assumed to possess the key to liberation. The teacher reveals the truth and the students, once they witness it, automatically give their assent. There is a kind of political evange-

lism here; and while this may occasionally explain some of the learning experiences students have, it remains a drastic oversimplification of the complex
and messy realities of classroom practice. Especially when it comes to the
areas with which media education is so centrally concerned – with what students see as their own culture and their own pleasures – they may well be
inclined to resist or reject what teachers tell them. This is particularly true if
such teaching is perceived to be grounded on ignorance about popular culture,
or if the study of the media is being used as a covert means of gaining students'
assent to positions that are seen to be 'politically correct'.

Questions of cultural identity and cultural difference are obviously central to this approach; yet both in media education and in anti-racist and anti-
sexist teaching, experience has shown that rationalistic forms of analysis are
a very limited means of 'changing students' consciousness', and that they
often prove counter-productive (see Cohen, 1988; Moss, 1989; Rattansi, 1992;
Williamson, 1981/2). While it may be comparatively easy to police the ways in
which students talk or behave, to make them conform in a superficial way to
particular forms of language or behaviour, it has proven much harder to make
long-term changes in the way they think, or in their identities. Such research
has provided a salutary – and somewhat chastening – challenge to the fantasies
of 'empowerment' and 'liberation' which still appear to infuse the discourse of
radical pedagogy.

Finally, while all of this work has been theoretically informed – primarily
by perspectives from Cultural Studies, feminism and poststructuralism – new
theoretical developments also pose important challenges for teachers. Carmen
Luke's chapter here offers a concise overview of these developments, which
are taken up in different ways in the more concrete studies which follow. Much
of the theoretical work discussed in Chapter 2 has yet to reach teachers in
schools, although in our view it has a great deal to offer to the analysis – and
indeed to the rethinking – of pedagogic processes. Yet the spirit of this collection – unlike that of a great deal of work on critical pedagogy – is one in
which theory is held to account against the evidence of practice. Rather than
regarding academic theory as a repository of truth, our commitment here is to
praxis – in other words, to a dialectical relationship between theory and
practice. Indeed, we would argue that any meaningful pedagogic theory has to
be able to take account of the experience of classroom practice; and that
practice is a site on which new theoretical insights and challenges can be
generated.

An Outline of the Contributions

The aim of this book, therefore, is to move *beyond* the limitations of the
somewhat abstract debates which have hitherto characterized discussions of
radical pedagogy. All the contributions here are based in a critique of previous
approaches, but they are also grounded in empirical analyses of practice, and

they seek to offer constructive alternatives (however tentative) to the radical orthodoxy. At the same time, the book does not intend to prescribe a singular version of what might lie beyond. The contributors draw on a range of theoretical approaches, including poststructuralism, postmodernism, neo-Vygotskyan theory, Cultural Studies, anti-racism, and feminisms. The collection is international in scope, with contributions from Australia, Canada, the UK and the USA, and covers educational sectors from primary schools right through to higher education – each of which clearly offers different constraints and possibilities. By bringing such diverse studies together, it seeks to generate a more rigorous debate about the future of radical educational practice across a broad range of constituencies and institutional contexts.

In Chapter 2, Carmen Luke provides an overview of the range of contemporary social theories which have been employed by radical educators in this field. She offers succinct outlines of the contributions of various forms of feminism, Cultural Studies, poststructuralism and postmodernism, illustrating their potential for pedagogical practice. While her principal focus is on higher education, many of the strategies she discusses can also be applied to the work of students in schools. Significantly, in the light of the overall aims of the book, Luke then moves on to question and challenge some of the implications of these approaches, building on recent feminist debates about pedagogy. She draws attention to the limitations of 'good girl feminism', and the dangers of feminist teachers simply falling back into a nurturing role. Finally, Luke questions the notion of the feminist classroom as a non-hierarchical space, arguing that pedagogical authority is both unavoidable and politically necessary.

Compared with the pedagogic security apparently offered by critical analysis, students' media production work has often been seen to have potentially dangerous ideological consequences. In Chapter 3, Donna Grace and Joseph Tobin explore some of these issues through their analysis of a video production curriculum developed in an ethnically diverse Honolulu primary school. Their account focuses particularly on the tensions that arose as the researchers, teachers and students negotiated the contents of the videos – and particularly the more 'subversive' elements such as 'butt jokes', parodies of teachers and representations of violence. Using Bakhtin's concepts of the carnivalesque and the dialogic and Barthes' writings on *plaisir* and *jouissance*, the chapter argues that video production in schools opens up an ambiguous space, a terrain where the authoritative discourse of teachers meets the potentially transgressive discourse of children's popular culture.

These issues are developed further in Chapter 4, where I offer a critique of previous debates about the relationships between theory and practice in media teaching, and discuss some of the ways in which teachers have attempted to resolve them. The chapter then moves on to consider two case studies drawn from research into media education in London secondary schools, focusing particularly on the role of imitation and parody in students' production work. Through an analysis of the generic form of students' work (a situation comedy and a women's magazine), and of the social relationships that surrounded its production, it identifies the fundamental ambivalence and evasion that often characterizes such work, and its ambiguous political consequences. While emphasizing the importance of critical reflection, this chapter questions the insistence on producing rationalistic, 'politically correct' discourse as a means of effecting change in students' political consciousness.

In 1981, Judith Williamson first asked the question, 'How does Girl Number Twenty understand ideology?' Confronted by a mixed class, she found the boys all too eager to condemn the girls' tastes in popular culture, and the girls unwilling to participate in classroom debate about texts supposedly addressed to them. This impasse led her to an understanding that teaching about the media must begin, not with abstract theories, but with the personal engagement of the students, and that this entails a risk for all. In Chapter 5, Sue Turnbull revisits Williamson's insights from a contemporary Australian perspective, in order to consider the risks involved for a group of 16-year-old girls from diverse ethnic backgrounds in revealing their media practices. She points to the contradictions which are entailed by the forms of 'empowerment' which are often offered to students, and to the need for an approach which acknowledges the aesthetic dimensions and the personal investments which characterize students' uses of popular culture.

In Chapter 6, Robert Morgan offers a broad-ranging account drawing on his research into media literacy teaching in Canada. He begins by focusing on the problems which arise as a result of the placement of media courses within the subject of English, both in terms of the expectations of students and in terms of the status of the subject. The account then moves on to consider the motivations of media teachers, which Morgan argues still rely on a view of students as helplessly manipulated by the media, and hence appear to adopt a defensive or protectionist stance. In emphasizing the limitations of these perspectives, he argues for an approach which goes beyond ideological critique and the literary fixation on texts. Drawing on the work of Bakhtin, and on recent studies of the ethnography of media consumption, he argues for an approach which connects educational practice with the everyday routines of media use and which extends beyond the confines of the classroom.

This latter point is developed further in Chris Richards' chapter, 'Beyond Classroom Culture'. Drawing on his research into teaching about popular music in two London secondary schools, and on extensive interviews with teachers, Chapter 7 considers the extent to which the classroom can still appropriately be defined as the locus of significant learning. Noting the contrasts between working-class students' perceptions of teachers and teachers' own accounts of their formation, their competence and their working lives, Richards argues that the present configuration of school identities, settings, routines of work and curricular prescriptions imposes impossible constraints on the possibilities of a radical pedagogy, and that changes in the relationships between forms of work and their associated social identities might suggest more productive possibilities for educational practice.

In Chapter 8, Phil Cohen discusses some of the possibilities and problems of using popular cultural materials in teaching about 'race', ethnicity and identity. Challenging rationalistic approaches to anti-racist and multicultural education, he points to some of the contradictions of an emphasis on 'positive images' and of appeals to an illusory 'authenticity'. His case study accounts are based on the use of the visual arts as a means of exploring how familiar story and image repertoires from the mass media shape and reflect commonly held prejudices, and how the everyday cultural practices of young people both relay and resist those representations. As Cohen indicates, this approach can cause difficulties for teachers who are still locked into traditional frameworks of multicultural and anti-racist education; although it can also enable students to explore the complexity and diversity of their cultural identifications and to generate new frameworks and narratives.

In the concluding chapter, 'Teaching for Difference', Bill Green provides a more theoretical formulation of some of the central dilemmas and contradictions of radical pedagogy, and lays out the ground for a more productive approach, bringing together the work of the 'London' tradition, with its characteristic focus on the everyday negotiations of classroom practice, with new work deriving from poststructuralism and postmodernism. Through a critical rereading of earlier texts in 'critical pedagogy', and a discussion of the central concept of pedagogy itself, Green points the way beyond a simplistic polarization between radical forms of transmission teaching and the limitations of an easy progressivism. Appropriately, Chapter 9 ends by looking forward to the future challenges of the 'semiotic society' – challenges which, Green argues, will call for new forms of educational and cultural practice.

For some, no doubt, this book will be seen as a further indication of a widespread loss of faith in the certainties of radical theories and educational strategies; in this sense, it might be accused of displaying a political agnosticism which is symptomatic of its time. Needless to say, that is not how it seems to us. On the contrary, we hope that the book will be seen as part of a necessary *rethinking* of some of those initiatives, not least in the light of their continuing contradictions and failures. Our aim is to move *beyond* radical pedagogy – not back to the rhetoric of progressivism, but forward to approaches which are both more inclusive, and more empirically grounded.

Notes

1 For a fuller account of these debates, both in general and specifically in relation to media education, see Buckingham (1996a).
2 For a fuller account of this history, see Buckingham (1996b).

References

ALVARADO, M. and BOYD-BARRETT, O. (Eds) (1992) *Media Education: An Introduction*, London: British Film Institute and the Open University.

ANYON, J. (1994) The retreat of Marxism and socialist feminism: Postmodern and poststructural theories in education. *Curriculum Inquiry*, **24** (2), 115–33.

BREHONY, K. (1992) What's left of progressive primary education?, in RATTANSI, A. and REEDER, D. (Eds) *Rethinking Radical Education*, London: Lawrence and Wishart.

BUCKINGHAM, D. (1986) Against demystification, *Screen*, **27** (5), 80–95.

BUCKINGHAM, D. (Ed.) (1990) *Watching Media Learning: Making Sense of Media Education*, London: Falmer Press.

BUCKINGHAM, D. (1993a) *Children Talking Television: The Making of Television Literacy*, London: Falmer Press.

BUCKINGHAM, D. (1993b) *Reading Audiences: Young People and the Media*, Manchester: Manchester University Press.

BUCKINGHAM, D. (1996a) Critical pedagogy and media education: A theory in search of a practice, *Journal of Curriculum Studies*, **28** (6), 627–50.

BUCKINGHAM, D. (1996b) *Media Education*, MA Mass Communication Course Unit, University of Leicester.

BUCKINGHAM, D., FRASER, P. and MAYMAN, N. (1990) Stepping into the void: Beginning classroom research in media education, in BUCKINGHAM, D. (Ed.) *Watching Media Learning*, London: Falmer Press.

BUCKINGHAM, D., GRAHAME, J. and SEFTON-GREEN, J. (1995) *Making Media: Practical Production in Media Education*, London: English and Media Centre.

BUCKINGHAM, D. and SEFTON-GREEN, J. (1994) *Cultural Studies Goes to School: Reading and Teaching Popular Media*, London: Taylor and Francis.

CENTRE FOR CONTEMPORARY CULTURAL STUDIES, EDUCATION GROUP II (1991) *Education Limited*, London: Unwin Hyman.

CHITTY, C. (1992) From great debate to great reform act: The post-war consensus overturned, 1976–88, in RATTANSI, A. and REEDER, D. (Eds) *Rethinking Radical Education*, London: Lawrence and Wishart.

COHEN, P. (1988) The perversions of inheritance, in COHEN, P. and BAINS, H. (Eds) *Multi-Racist Britain*, London: Macmillan.

DEWDNEY, A. and LISTER, M. (1988) *Youth, Culture and Photography*, London: Macmillan.

EDWARDS, D. and MERCER, P. (1987) *Common Knowledge*, London: Methuen.

ELLSWORTH, E. (1989) Why doesn't this feel empowering? Working through the repressive myths of critical pedagogy, *Harvard Educational Review*, **59** (3), 297–324.

ENTWISTLE, H. (1979) *Antonio Gramsci: Conservative Schooling for Radical Politics*, London: Routledge and Kegan Paul.

David Buckingham

Galton, M., Simon, B. and Croll, P. (1980) *Inside the Primary Classroom*, London: Routledge and Kegan Paul.

Giroux, H. (1992) *Border Crossings: Cultural Workers and the Politics of Education*, New York: Routledge.

Giroux, H. (1994) *Disturbing Pleasures: Learning Popular Culture*, New York: Routledge.

Gore, J. (1993) *The Struggle for Pedagogies: Critical and Feminist Discourses as Regimes of Truth*, New York: Routledge.

Hall, S. (1983) The great moving right show, in Hall, S. and Jacques, M. (Eds) *The Politics of Thatcherism*, London: Lawrence and Wishart.

Hodge, B. and Tripp, D. (1986) *Children and Television: A Semiotic Approach*, Cambridge: Polity.

Hunter, I. (1994) *Rethinking the School*, Sydney, New South Wales: Allen and Unwin.

Jones, K. (1989) *Right Turn: The Conservative Revolution in Education*, London: Hutchinson.

Jones, K. (1994) A new kind of cultural politics? The 1993 boycott of testing, *Changing English*, **2** (1), 84–110.

Leavis, F.R. and Thompson, D. (1933) *Culture and Environment*, London: Chatto and Windus.

Luke, C. (1992) Feminist politics in radical pedagogy, in Luke, C. and Gore, J. (Eds) *Feminisms and Critical Pedagogy*, New York: Routledge.

Luke, C. and Gore, J. (Eds) (1992) *Feminisms and Critical Pedagogy*, New York: Routledge.

Lusted, D. (1986) Why pedagogy?, *Screen*, **27** (5), 2–14.

McLaren, P. (1995) *Critical Pedagogy and Predatory Culture*, New York: Routledge.

McLaren, P., Hammer, R., Sholle, D. and Reilly, S. (1995) *Rethinking Media Literacy: A Critical Pedagogy of Representation*, New York: Peter Lang.

Masterman, L. (1980) *Teaching About Television*, London: Macmillan.

Moss, G. (1989) *Un/Popular Fictions*, London: Virago.

Orner, M. (1992) Interrupting the calls for student voice in 'liberatory' education: A feminist poststructuralist perspective, in Luke, C. and Gore, J. (Eds) *Feminisms and Critical Pedagogy*, New York: Routledge.

Rattansi, A. (1992) Changing the subject? Racism, culture and education, in Rattansi, A. and Reeder, D. (Eds) *Rethinking Radical Education*, London: Lawrence and Wishart.

Sharp, R. and Green, A. (1975) *Education and Social Control*, London: Routledge and Kegan Paul.

Simons, H. (1994) Teaching the pedagogies: a dialectical approach to an ideological dilemma, in Simons, H. and Billig, M. (Eds) *After Postmodernism: Reconstructing Ideology Critique*, London: Sage.

Walkerdine, V. (1984) Developmental psychology and the child-centred pedagogy: The insertion of Piaget into early education, in Henriques, J.,

HOLLWAY, W., URWIN, C., VENN, C. and WALKERDINE, V., *Changing the Subject*, London: Methuen.

WILLIAMSON, J. (1981/2) How does girl number twenty understand ideology?, *Screen Education*, **40**, 80–7.

WILLIS, P. (1977) *Learning to Labour*, London: Saxon House.

WILLIS, P. (1990) *Common Culture*, Milton Keynes: Open University Press.

Chapter 2

Pedagogy and Authority: Lessons from Feminist and Cultural Studies, Postmodernism and Feminist Pedagogy

Carmen Luke

How is knowledge produced and reproduced in the emancipatory classroom of the 1990s? During the 1980s, a substantial body of literature has produced an educational discourse variously named as critical or radical pedagogy. What it advocates is that an effectively inclusive pedagogy must give up unilinear transmission models and, instead, opt for a student-centred pedagogy which teaches with and toward students' cultural experiences and identities. In this way, so the argument goes, students traditionally marginalized by curricular knowledges which exclude them, and silenced because of their status and identity differences, will be given voice and their cultural differences affirmed. Feminist pedagogy and media pedagogies, particularly those based on British cultural studies models, also share this vision. Media education is seen as a form of critical practice, as conducive to dialogue, and as necessarily entailing forms of non-authoritarian, process-based and cooperative learning which draw on students' experiences with and pleasures derived from texts at which they are expert. Media studies teachers commonly claim that the media and popular culture curriculum invites rather than deters different student voices and interpretations. Hence dialogue is more readily enabled than, say, in a maths, physics or literature class because in those knowledge domains, the teacher is usually the expert and authority. Feminist pedagogy makes similar claims about critical practice and dialogue; the curriculum content of feminist knowledges is seen as reversing women's silences, and as conducive to generating non-competitive dialogue among women about their shared and different experiences.

Current models of transformative pedagogies that have attempted to politicize the construction, production and reproduction of knowledge and identities in educational contexts – whether the school or university classroom – share theoretical allegiances with contemporary social theories such as poststructuralism, postmodernism and feminism. Mindful of the many interpretations of and variations within each of these theoretical models, my intent in this chapter is to map and draw together various strands from each theory as they relate to issues of knowledge, identity and pedagogy. This mapping will enable me to show how, in the formulation of pedagogies for critical media and cultural studies, each can contribute to a theory-based guide for pedagogical practice. Moreover, since my focus is on feminist pedagogy, I will discuss some conceptual limits within feminist pedagogy discourse which, I argue, constrain the potential for generating critical, self-reflexive and emancipatory knowledge through pedagogy.

I begin with an outline of aspects of contemporary social theories which I consider salient to a media and cultural studies pedagogy. I will take up the contributions of feminist and cultural studies theories first and then outline three aspects of postmodernism relevant to a theorization of media literacy pedagogy. Throughout this first section I provide relevant examples, where appropriate, of teaching strategies for media and cultural analysis, particularly in the context of higher education. I then turn to feminist pedagogy to discuss how it ties in with some conceptual features shared by cultural studies, feminist theory and postmodernism in the production of student knowledges within a critical media literacy agenda. I close with a discussion of the 'not-said' in feminist pedagogy. That is, I discuss some of the conceptual contradictions of feminist pedagogy theorizations and practices, and their political consequences for classroom knowledge and identity production.

Feminist and Cultural Studies

Feminist theory has contributed much to current understanding of the masculinist (mis)representation of the feminine as 'other' in media texts and imagery, in social and natural science, and in literary and philosophical discourses (deLauretis, 1987; Gamman and Marshment, 1989; Haraway, 1992; Kaplan, 1986; McRobbie, 1994; Modleski, 1991; Morris, 1988). Central to feminist theoretical arguments against male textual authority is the near seamless historical repression of a female authorial voice. This argument claims that such representations, whether in print or visual texts, have been primarily male authored versions of girls, women and 'things feminine'. The historical silencing of female authorship–authority, in turn, has led to a fetishization and objectification of 'the feminine' which, in various cultural forms, is said to reflect a collective male gaze and desire. Cultural industries have a long history of male cultural productions of feminine stereotypes and misrepresentations which conceptualize women primarily either as objects of male adornment, pursuit and domination, or as mindless domestic drudges, brain-dead bimbos or saintly supermoms. The politics and economies of representation, feminists argue, extend and legitimate historically-situated and male-authored 'regimes of truth' – what Foucault termed institutionalized disciplinary knowledges. Feminist scholarship has repeatedly shown over the past two decades that, whether through the eye of the camera or the eye of theory, the socially situated epistemological standpoint of masculinity dominates the making of knowledge, history and the present: materially, textually, visually and symbolically.

Feminist cultural studies has a number of collocations within cultural studies and within feminism or women's studies. Mindful also of the differences in theoretical and research orientation within American, Australian and British cultural studies, I draw here only broad outlines of feminist cultural studies in order to map connections among feminism, cultural studies and postmodernism. This shared theoretical ground enables us to move beyond the specific concerns of each field of inquiry and to develop an understanding of pedagogy based in an epistemological standpoint which acknowledges differences of identity, the cultural constructedness of Theory, History and Truth, and the cultural dynamics of our own labour as academic researchers and teachers. This epistemological standpoint is a self-reflexive position which takes its theoretical maxim from Foucault's work on power/knowledge regimes as constitutive of the social constructedness of knowledge and the human subject, and from feminism's commitment to a politics of transformation.

Feminist cultural studies is inflected with the poststructuralist methodological and analytic agenda of deconstruction. In the liberal arts classroom, pedagogies of critical analysis have long been commonplace: critical readings of research studies, literary or legal texts, transcripts or policy documents, are commonplace student assignment and evaluation fare. However, what differentiates feminist from progressive pedagogies, or cultural studies from traditional criticism, is feminism's insistence on differences in identity and thus reading positions, and cultural studies' insistence on the cultural location of all texts, all readings and all models for 'critical' readings.

Foucault's premise that the human subject, social practices and institutions are products of historically situated discourses, social practices and (embodied) author–authorities, underlies much feminist and cultural studies theorizing. The speaking and reading subject of feminism is seen as both a cultural product of master discourses and a cultural agent in negotiating and/ or contesting the meanings about her, given in the discourses available to her. Women's complex and multiple identities, experienced *in* and *through* the discourses that define feminine gender identity, sexuality, ethnicity, class or culture, suggest that an understanding of women and the concept of femininity cannot be articulated in universal principles, but must come from women's individual voices articulated from specific social and cultural locations. Hence, in feminisms generally and in feminist pedagogy specifically, the importance of 'positionality' (Alcoff, 1988; Ferguson, 1993; Flax, 1990; Haraway, 1988) of voice and experience are paramount. The gendered politics of speech and silence in the university classroom are thus central theoretical, political and practical concerns for feminist educators (Belenky *et al.*, 1986; Bunch and Pollack, 1983; Gabriel and Smithson, 1990; Gore, 1993; Lather, 1991; Lewis, 1993; Luke, 1994; Luke and Gore, 1992; Maher, 1987; Mahoney, 1988; Middleton, 1993; Pagano, 1990; Stone, 1994; Weiler, 1988). However, the extent to which individual voice and experience can be taken as legitimate epistemological grounds for knowledge and for the formulation of normative criteria, remains hugely problematic for feminists (Alcoff and Potter, 1993; Bondi, 1993; Brown, 1991; Fraser and Nicholson, 1990; Fuss, 1989; Love, 1991; Luke, 1996; Martin, 1994; Shor, 1989). I take up this point in further detail later in the chapter. Feminist cultural studies and feminist pedagogy, then, can inform critical practice in the media studies classroom in a number of ways. Below I briefly outline a few strategies before moving on to discussion of cultural studies and postmodernisms.

Many women students in higher education, particularly mature-aged women, international students, and women from ethnically and culturally different backgrounds from the host country, often find the highly specialized discourse of western academic texts daunting and alienating, in ways which can erode their intellectual self-confidence. As Sandra Lee Bartky (1996) points out, many women bring into the university classroom a life-time social-ized repertoire of guilt and shame, of self-denigrating and self-invalidating ways of positioning their intellect and academic work as inferior, inadequate and 'shameful'. Many women find ways of invalidating their work through linguistic disclaimers, in their failure to take credit for good work, or by prefacing assertions or classroom contributions with self-denigrating com-ments such as 'I'm not sure that I'm right but . . .'; 'I don't know too much about this but . . .'; 'I typed this paper up badly . . .', and so forth.

One way to develop confidence and courage among women is to give them the opportunity to work with textual forms and content which may be more culturally amenable to women. A communications class, for instance, may give women the option of studying or preparing a research paper on the historical styles of women's communications and storytelling: from weaving, quilt making or pottery, to poetry, music or gardening (cf. Walker, 1984). For example, a cross-cultural investigation into different social, organizational and aesthetic features of women's weaving (from such as Navajo, Thai, Maori) would enable not only a feminist study of communications and cultural story-telling, but would invariably require critical theoretical and analytic attention to cross-cultural difference, the gendered division of labour, issues of repre-sentation, and so forth. Key here is to draw students' attention to the dynamics of cultural forms as cultural content rather than merely viewing culture as representational content. Other student research topics can include women's use of the VCR (Gray, 1992); telephone, computer networks and technologies (Kramarae, 1988, 1995; Sandoval, 1995; Spender, 1995; Wajcman, 1994); rural women's use of TV (Luke, 1993); women's viewer communities (Brown, 1990; Press, 1991; Walters, 1992); the history of TV as a domestic appliance (cf. Spigel, 1992; Spigel and Mann, 1992); or the organization of women's social networks and communication patterns in the cultural geography of place and space (Massey, 1993; Rose, 1993; Shurmer-Smith and Hannam, 1994; Spain, 1992; Thompson, 1994). A poststructuralist feminist approach to such research topics would also encourage students to look critically at the communications, historical or anthropology texts they consult for their research projects with a view to analyzing how women, women's contributions, or other cultures, are constructed in those texts. Their absence or marginality might well teach students larger philosophical and political lessons about patriarchy, cultural imperialism, historical author–authorities, the myths of 'scientific' research and the rhetoric of texts.

One need not essentialize gender differences to assert that girls and boys are socialized early into very different and highly gendered interests through play and games, adult behaviours and expectations organized around gender categories. These differences are as apparent in the university as in the elementary school classroom. Consider, for instance, that some male students may well be more interested than women in research or assignment topics on the political economy of media industries, the corporate and representational organization of sports, sports 'heroes' or sportscasters on TV, or the structuring of 'fact' in news, current affairs and documentary programmes. Some women, on the other hand, might well prefer options that enable them to research issues of concern to them such as: the construction of women's discourse in daytime talk shows, soaps or home shopping infomercials; children's programming, advertising and legislation; or children's popular culture, toy, clothing and videogame industries. Relatedly, lesbian and gay students need a speaking and research forum in which to critique homophobia through, for example, analyses of lesbian and gay representations in various media forms (cf. Ellsworth, 1988). In classes with large numbers of migrant and/or international students, readings and assignments can open up debate and research on media uses in migrant families and communities (cf. Gillespie, 1995), the globalization of media and popular culture, or on the conceptual and visual media treatment of non-western nations as 'foreign', alien and, not infrequently, as a 'threat'. Further, such class debate and investigation can lead to political analyses of concepts of nation, 'development', racial stereotyping, all of which can be framed in and introduce students to aspects of postcolonial theory. Hence, to open up inquiry into areas that are of particular cultural and political interest to students is a core aspect of feminist pedagogical practice with direct applications to cultural studies and media pedagogy across diverse disciplinary areas.

Cultural studies has some similarities with feminist theoretical concerns. However, like all other interdisciplinary fields of inquiry, cultural studies is not a seamless and unified discourse. Differences among cultural studies scholars continue to abound over definitions, methodology and analytic–theoretic approaches. Key concerns include the selection of culture-appropriate and media genre-appropriate methodologies, definitions of culture, and whether culture can be treated analytically as a language (cf. Franklin, Lury and Stacey, 1991). In other words, since speaking and reading *are* fundamentally about interpretation, meaning making and constructions of the self, and since these occur primarily through language and in language communities, should cultural analysis be grounded in linguistic theories? These concerns remain unresolved, but they do have some affinity with theoretical debates over voice, meaning and representation currently under scrutiny within feminisms, particularly within feminist cultural, psychoanalytic and film theory (cf. Erens, 1990). Although cultural studies remains primarily in the theoretical custody of men, it is, like feminism, concerned with the *specificity* of reading positions and cultural productions on the one hand and, on the other, concerned with the politics of power/knowledge regimes in the media(ted) construction of identities and knowledge.

What this convergence suggests, then, is that epistemologically both feminism and cultural studies question the relations between power and knowledge in the production of universal 'truths', commonsense understandings and everyday practices, and both insist that differences in identity and location are the only legitimate site from which to authorize the self. Both reject the theoretical products of modernist discourse: the (male and European) universal subject, objectivist inquiry and knowledge, and the transparency of language. In that regard, questions of how persons take up cultural texts or how women interpret patriarchal narratives of femininity, are fundamentally concerned with the textual deconstruction of received 'truths' – whether these be labelled discourses, ideologies, mythologies or empiricism. This emphasis in feminisms and cultural studies on critical deconstruction and the politics of identity and location has much in common with current theoretical concerns in several strands of postmodernism which I take up next.

Postmodernisms

Aspects of postmodernist theory relevant to my discussion here fall roughly into three areas: philosophical, cultural and economic postmodernism. I outline each briefly, fully aware that such a brief survey cannot adequately address the complexities of various strands within postmodernist thought. Philosophical postmodernism rejects Enlightenment totalizing theories and cultural stories which, as framed in modernist narratives, explained the world from a centred and privileged position of male power and knowing. Those master narratives historically associated with the supremacy of the white, male bourgeois subject (for example, high culture and 'Art', objectivity, universalisms, detachment, industrial and military rationality, etc.), have come under the critical scrutiny of both feminist and postmodernist scholars. This strand within postmodernism claims that modernist explanations could only account for all those not marked as white, male and of European descent, by defining them as *less* and *other* than the centred object of study of their own theories which spoke to and for those who authored those discourses in the first place.

Like feminist and cultural studies, postmodernism rejects the master narratives of modernity and, instead, argues for multiplicity, difference, heteroglossia and specificity. This focuses theory and political action on local sites, on micro-capillaries of power and oppression, and on the multiple differences that characterize specific contexts and persons. The postmodernist human subject is seen as situated in a collective social body which is constituted through and in differences of identity and location – not in sameness. In the media studies classroom, teaching students about the politics of identity formation, difference(s) and reading positions as a prelude to image and text analysis, is essential and can be tied into this epistemological framewofk with strands in feminism, cultural studies and postmodernism. Unless the usual image-text analysis of media studies pedagogy is linked to a theoretical understanding of how media and popular cultural texts enable both hegemonic and excentric subject and reading positions – how we actively and continuously (re)make ourselves in the image, and (re)make the image at the instant of reading/consumption – then students are given little more than analytic tools with which to deconstruct false consciousness, textual mythologies and the cultural/consumerist wool pulled over duped viewers' eyes.

Cultural postmodernism views contemporary culture metaphorically as a house of mirrors. The mass media technoculture of the present is seen as an infinite house of electronic mirror-screens, each deflecting and yet projecting images and symbols of desire and identity onto human subjects. The human subject is the screen upon which electronic imageries project symbolic identities, imaginary needs and wants (Grossberg, 1984). The subject is seen as a product of cultural symbols and signification systems which are said to have no referent to any concrete 'real' material objects or relations in the world. Images and signs are seen by postmodern cultural theorists to refer only to other images and signs, and it is within this cross-referential system of culturally constructed meanings that the social subject is situated and acts in the world (Baudrillard, 1983).

For Baudrillard, there is no 'real' dimension to social experience, only *simulated* experiences and identities. The 'real' time and social relations constructed around watching TV, shopping in malls, constructing an identity through designer labels, or kids playing with Barbie, Ninja Turtles or Power Rangers, are simulated experiences which have no concrete referent in the 'real' world, as understood in Enlightenment humanist discourse. In this regard, the cultural postmodernist position argues that the subject of postmodernity is nothing more than a 'simulacrum' – a simulation (Baudrillard, 1983). The social subject thus is a cultural artefact and bodily-material ground for the inscription and embodiment of mass produced symbolic meanings and the tie-in commodities which make those meanings concrete through purchase and ownership. What Baudrillard and other cultural postmodernists argue, then, is that the 'real' has slipped from its Enlightenment anchor of *de re* metaphysical certainty – essential properties and real things.

The postmodern rejection of metanarratives, totalized knowledges and a universal subject has been supplanted by an insistence on local and multiply constituted subjects and differences of identity. This turn to specificity – to a totality of difference, to a universe of different but allegedly equal voices, perspectives and experiences – runs serious theoretical and political risks.

Most crucial is its potential to undermine, indeed eradicate, any political and ethical grounds from which to claim the authority of moral, social or legal norms. Views and voices from everywhere are potentially views and voices from nowhere. In other words, without normative benchmarks, which criteria can we invoke to distinguish between morally defensible and indefensible positions? What moral and ethical criteria do we use to censure patently oppressive knowledges such as those (also called 'science') which spawned eugenics, colonial genocide or ethnic cleansing? Or, to what extent are semiotic constructions of the self, through available cultural significations, 'real' or 'simulated' markers of political and cultural identities? Are our identity statements – whether in-group colours or subcultural dress – simulated or 'real' representations of who we are? If cultural experience and identities are mere quotations and floating signifiers, where and how do we claim a standpoint in which to ground identity and difference claims? How, in the production of knowledge in classroom encounters, does the teacher claim a standpoint of authority on issues of identity difference, reading positions and what counts as discriminatory and offensive cultural representations or student readings? Is one student's critical interpretation more or less valid than another's? How does a teacher arbitrate what Dianne Fuss (1989) calls the 'hierarchy of oppressions' that often surface among students in identity-based knowledge productions?

These are practical pedagogical, political and ethical questions about knowledge, identity and authority which are not easily resolved from the theoretical standpoint of an endless deferral to difference. Critical and feminist pedagogies often pride themselves on flattened hierarchy models of instruction, and claim to relinquish normative benchmarks (commonly associated with 'canonical worth' as defined by master narratives) when making judgments and assessments, attempting to affirm students' different but equal voices, experiences and abilities; yet in the process, they can potentially uncouple pedagogy from its productive potential – that is, its potential for leading students to understand themselves and the world through different, more enlightening, lenses.

The third theoretical dimension of postmodernism relevant here, is best exemplified by Harvey (1989, 1993a,b), Lash (1990) and Lash and Urry (1987), who explain the post-industrial moment as a form of post-capitalism or economic postmodernism. The logic of modern capitalism was based on centralization of human and industrial resources; the logic of postmodern capitalism is based on off-shore and decentralized human and resource investments. The worker under industrial capitalism invested in lifetime specialization of skills whereas the postmodern worker is multi-skilled. Under modernist capitalism, workers laboured under an industrial regime producing the hardware of an industrial economy. Postmodern capitalism, by contrast, is now widely characterized as an information economy in which the primary object and medium of labour and social relations is information. In the postmodern age, the software of information is *the* privileged currency of exchange. And, unlike print, its simulated, soft- and hardware dependent, electronic character makes it highly permeable across time and space. The intensity, globalization and inter-textuality of information regimes, such as stockmarkets and banking, entertainment media, advertising, render information the core commodity of contemporary capitalist logic.

How, then, do these various postmodernist theoretical positions support arguments for a critical literacy of media and cultures? One key aspect of postmodernist theory relevant to a media and cultural literacy is the elimination of the high culture/low culture distinction which has characterized the study of popular culture and culture industries since the 1930s (see Horkheimer and Adorno, 1972). With the postmodernist turn away from Eurocentric notions of 'high culture' and 'high theory', academic inquiry – itself a labour of 'high culture' (Bourdieu, 1984) – has finally begun to take seriously those mass cultural knowledges, artefacts and practices which are of daily relevance to most people.

A second important insight of postmodern theory is the shift from centrist and relatively static notions of culture to global, corporate and electronic culture which is in a constant state of renewal and reinvention. That is, the acceleration of change in style, 'the look', and the commodities which enable continuous personal reinvention, is primarily achieved through increasingly globalized and standardized media messages, all of which refer to other sign systems (of status, success, 'in'-groupness). This shift in transferability and marketability of cultures is enabled and sustained by post-industrial capitalism which has given rise to postmodern economies of culture; anyone anywhere can buy into countless variations of innumerable cultural styles. Hilltribe kids in rural Thailand or Burma wear Chicago Bulls hats, Soviet kids wear Nike or OJ t-shirts (Homer Simpson t-shirts are still sighted in New Guinea), and women in the American midwest sport 'ethnic dress'.

Despite important theoretical differences among modernist and postmodernist cultural theorists, they do agree on the increasingly central role of electronic imageries which appear in growing intensity and exponential geographic expansion. The pastiche of contemporary cultural life is no longer confined to the urban landscape but has extended its reach into the everyday life and consciousness of persons located in the most far flung regions around the globe. Coke or Mattell toy ads beam into the most remote hamlets. In remote Australian Aboriginal or Guatemalan highland communities, people gather around the glow of the screen to watch old re-runs of *Rambo* or *Terminator, Beverly Hills 90210*, the Academy Awards or Miss Universe, brought to you by Pepsi, Coke, Nike or Toyota. Paradoxically, the intensity and global proliferation of primarily western cultural signs and symbols seem on one level to de-emphasize national cultural differences and interests. Yet the pan-global commodification of cultural symbols and meanings (associated primarily with soft drink, toy, fast food or entertainment empires) also appear to generate increasing resistance to the globalization of culture and increasing insistence on national and ethnic difference and identity.

As I noted above, part of the postmodern moment in academic inquiry is the turn away from the canonization of *great* books, *great* authors and *great* art precisely because those texts variously served as normative benchmarks with which to invalidate, exclude or marginalize all those knowledges and groups other than those classified as European, male and heterosexual. The collapse of distinctions between high and low culture, and the demystification of high culture as a self-referential masculinist myth of self-glorification, has also begun to cast some light on the modernist preoccupation with print text – with 'good' books – in educational institutions. Modernist pedagogy, after all, *is* organized around print knowledge and print literacy skills which are seen as applicable to and indispensable in a predominantly print culture. However, as we move from an industrial to a post-industrial information economy, one in which print literacy is not obsolete but certainly substantially transformed, then surely we need broader definitions of knowledge, literacy and pedagogy which will include study of the intertextuality of imageries, texts, icons and artefacts of new information economies, of media and of popular culture.

Feminist Pedagogy

I now turn to feminist pedagogy in attempting to link teaching–learning practices to the theoretical agendas of feminism, cultural studies and postmodernism. My aim in this section is to look more closely at the theoretical and pedagogical ramifications of assumptions underlying claims of voice, difference, identity, and non-hierarchical teaching and knowledge. Although my focus is on feminist pedagogy models, my discussion has applications to other critical and progressive models of pedagogy adopted in media studies (see for example: Alvarado and Boyd-Barrett, 1992; Buckingham, 1993a,b; Buckingham and Sefton-Green, 1994; Hart, 1991; *Journal of Communication Inquiry* 1994 special issue on critical media pedagogy; Kellner, 1995; Lusted, 1991).

The primary principle of feminist pedagogy is to enable ways of learning which foreground women. First, it foregrounds women's specific social and learning needs as women and as students in terms of their status and identity within a profoundly masculinist university culture. Second, it foregrounds feminine scholarship as a way of centering feminist epistemology and critical practice in efforts to connect women's experience to knowledges which validate, theoretically extend, and politicize women's life trajectories and possibilities. Third, because of feminism's sensitivity to the impossibility of *Woman* and its commitment to the plurality of *women*, differences among women students are taken into account through inclusive content delivery in teaching and assigned readings, term assignments and evaluation strategies.

A central but problematic tenet of feminist pedagogy is the demystification of the teacher–student relationship, and the politicization of knowledge (Luke and Gore, 1992). As Jennifer Gore (1993:5) puts it, it is a 'focus on the processes of teaching that demands that attention be drawn to the politics of those processes and to the broader political contexts within which they are situated. Therefore, instruction and social vision are analytical components of pedagogy.' Gore is correct in drawing our attention to 'the processes of teaching . . . [and] the politics of those processes' because, although feminist educators may claim to have changed power, authority and the master (teacher)–slave (student) dichotomy of pedagogical relations, the institutional embeddedness of feminist pedagogy suggests that there can be no 'pure' space outside of power and institutionally authorized authority. Feminist educators as subjects of feminist pedagogy discourse *are* institutionally authorized because they are judged and named, at the moment of hiring, as authorities of knowledge. Hence, their institutional status is based on their institutionally legitimated claims to knowledge which gives them both *de facto* and *de jure* intellectual authority and institutional power.

Feminist pedagogy disavows much of what is taken for granted as part of university culture and ethos. It refuses hierarchical elitism, competitive scholarship, and disclaims the kind of theoretical specialism which might be used to interpret women's allegedly undertheorized experiences (Belenky *et al.*, 1986; Bunch and Pollack, 1983; Cully and Portuges, 1986; Lewis, 1993; Luke and Gore, 1992; Maher, 1987; Mahoney, 1988; Middleton, 1993; Pagano, 1990). Hence, the feminist classroom tends to be more of a bottom-up than top-down knowledge exchange. In other words, the feminist pedagogue refuses the common equation of teacher as knower and student as unknowing and theoretically naive. The feminist pedagogue, so the literature claims, does not see herself as authoritative arbiter of student interpretation and understanding. Instead, she emphasizes her own situatedness, her own partial 'take' on the world, and thus acknowledges her own experience and knowledge as no more and no less valid, better or authentic than the diversity of students in her class. What she does offer are a range of knowledge options for her students – from course content to analytic tools, research topics and strategies – in efforts to connect women's interests, learning styles, social locations and identities to a range of feminist discourses. Pedagogically, what follows from this standpoint is a way of teaching which focuses on women's differences, and on her own situatedness as academic teacher–scholar within that grid of differences. It makes knowledge production a collaborative class effort in which the feminist pedagogue has a specific body of knowledge to offer alongside other women's equally situated knowledges and experiences.

This characterization of feminist pedagogy is its public face. That is, in nearly all feminist scholarship on pedagogy, collaborative knowledge production and a disavowal of teacher authority are presented as key political practices in the emancipatory project. It is both an ideal vision of what ought to be and a collective stance and testimony among feminist educators. However, as Jane Gallop (1994) among others has pointed out, what follows from this is a dangerous depoliticization of the sexual and institutional politics operant within the feminist classroom. I wish to take up this point in detail here because I believe this to be an important counter-argument to feminist pedagogy's slippage into one side of the nurture–authority dichotomy. Moreover, it also has related implications for similar claims in critical media pedagogy of non-authoritarian teaching and equal valuing of student readings and interpretations.

In my own teaching I have repeatedly experienced the impossibility of the kind of flattened hierarchy and non-authoritarian model of pedagogy professed by feminist pedagogy discourse. Despite my best efforts to demystify the student–teacher relationship, the politics of knowledge production, credentialling and credential inflation in the academy, in the end I still have to exert authority and power by judging student work, assigning grades, vetting grant, scholarship or promotion applications, and mediating the 'hierarchy of oppressions' (Fuss, 1989) that so easily creep into identity-based classroom debate. Consider the following example from Kathleen Jones' 'The Trouble with Authority', which is worth citing at length. She talks about teaching a large class of diverse students who are deconstructing an ad for the Four Seasons Hotel which features a woman from a 'small Chinese village' who now works for the hotel. She is depicted 'crisply uniformed, and holds two enormous, clean fluffy towels like gifts in her arms'. Part of the caption reads 'Marlene is the very soul of concern. She cannot sleep well at night unless she is certain that you will.' Jones continues:

> You ask the class to respond to this ad. Many have already gasped or snickered in shock. A vigorous discussion ensues, with people who have never spoken before in class offering their analyses. Then, one young Asian–American woman raises her hand. 'My mother is like this woman . . . She would not have been able to sleep unless she knew that everyone else was happy. I understand the point you're trying to make, but in my culture, much as I myself am now critical of it, this image is not derogatory.' You respond by calling attention to who is 'owning' the image – the Asian–American population or American capitalism – but you wonder whether, by using this ad to illustrate a point about the politics of gender images, you have assumed an ethnocentric interpretation of exploitation . . . Feminists have challenged the authority of the 'fathers' and their great works. Yet we also have claimed authority for our own texts. Moreover, critiques of feminism as a new 'master narrative' that arbitrarily postulates women's universal subjugation . . . has dissolved the category Woman into women so that even the category women seems to have lost its coherence. No more authority; no more women (1991:165–6).

We might ask: does this student's reading invalidate the teacher's and other students' readings, or are they all 'equally valid' readings depending on the situatedness of student identities and experiences? If all student readings are considered equally valid, then what is the point of the lesson if the image both is and isn't derogatory and subjugating? What is the teacher's position *vis-à-vis* the image and the student readings? Surely there is more at stake here than exposing students to textual polysemy or the politics of meaning making. If we accept this text as empowering and culturally affirming for some groups, then on which political and moral grounds can the teacher claim authority, and which normative criteria can she invoke, with which to argue that this text does indeed exemplify cultural, racial and gender stereotyping, an orientalist reading or the corporate interests of capital? How can we sustain critiques of injustice, subordination, imperialism or exploitation without reference to some forms of normativity, benchmarks or feminist 'master narratives'? This is what Jones sees as feminism's 'trouble with authority'.

Feminism is still fundamentally about transformation and enlightenment and, therefore, feminist educators still attempt in their teaching to give students access to 'better', more inclusive and non-exploitative knowledges. But in doing so, they require reference to criteria of moral, ethical and political worth in order to make value judgments in their teaching: from arbitrating students' commentary, evaluating their work and selecting course readings and classroom materials, to teaching aspects of feminist knowledge as 'better' than patriarchal knowledge, as well as making theoretical and political value distinctions among feminist theories. Moreover, because our work is authorized within the profoundly masculinist culture of the university, we repeatedly run up against the same dilemma regarding our professed commitment to destabilizing male models of power and authority invested in us, and yet being bound to an entrenched patriarchal intellectual and bureaucratic ethos of normative procedures, criteria and power relations through which we exercise our power over students and authority over knowledges. Anna Yeatman makes a similar point about the tensions 'subaltern intellectuals', such as feminists, encounter by virtue of their dual and often incommensurate accountability to their constituencies (women), and the institutional apparatus of the university, both of which position and challenge her authority in different ways:

> For these intellectuals, there are unresolved tensions between demands for accountability to the academic authorities for the quality of the academic performance their work represents, and demands for accountability to the subaltern constituencies in which their politics is entailed ... What matters is how they practice their authority as an intellectual and whether they open it up to being both problematicized and made accountable to different audiences (1994: 36–7).

The tensions and contradictions inherent in the multiple locations and forms of authority, accountability and power experienced by feminists are wide-ranging across the intellectual and institutional spectrum. Jane Gallop,

Marianne Hirsch and Nancy Miller (1990), for instance, talk about 'established' senior feminists in authority, 'getting trashed' and 'attacked' in print or at conferences by other feminists, male theorists or graduate students in order 'to score points'. bell hooks (1990) makes similar points about feminist struggles over authority and power within the intellectual 'star system' of 'third world diva girls' which spans black and 'third-world' feminisms. The flipside of these kinds of public and visible tensions over intellectual authority and institutional power can be found in the innumerable instances of university committee or similar meetings where feminists often are disempowered and de-authorized by the (usually male, sometimes female) discursive techniques of silencing, exclusion, and other 'vanishing acts'. Not least, the feminist classroom is one site where feminine authority and power are often actively and explicitly denied by women themselves. This disavowal of power and authority is structured into what Jane Gallop (1994, 1995) refers to as 'good girl feminism' which characterizes much of feminist pedagogy theory and epistemology, and the intersubjectivity of pedagogical relations.

A purported absence of pedagogical authority runs a two-fold risk. On one level it positions persons in pedagogical relations as equals-in-difference. This provisional equality – the momentary bracketing of patriarchal knowledges which hierarchize differences – imbues the female teacher with the subject position of nurturer (in place of masculine power and authority), and the student as object of nurturance. This risks masking the substantively differential access to and deployment of power between student and teacher since the very identity of teacher (as embodied signifier of the knowing subject) and student (as embodied signifier of the un-knowing object – the teacher's other) is institutionally produced and named. On another level, the disavowal of authority potentially works much like Foucault's disciplinary regimes of truth whereby authority, discipline and truth statements (judging student voice or ranking student work) are deployed from faceless, panoptic centres of control. Pedagogy without a locus of authority thus risks deceit: embodied difference and differential power access are camouflaged under a false pretence of allegedly equal subject positions. Knowledge production through teacher and student voices – in speech and in text – thus becomes a masquerade of ostensibly 'authentic' voices and knowledges shared among equals. This assumption invokes Habermas' model of communicative intersubjectivity, specifically his concepts of communicative competence and the ideal speech situation. Habermas' rationalist–idealist conceptualization has been challenged – not least by feminists – on its epistemological blindness towards embodied (i.e. sexual) difference, and its failure to theorize the power relations underlying all communicative exchange and identity politics (see Fraser, 1989).

Critical and feminist pedagogies, then, which attempt to transform top-down transmission models of knowledge by reconceptualizing the teacher role as 'equal' to the diversity of student differences, run the risk of giving up authority over and claims to knowledge altogether, or else masquerading as an ideal speech situation wherein all participants allegedly have equal speaking status and equally valued cultural and linguistic resources with which to make knowledge claims and seek consensual understandings of different knowledge claims. This position is theoretically untenable for two reasons: first, it contravenes feminism's cherished claims of having more fine-grained and morally defensible conceptions of ontology and epistemology than patriarchal models; second, rendering differences as equally situated unifies them into a principle of sameness which contradicts feminism's commitment to difference(s) of identity, location, history and experience. Feminism began with a critique of the many inequalities structured into patriarchal knowledges and institutions under the guise of categories of sameness: man, humanity, human nature, others. And yet what has become of feminism's critical practice is that feminist pedagogy disavows differences of authority, power and knowledge among women, and celebrates an almost dogmatic anti-essentialism which totalizes difference through false generalizations about women's inexhaustible and irreducible differences (cf. Luke, 1996; Martin, 1994).

Once 'woman' or 'experience' or 'reading position' are individuated to the point where commonalities are impossible, and 'authenticity' of voice, identity or experience are conceptualized as more or less equally valid but different, then differences and structures of power are ignored and, in a world of nothing but difference, diversity is given a uniformity and dangerous sameness (Luke, 1992). The contradiction here between the practical teaching project of academic feminism (denial of sovereign and foundational authority; equal differences; individuated voice/identity) and its professed theoretical and political standpoints (critique of sovereign and foundational authority; critique of myth of equality and exclusion of difference; universal voice/ identity) undermines feminism's commitment to honest, honourable, and ethical engagement with the politics of knowledge production, and the conduct of teacher–student relationships. That is, to treat power and authority as absent or illusory in the feminist classroom, as an exclusively male evil or attribute of 'bad girl' feminism, is to deceive students and masquerade a performance of 'good girl' feminism (cf. Gallop, 1994). Liz Bondi comments on this conceptual pluralism with reference to the category 'women':

> Taken to its logical conclusion, the category 'women', upon which feminism is based, becomes a free-floating sign apparently able to take on any meaning we give it. The materiality of social relations is, in effect, ignored, in favour of a domain of representation in which structures of power are treated as illusory (1993:94).

Feminism's insistence on dissolving patriarchy's oppositional logic has led much feminist thought to buy into one side of a litany of conceptual dualisms. In contesting phallocentric models of knowledge and the subject – wherein male/rationalist/objective knower is counterposed to female/affective/subject of knowledge – feminist pedagogy has located itself, perhaps unwittingly, on the maternal–nurturance side of humanism's classic dualism. Concepts of nurturing invoke maternal images: an ethics of care, ontology and intersubjectivity as relational, groupness and cooperation rather than individualism and competition. Transposed to pedagogy, this image and social vision is potentially disastrous because it reinstates and legitimates the asexual, maternal and disempowering image of the self-effacing, benevolent school-marm. Teachers with authoritative knowledge and in authority have traditionally been male, and the historical record, beginning with Socrates, and popular cultural narratives are filled with images of 'great' and 'illustrious' male teachers (for example, *Dead Poets Society*, *Blackboard Jungle*, *Stand and Deliver*, *Educating Rita*; or compare Mr. Kotter with *Our Miss Brooks*). In short, the public image of female and feminist teachers is one of 'good girl feminism': asexual, benign, powerless, 'nice'. As Gallop puts it:

> In the discourse of feminist teaching, the bad girl has been at best an object, at worst invisible, never a speaking subject. Although feminist pedagogy has sometimes promoted the bad-girl student, feminists as teachers have almost always spoken from the place of the good woman. Perhaps because teaching itself has been associated, since the common school movement of the early nineteenth century, with traditional 'good' femininity, that is, with selfless, sexless nurturance (1994:6).

One consequence of 'good-girl' feminist pedagogy is that the sexual politics of the feminist classroom (or of desire), whether in single-sex or co-ed classrooms, have hardly been taken up by feminist or educational scholarship. I suspect that there are two reasons for this. First, feminism's moral discomfort with claiming individual power and authority (Jones, 1991), has produced a concept of the feminist teacher characterized by a series of lacks, including lack of ('bad girl') authority and sexual identity. Her refusal to claim power or authority over others or knowledge, evacuates her identity of any authoritative knowledge claims and claims to institutional power – or at least, not to use power and knowledge in traditional male ways. Second, because her role as teacher is conceived in 'good girl feminism' – selfless dedication and nurturance of her students – her identity is desexualized and repackaged as the nurturing maternal subject. The teacher as maternal signifier reverses the historically formalized student–teacher relationship: the masculinization of the teacher–father and feminization of the student–child (Kirby, 1994:25). To take this argument one step further, one can argue that the reversal of the historically eroticized male-teacher female-student relationship through displacement of the paternal-authority teacher signifier by historically infantilized women leaves no conceptual room, within the patriarchal discourse of the academy, other than to mark the female teacher as a desexualized, non-desiring, nurturing maternal signifier.

In this theoretical scenario, the feminist pedagogue does not give up desire, but it is disconnected from sexual identity politics (a current theoretical preoccupation in all other branches and brands of feminism) and reclaimed by maternal desires: 'the maternal guise of benign innocence, purity of purpose and desire, natural devotion and selflessness' (Kirby, 1994:18). Her desire becomes devotion to socialize, nurture and transform her students through the feminist lenses she offers, with which they can reinterpret and potentially liberate themselves from a litany of patriarchal injustices. And, as feminist scholarship has thoroughly documented, those multiple injustices are written into the forms and content of patriarchal knowledges which are the very metanarratives and ways of knowing that feminism and feminist pedagogy seek to contest and subvert.

Importantly, however, the feminist teacher's desire to change, convince and enlighten her students through contestation of the masculine canon, by definition has to rely on some normative criteria by which one set of (patriarchal) knowledges are explicated as inadequate and inferior to the (feminist) knowledges she usually claims as superior to patriarchal regimes of truth. Pedagogy and feminism are fundamentally hermeneutic and hermeneutics functions from its exteriority – that is, its appeals to normative discourses, whether these be normative feminist claims of 'the good' for women, normative moral claims in educational discourse about 'meritocratic' equity or ethical conduct in student–teacher relationships, or the many discipline-based 'truth' claims that guide teaching and interpretation across the curriculum. Appeals to normativity – even if an ideal-type model of social justice were available based on normative principles of situated heterogeneity (Young, 1990) – invoke issues of authority at the level of discourse (the 'sovereign' authority of normative criteria), and at the level of discursive practice (the speaking subject who invokes and is governed by normative criteria). And the 'trouble with authority' for feminists, as Kathleen Jones aptly puts it, is that

> Authority has become both totem and taboo: we consider those who claim authority to be powerful and controlling and . . . Yet the antifoundationalism of the postmodern critique undercuts the theoretical coherence of authority itself. Consequently, feminists are confronted with a paradox: claiming that authority is the practice most necessary for all women – and all 'others' . . . while simultaneously deferring the question of writing [and speaking] authoritative texts in favor of a theoretical position supporting a veritable cacophony of voices. I contend that we remain trapped in and immobilized politically by a peculiar discourse on authority (1991:107–8).

Given feminism's inheritance of metanarratives written in the language of the father, and taught by the rule and authority of the teacher–father, it is little wonder that feminist pedagogy would be based on a conceptual and practical reversal of masculinist forms of knowledge production and transmission. Yet the conceptual logic and political practice of feminism's opposition to the male legacy of authority, power and knowledge – specifically as that opposition is practiced and theorized in feminist pedagogy – has potentially self-invalidating and politically disabling consequences for women.

Conclusion

The problems with postmodernist and feminist notions of difference, and critical, progressive pedagogy's formulation of the teacher as benign, neutral, non-authoritative, and non-authoritarian, should now be clear. The contradictions of knowledge production in critical or feminist pedagogy models – whether in the media, cultural or women's studies classroom – have not received careful theoretical scrutiny. I suspect that, among feminist pedagogy theorists, the lack of self-reflexive critique of issues of female power, authority and sexual politics has to do with fear of crossing the line from good girl to bad girl feminism. But clearly, some theory-based, politically and ethically defensible criteria are needed with which to formulate 'an *ethics* of pedagogy' (Gatens, 1994:15) which do not reproduce the tyranny of authoritarian transmission models, but at the same time avoid slipping into a vacuous celebration of difference and rampant pluralism. What this suggests is that, despite our discomfort with foundational and institutional authority, we may need to re-engage with the Foucauldian project of making our own power and authority visible and political. Feminists should resist the silent authority – the hidden hegemony of feminism itself – that keeps feminists from engaging in constructive criticisms of some of feminism's most cherished tenets.

I have taken an extended route to argue two cases. First, feminist theories of representation and recent work in feminist pedagogy provide the conceptual support for analyzing the politics of knowledge production, voice, standpoint and authorship, exclusion and inclusion, and the cultural productions and representations of the popular, popular sentiment, gendered desires and identities. Media, cultural and feminist studies are fundamentally about critical practice and interpretation, and critical pedagogy foregrounds the importance of teaching with and about cultural texts, images and icons that are relevant to a diverse student population. Strands in postmodern thought support arguments for the curricular inclusion of cultural and media studies and a pedagogy based on concepts of the postmodern subject as multiply constituted, culturally situated and produced in and through intersecting discourses. Second, critical, particularly feminist, pedagogies offer useful templates for engaging students in the production of knowledge that value diverse experiences, identities and reading positions. I have tried to caution, however, of the pitfalls implicit in the postmodern and feminist turn to difference.

Teachers need to acknowledge and take seriously students' different readings of and pleasures derived from popular culture, while guarding against potential slippage into a vacuous celebration of individual 'taste', 'pleasure' or 'personal response'. As I have argued, this is not an easy task since so much of progressive and feminist pedagogies valorize the politics of personal voice and difference. However, the postmodern turn to difference, heteroglossia and heterogeneity does not mean that 'anything goes' (Luke, 1992). What it does mean is that a commitment to social justice and equity principles should guide the media educator's work in enabling students to come to their own realizations that, say, homophobic, racist or sexist texts or readings, quite simply oppress and subordinate others. In pedagogical terms, this may mean a renewed emphasis on theory rather than over-reliance on the testimony of experience and 'personal response'. To provide students with theoretically grounded frameworks with which to analyze and politicize cultural and textual constructs of meaning, gives students the discourse analytic tools with which to interrogate how socio-culturally and historically contingent texts, social sites and practices of consumption and production, construct and hierarchize identity differences, shape patterns of exclusion and marginalization, situate subjectivities, interpretations and meaning, and legitimate and destabilize power/knowledge regimes. In short, the discourse analytic skills taught through media and cultural studies can enable students to politicize their own culturally and historically situated experiences and identities, and question wider issues concerning the politics of knowledge embedded in the narratives of theory, conceptual categories, disciplinary regimes of truth, and what pass as empirical givens such as 'society', 'individual', 'race', 'sexuality', 'experience', 'voice', 'History', and so on.

In my estimation, feminist and otherwise progressive educators need to disengage from their anxieties about authority and power. Feminist educators particularly need to find ways to interrogate the assumptions and consequences of our critical practices, so that we might begin to let go of our feminized attachments to a learned powerlessness and scepticism of authority (cf. Gallop, Hirsch and Miller, 1990). In closing, I would argue that, first, we do need to take both intellectual and institutional authority – or at least, make explicit that we already embody and exercise authority even in its camouflaged veneer of pastoral nurturance. Second, we do need to acknowledge and theorize the power we variously exercise in order to come clean on the ethical and political dimensions of feminist work in the academy, and in order to stake public claim on the knowledge domains and institutional practices we want to transform according to feminist normative visions of 'the good' and socially just. And, doubling back on what I have argued here, such critical interrogations and self-reflexive practices should focus not only on cultural texts, social identities, meaning and interpretations, but need to be turned on our own knowledge-producing labour: the academic journal and textbook readings we assign, the media and cultural texts we select for analysis, the analytic frameworks we offer, the authority over knowledge and students we enact or mask, and the pedagogical choices we make.

Note

Parts of this chapter were previously published as Luke, C. (1994) Feminist pedagogy and critical media literacy, *Journal of Communication Inquiry*, **18** (2), 30–47.

References

ALCOFF, L. (1988) Cultural feminism versus post-structuralism: The identity crisis in feminist theory, *Signs*, **13** (3), 405–36.

ALCOFF, L. and POTTER, E. (Eds) (1993) *Feminist Epistemologies*, New York: Routledge.

ALVARADO, M. and BOYD-BARRETT, O. (Eds) (1992) *Media Education: An Introduction*, London: British Film Institute and the Open University Press.

BARTKY, S. L. (1996) Pedagogies of shame, in LUKE, C. (Ed.) *Feminisms and Pedagogies of Everyday Life*, Albany, NY: State University of New York Press.

BAUDRILLARD, J. (1983) Simulations, *Semiotext(e)*, 1–13, 23–49.

BELENKY, M., CLINCHY, B., GOLDBERGER, N. and TARRULE, J. (1986) *Women's Ways of Knowing*, New York: Basic Books.

BONDI, L. (1993) Locating identity politics, in KEITH, M. and PILE, S. (Eds) *Place and the Politics of Identity*, New York: Routledge, 84–101.

BOURDIEU, P. (1984) *Distinction: A Social Critique of the Judgement of Taste*, New York: Routledge & Kegan Paul.

BROWN, M. E. (Ed.) (1990) *Television and Women's Culture: The Politics of the Popular*, Newbury Park, CA: Sage.

BROWN, W. (1991) Feminist hesitations, postmodern exposures, *differences*, **5** (1), 63–84.

BUCKINGHAM, D. (1993a) *Children Talking Television: The Making of Television Literacy*, London: Falmer Press.

BUCKINGHAM, D. (1993b) Going critical: The limits of media literacy, *The Australian Journal of Education*, **37**, 142–52.

BUCKINGHAM, D. and SEFTON-GREEN, J. (1994) *Cultural Studies Goes to School, Reading and Teaching Popular Media*, London: Falmer Press.

BUNCH, C. and POLLACK, S. (Eds) (1983) *Learning our Ways: Essays in Feminist Education*, New York: Crossing Press.

CULLEY, M. and PORTUGUES, C. (Eds) (1986) *Gendered Subjects: The Dynamics of Feminist Teaching*, New York: Routledge.

DE LAURETIS, T. (1987) *Technologies of Gender*, Bloomington, IN: Indiana University Press.

ELLSWORTH, E. (1988) Illicit pleasures: Feminist spectators and personal best, in ROMAN, L. G., CHRISTIAN-SMITH, L. K. and ELLSWORTH, E. (Eds) *Becoming Feminine: The Politics of Popular Culture*, Basingstoke, UK: Falmer Press, 102–22.

ERENS, P. (Ed.) (1990) *Issues in Feminist Film Criticism*, Bloomington, IN: Indiana University Press.

FERGUSON, K. (1993) *The Man Question: Visions of Subjectivity in Feminist Theory*, Berkeley, CA: University of California Press.

FLAX, J. (1990) *Thinking Fragments: Psychoanalysis, Feminism, and Postmodernism in the Contemporary West*, Berkeley, CA: University of California Press.

FRANKLIN, S., LURY, C. and STACEY, J. (Eds) (1991) *Off-centre: Feminism and Cultural Studies*, London: Harper Collins Academic.

FRASER, N. (1989) *Unruly Practices: Power, Discourse and Gender in Contemporary Social Theory*, Cambridge: Polity.

FRASER, N. and NICHOLSON, L. (1990) *Social Criticism Without Philosophy: An Encounter Between Feminism and Postmodernism*, in NICHOLSON, L. (Ed.) *Feminism/Postmodernism*, New York: Routledge, 19–38.

FUSS, D. (1989) *Essentially Speaking*, New York: Routledge.

GABRIEL, S. L. and SMITHSON, I. (Eds) (1990) *Gender in the Classroom: Power and Pedagogy*, Urbana/Chicago, IL: University of Illinois Press.

GALLOP, J. (1994) The teacher's breasts, in MATTHEWS, J. J. (Ed.) *Jane Gallop Seminar Papers*, Humanities Research Centre Monograph Series No. 7, Canberra, ACT: The Australian National University, 1–12.

GALLOP, J. (Ed.) (1995) *Pedagogy: The Questions of Impersonation*, Bloomington, IA: Indiana University Press.

GALLOP, J., HIRSCH, M. and MILLER, N. K. (1990) Criticizing feminist criticism, in HIRSCH, M. and FOX KELLER, E. (Eds) *Conflicts in Feminism*, New York: Routledge, 349–69.

GAMMAN, L. and MARSHMENT, M. (1989) *The Female Gaze: Women as Viewers of Popular Culture*, Seattle, WA: The Real Comet Press.

GATENS, M. (1994) Responding to Gallop: Feminist pedagogy and the 'family romance', in MATTHEWS, J. J. (Ed.) *Jane Gallop Seminar Papers*, Humanities Research Centre Monograph Series No. 7, Canberra, ACT: The Australian National University, 13–16.

GILLESPIE, M. (1995) *Television, Ethnicity and Cultural Change*, New York: Routledge.

GORE, J. (1993) *The Struggle for Pedagogies: Critical and Feminist Discourses as Regimes of Truth*, New York: Routledge.

GRAY, A. (1992) *Video Playtime: The Gendering of a Leisure Technology*, London/New York: Routledge.

GROSSBERG, L. (1984) I'd rather feel bad than not feel anything at all: Rock and roll, pleasure and power, *Enclitic*, **8**, 95–111.

HARAWAY, D. (1988) Situated knowledges: The science question in feminism and the privilege of partial perspective, *Feminist Studies*, **14**, 575–99.

HART, A. (1991) *Understanding Media*, New York: Routledge.

HARVEY, D. (1989) *The Condition of Postmodernity*, Oxford, UK: Blackwell.

HARVEY, D. (1993a) Class relations, social justice and the politics of difference, in KEITH, M. and PILE, S. (Eds) *Place and the Politics of Identity*, New York: Routledge, 41–66.

HARVEY, D. (1993b) From space to place and back again: Reflections on the condition of postmodernity, in BIRD, J., CURTIS, B., PUTNAM, T., ROBERTSON, G. and TICKNER, L. (Eds) *Mapping the Futures: Local Cultures, Global Change*, London/New York: Routledge, 3–29.

HOOKS, B. (1990) *Yearning: Race, Gender and Cultural Politics*, Boston, MA: South End Press.

HORKHEIMER, M. and ADORNO, T. (1972) *Dialectic of Enlightenment* (J. CUMMING, Trans.) New York: Herder & Herder.

JONES, K. (1991) The trouble with authority, *differences*, **5** (1), 104–27.

Journal of Communication Inquiry (1994) Special issue: 'Critical Media Pedagogy' (L. McLAUGHLIN, Ed.) **18** (2).

KAPLAN, C. (1986) *Sea Changes: Culture and Feminism*, London: Verso.

KELLNER, D. (1995) *Media Culture*, New York: Routledge.

KIRBY, V. (1994) Response to Jane Gallop's 'The Teacher's Breasts': Bad form, in MATTHEWS, J. J. (Ed.) *Jane Gallop Seminar Papers*, Humanities Research Centre Monograph Series No. 7, Canberra, ACT: The Australian National University, 17–22.

KRAMARAE, C. (Ed.) (1988) *Technology and Women's Voices*, New York: Routledge & Kegan Paul.

KRAMARAE, C. (1995) A backstage critique of virtual reality, in JONES, S. (Ed.) *Cybersociety: Computer-mediated Communication and Community*, Thousand Oaks, CA: Sage, 36–56.

LASH, S. (1990) *Sociology of Postmodernism*, New York: Routledge.

LASH, S. and URRY, J. (1987) *The End of Organized Capitalism*, Oxford, UK: Polity.

LATHER, P. (1991) *Getting Smart: Feminist Research and Pedagogy with/in the Postmodern*, New York: Routledge.

LEWIS, M. (1993) *Without a Word: Teaching Beyond Women's Silence*, New York: Routledge.

LOVE, N. S. (1991) Politics and voice(s): An empowerment/knowledge regime, *differences*, **5** (1), 85–103.

LUKE, C. (1992) The politicised 'I' and depoliticised 'we': The politics of theory in postmodern feminisms, *Social Semiotics*, **2** (2), 1–20.

LUKE, C. (1993) Television curriculum and popular literacy: Feminine identity politics and family discourse, in GREEN, B. (Ed.) *The Insistence of the Letter: Literacy Studies and Curriculum Theorizing*, London: Falmer Press, 175–94.

LUKE, C. (1994) Feminist pedagogy and critical media literacy, *Journal of Communication Inquiry*, **18** (2), 30–47.

LUKE, C. (1996) Feminist pedagogy theory: Reflections on power and authority, *Educational Theory*, **46** (3), 283–302.

LUKE, C. and GORE, J. (Eds) (1992) *Feminisms and Critical Pedagogy*, New York: Routledge.

LUSTED, D. (1991) *The Media Studies Book*, New York: Routledge.

McROBBIE, A. (1994) *Postmodernism and Popular Culture*, New York/London: Routledge.

MAHER, F. (1987) Toward a richer theory of feminist pedagogy: A comparison of 'liberation' and 'gender' models for teaching and learning, *Journal of Education*, **169**, 91–100.

MAHONEY, P. (1988) Oppressive pedagogy: The importance of process in women's studies, *Women's Studies International Forum*, **11**, 103–8.

MARTIN, J. R. (1994) Methodological essentialism: False difference, and other dangerous traps, *Signs*, **19** (3), 630–57.

MASSEY, D. (1993) Politics and space/time, in KEITH, M. and PILE, S. (Eds) *Place and the Politics of Identity*, New York: Routledge, 141–61.

MIDDLETON, S. (1993) *Educating Feminists*, New York: Teachers College Press.

MODLESKI, T. (1991) *Feminism without Women: Culture and Criticism in a 'Postfeminist Age'*, New York: Routledge.

MORRIS, M. (1988) *The Pirate's Fiancee: Feminism, Reading, Postmodernism*, London: Verso.

PAGANO, J. (1990) *Exiles and Communities: Teaching in the Patriarchal Wilderness*, Albany, NY: State University of New York Press.

PRESS, A. (1991) *Women Watching Television: Gender, Class and Generation in the American Television Experience*, Philadelphia, PA: University of Pennsylvania Press.

ROSE, G. (1993) *Feminism and Geography*, Cambridge, UK: Polity.

SANDOVAL, C. (1995) New sciences: Cyborg feminism and the methodology of the oppressed, in GRAY, C. H. (Ed.) *The Cyborg Handbook*, New York: Routledge, 407–22.

SHOR, N. (1989) The essentialism which is not one: Coming to grips with Irigaray, *differences*, **1** (2), 38–58.

SHURMER-SMITH, P. and HANNAM, K. (1994) *Worlds of Desire, Realms of Power: A Cultural Geography*, New York/London: Edward Arnold.

SPAIN, D. (1992) *Gendered Spaces*, Chapel Hill, NC: The University of North Carolina Press.

SPENDER, D. (1995) *Nattering on the Net: Women, Power and Cyberspace*, Sydney, New South Wales: Spinifex Press.

SPIGEL, L. (1992) *Make Room for TV: Television and the Family Ideal in Postwar America*, Chicago, IL: University of Chicago Press.

SPIGEL, L. and MANN, E. (Eds) (1992) *Private Screenings: Television and the Female Consumer*, Minneapolis, MN: University of Minnesota Press.

STONE, L. (Ed.) (1994) *The Education Feminism Reader*, New York: Routledge.

THOMPSON, S. (1994) Suburbs of opportunity: The power of home for migrant women, in GIBSON, K. and WATSON, S. (Eds) *Metropolis Now: Planning and the Urban in Contemporary Australia*, Sydney, New South Wales: Allen & Unwin, 33–45.

WAJCMAN, J. (1994) Technological a/genders: Technology, culture and class, in GREEN, L. and GUINERY, R. (Eds) *Framing Technology*, Sydney, New South Wales: Allen & Unwin, 3–14.

WALKER, A. (1984) *In Search of our Mothers' Gardens: Womanist Prose*, New York: Harcourt Brace Jovanovitch.

WALTERS, S. D. (1992) *Lives Together, Worlds Apart: Mothers and Daughters in Popular Culture*, Berkeley, CA: University of California Press.

WEILER, K. (1988) *Women Teaching for Change: Gender, Class and Power*, South Hadley, MA: Bergin & Garvey.

YEATMAN, A. (1994) *Postmodern Revisionings of the Political*, New York: Routledge.

YOUNG, I. M. (1990) *Justice and the Politics of Difference*, Princeton, NJ: Princeton University Press.

Chapter 3

Butt Jokes and Mean-teacher Parodies: Video Production in the Elementary Classroom

Donna J. Grace and Joseph Tobin

It is a sunny October morning in Pearl City, Hawaii. The third-graders at Waiau Elementary School are seated on the floor, ready to watch the videos they have made. As the room is darkened and the monitor lights up, the students' eyes widen and grins appear. The children giggle, squirm and nudge one another as they recognize faces on the screen.

The first video, *The Dog Who Knew How to Play Tricks*, is about a dog and a cat who enter a talent show. Enjoying seeing their peers pretend to be animals, the children chuckle at the silly antics performed before the camera. Next, there is *The Planet Knick-Knack*, a musical about a dog named Beethoven, who runs away from home and gets lost. The video closes with the cast singing the familiar childhood song 'This Old Man'. The audience spontaneously joins in a chorus of slightly off-key voices. The third piece is called *Chase Master Monster*. The video opens with three boys playing the parts of little monsters who live on the very hot sun. They wake up one morning, put on their air-conditioned shoes, and begin playing the game 'Chase master monster'. The narrator then informs the viewers that the little monsters fall on their butts and burn them on the hot sun. On screen, the actors are running around in imaginary agony, swatting at their buttocks and shouting, 'Ooh! Ouch! Ooh! Ouch!' 'My buns are burning!' 'My buns are burning!' They keep running until they find some ice, which they rub on their burning rear ends. In the next shot, their eyes roll upward and they sigh with deep relief. Their expressions are those of pure bliss.

The class finds this scene hilarious. Performers and audience are fused in a surge of camaraderie, a spirit of oneness joined by laughter. The adults in the room exchange uneasy smiles. This festive moment is formed in relation to us, the authority figures, and fuelled by the knowledge that classroom norms have been transgressed. The moment passes, and the next video begins. The children are quiet, focused on the new images appearing before them. The adults, however, are left with lingering doubts and questions. The equilibrium of the classroom has been unsettled. Taken for granted boundaries have blurred before our eyes.

Video production in the Waiau classrooms provided an opportunity for students to incorporate their own interests, experiences and desires into schoolwork. A space was located where they could explore the limits of speech, behaviour and humour allowed in the classroom. In our three years of doing video work with children at Waiau, we found many examples of students pushing the boundaries and transgressing the norms of everyday life in school. Alongside the many entirely acceptable and nonproblematic scripts the children wrote, a number of more questionable scenes and storylines emerged. These pieces contained words, actions and situations that challenged classroom norms and decorum. For the children, these moments of curricular slippage and excess provided the opportunity to produce their own pleasures, on their own terms, in the classroom. Yet these same moments posed questions and gave rise to tensions for the teachers.

That children are frequently fascinated with things that adults consider to be rude, uncouth or gross comes as no surprise. Alison Lurie (1990) traces the subversive nature of many popular children's stories, rhymes and verses from the Grimm brothers on through the present day, and Tom Newkirk (1992) writes of children's predisposition for poop jokes, farts and insect mutilation. Peter McLaren (1986) and Paul Willis (1981), among others, have documented ways students have found to subvert school control and authority. However, these behaviours usually occur outside of the school agenda. Significantly, the transgressions that emerged in the Waiau video project were organized and authorized *within* the curriculum rather than apart from it.

This chapter explores the issues and tensions that emerged during a three-year project in which the informal, unofficial and everyday interests of children were brought into the curriculum through the medium of video production. Drawing on Mikhail Bakhtin's writings on the carnivalesque (1968) and Roland Barthes (1975) concepts of *plaisir* and *jouissance*, we argue that video production opens up a space where students can play with the boundaries of language and ideology and enjoy transgressive collective pleasures. This boundary-crossing and pleasure-getting by the children in the midst of the curriculum pushes teachers to think about their authority in new ways.

The Study

A great deal is known about children as readers and writers in classrooms. Little, in contrast, is known about children as producers of video texts. Video production is a new form of literacy that integrates art, language skills, problem solving, technical proficiency and performance. Although there are manuals available on the technical skills involved, there has yet to be a critical, theoretically informed study of video production with young students. The small body of work that examines the process of production comes largely out of the United Kingdom and has involved older students (Buckingham, 1990; Buckingham and Sefton-Green, 1994; Buckingham, Grahame and Sefton-Green, 1995). With the use of video technology rapidly increasing in school systems worldwide, research is needed that can help us understand what happens to students and teachers when cameras are put in students' hands.

In light of these facts, we developed a video curriculum project with a group of teachers at an elementary school in Hawaii. In meetings with the teachers, it was decided to begin integrating video production into the curriculum, building upon the children's interests in and prior knowledge of television and movies. This was viewed as an unique opportunity to enhance the elementary language and literacy curriculum while increasing our understanding of children as communicators and meaning makers.

The video curriculum was tested in two third-grade classes during the spring of 1992. It was then introduced to grades 1–6 in the fall and continued for the next two school years. In all, eight classes of approximately 25 children actively participated in the video curriculum. This chapter focuses on work that emerged in grades 1–3.

Our role throughout the project was that of participant–observers, with the emphasis shifting over time from the former to the latter. During the pilot study and the first phase of video production, we were actively involved in developing and teaching the curriculum to both the teachers and the students. As the teachers and children grew more comfortable and confident with the process, our role turned more to that of observers.

Our research method is an ethnographically informed case study of children as videographers. We do not view children as a distinct cultural group separate from adults, but as an interpretive community, a subgroup within the larger culture, with shared interests, experiences and understandings, reflecting their age, generation and situation as students. As Anne Dyson (1993) writes, school children operate in a social world of peers which is framed by a sense of being in this together (1993:3). Their responses to school authority often include attempts to claim a space for themselves in the classroom and to assert their collective identity as children. Bringing the unofficial into the official is one way of establishing territory of their own and forming networks of peer relationships in the process.

Child-centred Pedagogy

During the pilot phase of the student video production project, we spent two to three days a week working with the children in Waiau classrooms on scripting, storyboarding, using video equipment and producing. The children in each classroom were then placed in groups and asked to retell, script, storyboard and tape a familiar story. The resulting productions included such favorites as *Chicken Licken*, *Snow White*, *Jack and the Beanstalk*, *Henny Penny*, and *The Princess and the Pea*. From an adult standpoint, these productions tended to lack creativity. However, they functioned as good entry points into video production. The retellings seemed to offer the children some safety, security and predictability while they were working in this new medium with unfamiliar technology. In the second phase of the project, we decided to give the children free choice in content and genre, putting many of our teacherly beliefs about classroom control and the curriculum to the test.

Progressive educators speak of giving children choice, building on their interests, background knowledge and experiences, and making learning fun. These pedagogical assumptions underlie student-centred, inquiry-based, whole-language and constructivist approaches to curriculum and instruction. Most often, when teachers tell students 'You can write on anything you want to', the students interpret this invitation to mean 'anything you want to that I, a teacher and an adult, will consider appropriate for a school assignment.' Yet occasionally, moments arise in the classroom when students do work that ignores, transgresses or exceeds teacherly, adult notions of appropriateness. Such moments may occur in a writing assignment, a literature circle, an art project or a science experiment. At Waiau we learned that there is something about video production that produces an outpouring of transgressive, excessive moments which push us to question how comfortable we are when the curriculum becomes child-centred.

Giving Children Choice

Our intent was to give the students considerable latitude in the content of their videos. The teachers, however, had a hard time relinquishing their right and inclination to guide, shape and influence these choices. In order to see what would happen if students' unrestrained choices were authorized in the classroom, we asked the teachers to give the children as much leeway as they felt they could.

As video production got underway, it became apparent that the scripts created by the children were strongly influenced by popular culture. They included X-Men, ninjas, and characters from the television shows *Saved by the Bell, The Simpsons, Full House* and *Ghostwriter*, and from such movies as *Cop and a Half, Airborne* and *Jurassic Park*. Themes and characters were also occasionally drawn from more controversial television programmes and movies including *Beavis and Butthead, Studs, Child's Play* and *Friday the 13th*. Tensions arose. Although the children were reading, writing, storyboarding, editing and gaining technical proficiency in their video work, notions of normalcy in school were being challenged. As popular culture entered the classrooms, the unofficial interests of the children shifted from the periphery of classroom life to centre stage.

Fear of the Interests and Knowledge of Children

Although child-centred curricula emphasize connecting the world of school to the lives of the children, many of their everyday pleasures and interests lie

LIBRARY , UNIVERSITY COLLEGE CHESTER

untouched and untapped in the classroom. Movies, television, videos, popular magazines, fiction and video games contribute to the shaping of student experiences and subjectivities. However, these interests must typically be left on the doorstep when arriving at school each day.

As Buckingham (1990; Buckingham and Sefton-Green, 1994) points out, there are many reasons for the failure to incorporate the popular culture of children into the curriculum. Many educators, of all moral and political persuasions, are concerned with the negative effects of the media on children. Where the Right faults the media for undermining the morals and values of the dominant society, the Left blames the media for perpetuating them. Yet in both cases, children are seen as passive and powerless mini-consumers, duped by the culture industry. The children's video work in our project provided evidence to the contrary. We found that they played with the meanings and messages of the media, rather than absorbing them uncritically.

A second reason for the exclusion of popular culture from the curriculum is the threat to teacher supremacy. Teachers like to feel that they are standing on secure ground when it comes to curriculum. Students often know more than their teachers do about popular television shows, movies and video games. In this domain, the children are the experts.

A third reason relates to the fear of erasure of boundaries. When popular culture is brought into the curriculum, lines are crossed between the high and the low, the official and the unofficial, the authoritative discourses of the school and the internally persuasive discourses of the children. The canon is compromised.

In the face of these concerns, we nevertheless insist that popular culture should be brought into the primary school curriculum. Because school privileges the written word, the knowledge children bring to school about plots, characters, genre is often underestimated in the classroom. Including children's knowledge of popular culture in the curriculum provides another avenue for children to enter school literacy, especially for those who have had limited experiences with reading in the home. We also support teaching about movies and television in the primary grades because the role of pleasure has long been overlooked and neglected in schooling. Most children find great pleasures in popular culture. Making a place for such pleasures in the classroom can enrich the school lives of children.

We are aware, however, that by bringing popular culture into the official curriculum, there is the danger that adults will colonize one of the last outposts of children's culture. Bringing popular culture into the school curriculum may serve to rationalize and regulate it. Once transported into the domain of the classroom, these outside interests are in jeopardy of being purified, homogenized and reconstituted as curriculum or motivational strategies. When popular culture is coopted by the teacher, aspects of pleasure associated with it may be destroyed. Our goal, therefore, should be to validate the popular cultural interests of children without appropriating them. Student video production provides an arena for this to occur.

Popular Culture and Video Production

The children's videos produced in our study were greatly influenced by the media and popular culture. But the videos do far more than mimic and imitate. Rather than simply replicate remembered plots and themes, children play with aspects of the familiar and conjoin them in imaginative and pleasing ways. In the children's videos, the world of popular culture is interwoven with the world of school. In *Zip and the Ninja Turtles*, for instance, a group of first-graders turned a favourite classroom book about a lost dog into a tale involving a runaway worm who is eventually rescued by three Ninja Turtles. Another group of children from the same class created a story entitled *The Nine Astronauts and the Revenge of the Slimy Earthlings*. This tale involves a shootout with drool-covered, earthling-eating aliens and ends with the cast singing a song they had learned in school about the planets. A third-grade group did a take-off on the *Wizard of Oz* called *Dorothy Goes to Candyland*, in which Dorothy visits a land where candy grows abundantly on trees. There she is threatened by a slime-breathing, rock-spewing blob that she eventually destroys with a magic candy gun. These are but a few examples of how children imaginatively combined their interests in movies and television with classroom literacy and knowledge.

These videos were not unlike the stories children might write when given free choice of content in a language arts assignment. However, the medium of video, along with the dynamics of the collaborative group process, worked to enhance children's sense of freedom to explore and transgress. The extra-linguistic elements of gesture, facial expression, sound effects and performativity carried the written words into a new and sometimes forbidden realm. As the students incorporated their own interests and pleasures into the videos, they pushed at the borders of propriety, reminding us of the fragility of classroom equilibrium.

Clearly, the children's sense of audience influenced the type of videos they produced. When the intended viewers included parents, relatives, or other community members, their videos took on quite different forms. This was demonstrated in videos the students created for the school's Open House, the sixth grade graduation and for competition in a video festival, all of which were very well received. However, when produced with their peers as the anticipated audience, the content noticeably strayed from adult-pleasing fare. Fuelled by the desire to surprise, amuse and entertain, the content of some of these videos was of questionable taste, including depictions of drool, burps, blood, dripping mucus, butt jokes, aggression, violence and occasional severed body parts. These scenes were enormously appealing to the children and the source of a good deal of transgressive excitement. What was most popular with the children tended to be unpopular with the teachers.

Video Production and the Carnivalesque

In analyzing the children's videos, it became apparent that they did not fit neatly into traditional categories. They hovered in a sort of literary homelessness in the classroom. Genres were collapsed and borders erased. Their videos, to use Bakhtin's term, were carnivalesque. In *Rabelais and His World* (1968), Bakhtin described the world of the carnival as one of laughter, bodily pleasures, hierarchical inversions and bad taste. Bakhtin categorized the manifestations of carnival humour into three forms: ritual spectacles (feasts, pageants and marketplace festivals), comic verbal compositions (oral and written parodies), and billingsgate (curses, oaths, slang, profanity). The laughter provoked by such humour was bawdy, crude and irreverent. Rank and privilege were temporarily overturned. The people portrayed kings as fools and peasants as royalty. It was the official world as seen from below.

Over time, the carnival of the Middle Ages was gradually suppressed. It became licensed, regulated and tamed. Its remnants survive today in Mardi Gras, the Carnival of Brazil, and Germany's *Fasching*. Elements of the ancient carnivals, Bakhtin reminds us, live on in our everyday life as well. These carnivalesque moments foreground freedom, pleasure and desire. They unsettle the existing order of things. They use satire and laughter to imagine how things might be otherwise. Mary Russo (1986) writes that the 'masks and voices of carnival resist, exaggerate and destabilize the distinctions and boundaries that mark and maintain high culture and organized society . . . They suggest a counterproduction of culture, knowledge, and pleasure' (1986:218).

Like the carnivals, fairs and marketplaces Bakhtin wrote about, the classroom may be viewed as a site of conflicting agendas and desires where the high (teachers and the curriculum) and the low (children and their interests and desires) meet. Carnival offered peasants opportunities to symbolically invert the usual hierarchies and imagine different roles and relationships. Video production at Waiau offered many such opportunities. With the click of a button, students could become rock stars, royalty or superheroes. Tiny children might portray giants or all-powerful rulers. The academically marginalized had the opportunity to choose roles as scholars, teachers or wizards. Serious children could play parts in comedies and parodies, and the quiet and shy could blossom under the guise of fantasy. Through the medium of video, the students were able momentarily to acquire the power of the represented.

The children's video productions often featured the parodic, the fantastic and horrific, the grotesque and the forbidden. These scenarios enabled the children to locate a space where collective pleasures were produced. As with carnival, however, there were also darker sides to the merriment. Without this darker side, carnival would lose much of its potency and seductive power. In our project, the darker side emerged when students discussed making videos involving cruelty and hurtful stereotypes. Topics in this category included portrayals of animal cruelty, racial caricatures, a stuttering singer and a blind man who stumbles into various objects around him. In some cases, the groups themselves dismissed these ideas, and in others the teachers exercised their veto.

Laughter and Parody

For Bakhtin (1981), parody, the laughing word, is a corrective of reality. Embodying dual intentions, it contains both the meanings of the author and the refracted meanings of the parodied text or situation (1981:324). Parody can bolster cultural barriers as well as break them down. In some situations, parody functions to release tension, thereby preserving the status quo. In others, it offers opportunities for opposition tempered by humour. Regardless of the outcome, parody provides a space for critique and change. It may pose questions, challenge assumptions and offer new possibilities.

Our students well appreciated the pleasures derived from humour and parody. In the wink of an eye, the serious became comical in their videos. The driving force in the children's scriptwriting was the desire to make the audience laugh. Several of the student groups incorporated parody in their videos. They produced ridiculing and humorous versions of television shows, movies, books, classrooms and field trips. Two videos parodied marriage (*The Three Stooges Get Married* and *The Rock and Roll Marriage*). A second grade group, which began quite seriously to script their research report on the Gila monster, wound up with the lizard eating the reporter. The third-grade production of *The Magic School Bus Visits Plant Quarantine* parodies a class field trip. The video begins with students sitting in a row, frowning and slumped over, with their heads in their hands. In a dreary, singsong monotone, they say in unison that school is boring and they want to go on a field trip. Miss Frizzle, played by a boy wearing an outlandish wig, agrees. They go to Plant Quarantine, where animals are held on their arrival in Hawaii. There, scenes such as a student getting his hand sliced off by a man-eating piranha alternate with very scholarly reports on toucans, flowers and fire ants. In other videos, laughter is produced through humorous depictions of tyrannical teachers, ridiculous rules and rebellious students.

The very ambiguity of parody is the source of the power and pleasure associated with it. Initially, the teachers wondered how such parodies should be taken. However, rather than view these scenes as threatening or subversive, the teachers eventually came to perceive them in a generally pro-social light. They were able to overcome their initial fears and join in the pleasures of the carnivalesque. The teachers eventually realized that the children were not attacking them or their school routines and practices – these teachers did not have deadly boring classes, nor had they sent children to sit in the corner; it was the stereotype, the comic-book representation of school that was the object of ridicule.[1]

The Fantastic and Horrific

Both horror and fantasy are linked to transgressive feelings of pleasure and desire. The student's videos demonstrated their fascination with these genres. They overwhelmingly wanted to make videos that were scary, funny or both. Their video plots were full of monsters, ghosts, aliens, beasts, werewolves and giant scorpions who frightened, threatened and eventually were conquered by the protagonists. Inevitably, these conquests provided an opportunity for the usually forbidden play-fighting and produced a great deal of transgressive excitement for the children. In portraying such awesome, fear-inspiring creatures and characters, the students experienced power, agency and control. Neither size nor gender determined who would play these roles. One of the smallest children in a first-grade class portrayed Magnito, a powerful villain and enemy of the X-Men, and girls frequently chose to play fierce ninjas, creatures from outer space, or mummies and vampires awakened from the dead. Although the hero and monster roles are traditionally figured as masculine (strong, brave, tough, fearless) in the movies and television programmes the children see, this was not necessarily the case in their own productions. Traditional masculinity and femininity were frequently muted and blurred in their video stories.

The horrific beings in these scripts usually wound up being more humorous than terrifying, more like the gay monsters of the Rabelaisian world and less like the terrifying creatures typical in films of this genre. They tended to be inserted into very childlike plots and in a context of play, providing the children the opportunity to explore their fears and fantasies in the safety of the group, surrounded by laughter.

The Grotesque Body

A central concern of carnival is the body. According to Bakhtin (1968), the grotesque carnival body represents a lowering of all that is that is high, privileged, sacred or ideal. In this oppositional form, the body serves as a site of resistance to regulation, social control and definitions of normalcy. The grotesque body is ugly and monstrous in comparison to the classical body, as represented in Renaissance statuary. Where the classical body is pure, clean, finished, beautifully formed and with no evident openings or orifices, the sensual, earthy, grotesque body is protuberant, excessive, impure, unfinished. It emphasizes the parts of the body that open up to the world: flared nostrils, gaping mouth, the anus, and what Bakhtin termed the lower bodily strata (belly, legs, feet, buttocks, genitals). The grotesque body is overflowing and transgresses its own limits. Bakhtin (1968:24) writes that these images, over time, have lost their positive dimension. However, in the Renaissance, they represented becoming and growth, a phenomenon in transformation, an unfinished metamorphosis. In this sense, the grotesque body has much in common with childhood. Not yet fully formed nor matured, children typically do not share the repulsion adults feel with sweat, runny noses, dirty bodies or germ-spewing sneezes and coughs. Rather, they are full of interest and curiosity about their bodily orifices and functions, as their videos make clear.

Images of the grotesque body were prominent in the students videos. Their works provided many examples of the gaping, oversized, overflowing body. Some scripts also contained suggestions of cannibalism, or the swallowing up of bodies by other bodies. Stam (1989) refers to this as the ultimate act in dissolving the boundaries between self and other (1989:126). In a first-grade production of *Chicken Licken Goes to Jupiter*, for example, the story ends with Chicken Licken getting eaten up by a mean space creature before she is able to complete her journey to reach the king. In *The Nine Astronauts and the Revenge of the Slimy Earthlings*, another group of first-graders created a script involving a confrontation between several astronauts and the aliens they encounter on the planet Saturn. Upon sight of the astronauts, the aliens begin rubbing their tummies, licking their lips and trying to capture the astronauts to feed to their babies. In enacting this script, the aliens worked up a healthy supply of saliva, which oozed profusely from their chomping, hungry mouths. Like all other examples of the grotesque body, such scenes produced the intended surprise, delight and carnivalesque laughter in their viewing peers.

The Forbidden

Scatological, parodic and grotesque elements in children's videos have the power to offend adult sensibilities, but they can be dismissed as typical amusements of childhood. We shake our heads and convey our disapproval but assume that with increased maturity such interests will fade. Fighting, aggression and suggestions of violence in children are more disturbing to adults. For example, in many homes and schools, play-fighting is forbidden, apparently on grounds of safety. Yet more children are injured by falling off playground equipment or participating in sports than in play-fighting. The fact that monkey bars, jungle gyms and ballgames are rarely banned suggests that something other than safety underlies adults' concerns about play-fighting. Aggressive behaviour in children taps into much deeper fears about crime, violence and moral decline in society as a whole. Something about children's delight in mock violence threatens adult authority and disrupts culturally constructed notions about childhood innocence. Thus, we impose rules and prohibitions and attempt to socialize children away from such behaviours.

Nancy King (1992) writes that in education the goal has been to create environments and situations in which children will produce only good play, consisting of socially approved behaviours such as rule-following, cooperation, turn-taking, inclusion, socially approved uses of imagination and conversation, and good sportsmanship. In other words, good play has little in common with the everyday, nonrestricted play of children. As any parent or teacher of young children knows, toy guns may be banned, but fingers can be used as pretend gun barrels; play-fighting may be prohibited, but rough and tumble activities rarely disappear.

A predisposition to play-fighting was clearly evident in the children's video stories. Group after group incorporated such scenes, usually involving some form of martial arts. These usually forbidden behaviours produced high levels of transgressive excitement in both the performers and their child audience. In a third-grade production of *The Four Ninjas* these scenes turned out to be the story's driving force. This tale began with fighting practice for the ninjas (three boys and one girl). Soon they discover that their father has mysteriously died, and their mother has been kidnapped. Preparing to avenge their father's death and rescue their mother, they go back to fighting practice. The next day, the enemy ninjas, played by two girls, invade the classroom, and the big battle begins. It goes on until the evil ninjas are eventually conquered. The four victorious ninjas end the night with a celebration at Pizza Hut.

In this video, as well as in others with similar themes, the fighting scenes were greatly elaborated. In each of these scenes, good triumphed over evil, and there was no intent to harm. Enacted in a spirit of play, these scenes have a comic character and begin and end with laughter. Bakhtin (1968) writes that in the carnivalesque, ruthless slaughter and death are transformed into a merry banquet, and bloodshed, dismemberment, burning, death, beatings, blows curses and abuses – all these elements are steeped in merry time (1968:211). In neither classroom nor carnival are such scenes meant to represent or transfer to the real. That children find pleasure in these mock battles does not mean that they enjoy violence in real life. As with the grotesque body, they find power, pleasure and opportunities for resistance in portraying these strong, bold and courageous characters.

In acting out hand-to-hand combat, the children were also able to engage in a physical closeness with one another that they are otherwise denied. The body-to-body contact characteristic of the carnivalesque crowd appeared to be a source of pleasure for the children in their video fighting scenes, allowing for bodily contact typically repressed by social codes in school. Once past the preschool hand-holding stage, students have few opportunities for touch. Yet such sensations are still needed, desired and enjoyed by them. Play-fighting provides a space for this while producing a very intense form of transgressive pleasure.

Another area of the forbidden that surfaced in the video projects was the notion of animal cruelty. This occurred as a third-grade group of two boys and two girls were trying to decide on a topic for their script. Portraying a mad scientist and doing crazy experiments had been suggested, so the group members were flipping through science books looking for ideas. One of the boys asked if they could do some animal cruelty, adding '... or is cruelty not allowed?' The rest of the group did not appear to be surprised, concerned or even interested in this query. They just shrugged and indicated that they preferred to go ahead with the mad scientist idea. As observers of this scene, we were seized by competing impulses. On the one hand, we wanted to question the boy as to his intentions. On the other hand, we were disturbed by what we had witnessed and wanted to erase ourselves from the scene. The taken-for-granted had been unsettled, and the familiar had suddenly become strange. This overheard bit of conversation had denatured the ordinary and brought us face-to-face with the tenuousness, contingency and uncertainty that lie just below the surface of classroom pedagogy and practice. Why had this boy suggested animal cruelty? Why weren't the others surprised by this suggestion?[2]

In contemplating the parodic, horrific, fantastic and forbidden elements in the students' videos, it is important to remember that they occurred in a playful, carnivalesque context. The video stories were not empty reproductions or mirror reflections of their perceptions of reality. They were more like funhouse mirrors, where all is exaggerated and distorted for comic effect. The very *unreality* of the children's stories contributed to the enthusiasm and enjoyment associated with them. The videos gave students the chance to represent their desires, work through their fears and concerns, and to play with their identity as children. In the process, collective pleasures were produced. The teachers, however, were less sure about what to do when school became not just fun but pleasurable.

Fun versus Pleasure in the Classroom

Schooling has traditionally been defined largely in instrumental terms. Along with the explicit goals of imparting knowledge, skills and information, the school has also been implicitly mandated to transmit the norms, language, styles and values of the dominant culture. School has typically been a place to learn, work hard and develop such traits as punctuality, perseverance, conscientiousness, self-discipline and initiative. In earlier times, fun in school was incidental. Play was considered frivolous, nonproductive and indulgent. However, discourses surrounding children in school have changed.

Today there is an emphasis on making learning fun through child-centred, play-like activities. Play is now considered to be an activity contributing to the cognitive, psychological and social development of children. Play is utilized to motivate and reward children. Typically play in school is defined, planned and monitored by teachers. Studies by Nancy King (1979) and Maria Romero (1989) have demonstrated that young children and teachers tend to have very different perspectives on play in school. Teachers define play as being creative, fun, pleasing and rather easy (Romero, 1989:406). Children consider activities play when they are voluntary and self-directed. All activities assigned or directed by the teacher are relegated to the category of work. Teacher talk of making learning fun masks play's motivational and disciplinary purpose and its intent of preparing the child for the later world of work. Play is rarely valued by teachers as an end in itself.

For the students, video tended to blur the lines between work and play. In their journals, they wrote repeatedly about the fun of video production, yet they often mentioned how much work was involved. Video production seemed to represent a type of work that was fun and in which the children located spaces to play. In their collaborative groups, they read, wrote, problem-solved and gained technical skills, yet they also found ways to produce pleasure in exploring the boundaries between rules and freedom. Such pleasure frequently moved beyond what we typically think of as fun in school. Spontaneous and sometimes transgressive, the students' videos privileged community, festivity and solidarity. The pleasures experienced in the video project existed in and of the moment and had a life of their own.

In *The Pleasure of the Text* (1975), Roland Barthes presents his two-fold notion of pleasure as *plaisir* and *jouissance*. *Plaisir* represents conscious enjoyment and is capable of being expressed in language. It is more conservative, accommodating and conformist than *jouissance*. Where *plaisir* is a particular pleasure, *jouissance* is more diffuse; it is pleasure without separation; bliss, ecstasy, pure affect. *Jouissance* is an intense, heightened form of pleasure, involving a momentary loss of subjectivity. It knows no bounds. Fiske (1989) sees the roots of *plaisir* in the dominant ideology. Where *jouissance* produces the pleasures of evading the social order, *plaisir* produces the pleasures of relating to it (p. 54).

In school, fun is much like that described as *plaisir*: conservative, connected to curricular purposes, and usually organized and regulated by adults. The intent is either to provide a momentary release of tension or to induce the students to engage in the activities on the academic agenda. Pleasure, like *jouissance*, is produced by and for the children, in their own way and on their own terms. It exhausts itself in the present: the human interplay is all that matters. Where *plasir* is an everyday pleasure, *jouissance* is that of special moments. At times, in the video work, *jouissance*-like pleasures were created. At these moments, the teacher's presence temporarily ceased to exist, and the children were united in a spirit of camaraderie, a celebration of otherness organized around laughter.

Is the Carnivalesque Transformative?

Several colleagues who read earlier versions of this chapter questioned our celebration of the carnivalesque classroom. One commented, 'So, some kids made butt jokes in a school project. That doesn't mean they've overturned the power structure of the school.' Another warned, 'I think you need to be careful not to idealize the transformative potential of the carnivalesque.' To avoid being misunderstood, we need to clarify our view of the significance of opening spaces for pleasure and the carnivalesque in the curriculum.

Our colleagues' concerns reflect a deep ambivalence and a long debate among progressive educators about the naughty, resistant and transgressive behaviours of students. Viewing schools as sites where capitalist, patriarchal societies crush and indoctrinate students, some theorists argue that playing with and even flaunting school expectations, norms and rules represents a meaningful and even desirable form of resistance (Britzman, 1991; D'Amato, 1988; McLaren, 1986). Other neo-marxist and feminist theorists are suspicious of such claims that naughtiness accomplishes anything.

In *Learning to Labour* (1981), for example, Paul Willis argues that the anti-authoritarian antics of the lads in a British secondary school work to support rather than overturn the anti-egalitarian structure of the school and more generally of the larger society. The scatological humour, sexual banter and, most disturbingly, the mock and real acts of violence that characterize the everyday lives of the lads in and out of school function in the end to further legitimize the school's authority and to sentence the lads to reproducing their families' position in the economic system as an inexpensive source of labour. By antagonizing their teachers and ignoring their school work, the lads take themselves out of competition, giving their better behaved middle-class peers a less contested path to educational opportunities and better jobs. The lads' transgressive talk and behaviour supports not just capitalism's need for a labour pool, but also patriarchy and misogyny, as their sexual banter supports the objectification of the girls in their school.

In a study set in a nursery school, Valerie Walkerdine (1990) finds the roots of patriarchal violence against women in the sexual banter of two 4-year-olds boys who verbally assault first a female classmate, and then their 30-year-old female teacher:

Terry: You're a stupid cunt, Annie.
Sean: Get out of it, Miss Baxter paxter.
Terry: Get out of it, knickers Miss Baxter.
Sean: Get out of it, Miss Baxter paxter.
Terry: Get out of it, Miss Baxter the knickers paxter knickers bum.
Sean: Knickers, shit, bum.

Walkerdine argues that such talk, though resistant and transgressive, is far from progressive or emancipatory. The boys succeed in resisting the authority of the teacher and the school, but only by reproducing the patriarchal power available to them as a male birthright.

Willis' and Walkerdine's arguments are disturbing and persuasive: there is nothing inherently emancipatory or progressive in students' acts of resistance and transgression. Nevertheless, it is our position that educators in general and media educators in particular have erred in discounting the significance and value of opening up space for transgressive and carnivalesque moments in the curriculum. Our argument is that children's sexual, grotesque and violent play and expression can be ways of working through rather than just reproducing dominant discourses and undesirable social dynamics, and of building a sense of community in the classroom.

Video projects that include representations of violence, racism and other objectionable subject matter may merely reproduce, or, through parody, undermine the sources they imitate. As Bakhtin (1981) argues, of all words uttered in everyday life, no less than half belong to someone else (1981:339). Applied to children's video production, this concept suggests that children's videos necessarily will imitate and cite images, plots and characterizations borrowed from popular cultural sources. But in the process of remaking a movie or television programme and imitating previous forms, there is also, always, an element of newness and thus the potential for transformation.

In her reflections on the pornographic memoirs of the gay African American writer Gary Fisher, Eve Sedgwick (1997) raises the possibility that even sado-masochistic relationships have the potential to be transformative. In a disturbing memoir, Fisher speculates that sexual encounters in which he was hit and called nigger by a white man did not just repeat the dynamics of slavery and racism, but also allowed him a chance to re-experience these dynamics and potentially to rework them. Performance (sexual as well as video) has the potential to be transformative – a way of coming to understand through doing/acting/reflecting. As Freud argued, the dream dreamt, remembered, and re-told simultaneously reproduces and transforms the emotional impact of disturbing life events.

We can use this logic to analyze a take-off on the television show *America's Funniest Videos* produced by a group of third-graders at Waiau. In *Waiau's Funniest Kids*, a sneezing, nose-blowing, mucus-dripping Master of Ceremonies presents segments featuring a blind girl who repeatedly walks into a wall, a stuttering boy who cannot get through his rendition of a popular song, and hula dancers who clumsily bump into one another, knocking off their grass skirts. These segments can be seen as performative attempts to acknowledge, comment on and work through issues and tensions of everyday life at Waiau. A full inclusion school, Waiau is home to a great variety of children, including some with physical, cognitive and emotional disabilities. Some visit the speech therapist to help them with stuttering. There are blind and deaf children, and children in wheelchairs. During the years of our project, Waiau was also home to the Hawaiian Language Immersion school-within-a-school. The children who made *Waiau's Funniest Kids* were in a classroom next door to a classroom of immersion children who spent the day speaking Hawaiian and who often performed the hula (although their skirts, to our knowledge, never fell off). The content of *Waiau's Funniest Kids* thus reflects what Bakhtin would call the stratified, heteroglot character of the school. The children's parodic, silly representations of disabled children and of Hawaiian culture are contrary in content and in tone to the authoritative discourse the school imposes on discussions of difference. When given the opportunity to make their own video, these children chose to deal with the variety of Waiau's student body in a satirical, irreverent way. Their representations made the adults who viewed the video uncomfortable. But whether they produced discomfort in their student audience, whether the disabled and Hawaiian children represented in the video felt gratified or abused by being included as characters, and whether the parodies reflect the presence of prejudicial feelings in the children, we do not and perhaps cannot know. The videos produced by the children at Waiau are complex social texts which cannot be tied to the beliefs of their producers or audience in any simple way.

Our sense is that in most cases, the video making and video watching brought the children and the school together. *Waiau's Funniest Kids*, and similar videos that lampooned boring teachers, befuddled kindergarteners, and school bullies, while not artistic hits, proved to be great audience favourites. These videos, by subjecting to the same parodic treatment the foibles of everyone from teachers to kindergarteners, worked to reduce, though not erase, distance and hierarchy. In the carnivalesque spirit of the video making, everyone could be laughed at and everyone could laugh. No disability was too terrible to be lampooned, no difference so great as to be unrepresentable.

These videos addressed the diversity and inequity of life at Waiau not in the modern liberal mode of full inclusion and democratic values under which no one should be laughed at or treated as different but in the Bakhtinian, carnivalesque mode in which everyone is laughed at and differences are to be freely acknowledged. There is a fear in schools, and in society in general, that if differences and inequities are frankly acknowledged, the already frayed social fabric will be torn further apart. In the carnivalesque atmosphere that reigned during the period of our video production project, in contrast, there was a sense of confidence that differences and tensions, even if talked about openly, would not harm the children's and teachers' sense of community.

Another example: in our first round of video making, as described above, most of the children did remakes of their favourite books and movies. Several of the groups chose to make versions of recent commercial films, with Disney cartoon features the most popular source material. The casting of these Disney remakes often made us uncomfortable, as the children tended to reproduce stereotypical views of race, gender and physical attractiveness. For instance, during a casting discussion for a second-grade production of *The Little Mermaid*, we overheard the following conversation: 'Tina is the prettiest, so she should be Ariel.' 'Yeah, and you're the fattest, Angela, so you be Ursula.' As adults and as teachers, our impulse was to intervene, perhaps by giving a lecture on how everyone is pretty in different ways, or on the importance of not hurting people's feelings by talking about their appearance. But the reality, which the children seemed to accept even if we could not, was that Tina was the prettiest and most petite girl in the group and thus the most like Disney's Ariel, and Angela was the fattest and thus the most like Ursula. The children know, as we do, that such realities govern how real movies are cast, animated characters drawn and notions of slimness and attractiveness work in our society. Nothing we could say or do could make it otherwise.[3]

In some instances, the children cast their movies against type, with little boys playing giants, girls playing men, native Hawaiians playing pilgrims, and African Americans playing Chinese brothers. In these productions, children gave each other latitude to play parts with or against physical, temperamental and racial type. But whichever way they handled it, the children seemed unafraid to acknowledge their differences, even when those differences are sources of unequal treatment in the larger society.

Marxist, neo-marxist, feminist and liberal democratic views of social stratification and inequality share an agenda of reducing difference by making people and the conditions they live and work under more alike. Bakhtin offers a different view of stratification and power, a view which while not inconsistent with an agenda of progress toward social equality, sees stratification and inequality as inevitable but not totalizing. In Bakhtin's worldview, power and status differentials are characteristic of all complex, stratified, heteroglossic societies; societies are better or worse not according to their degree of stratification, but to the quality and quantity of the interactions and the openness to dialogue that exists between high and low, and between diverse sub-cultural groups. Like the marketplace and the carnival, media projects can provide a safe place for satire, parody and social laughter. Such contexts where high and low meet in a stratified society make life more bearable and meaningful and work as a form of checks and balances on the power of those at the top. Classroom media projects no more erase the power differential separating teachers from students than do carnivals erase the power and wealth differential that separates the rulers from the people. But media projects, like carnivals, have the potential to bring the high and the low together. And in modern societies where the poor are kept not just down but also away from the middle-class and rich, increasing interaction between the powerful and the powerless is a significant accomplishment. Schools are highly stratified societies. They can be run like totalitarian states, banning satire, parody and protest, fearing the open discussion of difference, heterodoxy and inequality, and erecting emotional barriers between students and their teachers. Or they can be more like Bakhtin's vision of feudal societies, in which the rulers did not fear acknowledging their common humanity with the classes below them or creating spaces for dissent, satire and laughter.

Final Reflections

Over the course of this project, our thinking about children in classrooms was challenged and in many ways changed. As the unseen and unsaid in school life materialized, new questions were posed and alternatives presented. These instances represented a temporary break with the everyday and offered multiple possibilities and outcomes. The laughter of the carnivalesque set both the teachers and the children free and provided an interval in which the terrain of the classroom could be renegotiated. As borders were shifted and redrawn, the unofficial interests, pleasures and humour of children were acknowledged and given a more equal footing. As Bakhtin (1981) suggests, we are always creating ourselves and our world, moment to moment, in our speech and our actions. It is here that change takes place – not in sweeping waves, movements or mandates, but in the minute alterations in our day-to-day lives and relations.

Like carnival, video production has no essential nature. Classroom video endeavours play out and are interpreted in different ways at different times and places. As video production becomes institutionalized in school curricula, it is possible that these carnivalesque moments will be tamed, controlled or stamped out completely. Uncertainty and trepidation accompany the exploration of uncharted territories. However, the possibility for new understandings also exists. As the space is broadened for students to explore, experiment and construct their own meanings, we stand to learn more about the children, ourselves and the relationship between us. As we let go of some of our fears about children's behaviours and inclinations, the classroom may become not only a more democratic place but a more pleasurable one as well.

Our point is not to celebrate or romanticize the children's transgressions of classroom norms and values or to suggest that we should write them into our curricula, with, for instance, butt jokes scheduled right after morning recess. Rather, it is to validate the humour and everyday interests of children and to suggest that they have a place in the classroom, in the delicate, fragile and shifting balance between excess and constraint. Victor Turner's notion of spontaneous *communitas* helps to illuminate this position. Turner defines this term as freedom coexisting within structure (1977:129). He writes that *communitas* transgresses or dissolves the norms that govern structured and institutionalized relationships and is accompanied by unprecedented potency. Yet the immediacy of *communitas* gives way to structure in a dialectical fashion. He suggests that Wisdom is always to find the appropriate relationship between structure and *communitas* under the given circumstances of time and place, to accept each modality when it is paramount without rejecting the other, and not to cling to one when its present impetus is spent. Spontaneous *communitas* is a phase, a moment not a permanent condition. It is nature in dialogue with structure (1977:140).

Thus, these carnivalesque pleasures are ephemeral. They appear in unexpected places and begin to close at the very instance when they open. As soon as an attempt is made to rationalize and regulate them, they lose their essence and begin to vanish. Yet they will continue to materialize, for these pleasures have value and importance in the school lives of children. They are sites of energy and powerful affect and can be a rejuvenating and creative force for all involved. They can live briefly in the interstice between freedom and structure until their moment is spent, and pleasure can be enjoyed in and of the moment, for itself and nothing more.

Notes

1 All parodies and satires are not inclusive and harmless. Teachers have to use their intuition and judgment. We intervened, for example, to block the development of a proposal to make a video about Arnold Schwartzennigger. Perhaps this video would have ended up lampooning racists rather than African Americans. But we decided to veto it because our intuition suggested that the topic was more likely to turn out badly than well. Teachers must make case-by-case decisions. In this case, our prior experience at Waiau, a school with only a handful of African American students, suggested to us that this project was more likely to widen racial divisions than to narrow them. The other project we discouraged, based on our concerns about the need for separation of church and state, was a proposal to make a video about Jesus. In retrospect, we wish we had allowed this project to go forward.

2 Although the notion of animal cruelty affronts most adult, middle-class sensibilities (ours included), it is not an uncommon feature of games and sport. Cock fighting, dog fighting, rat killing, bull running and the baiting of wild animals were popular amusements in England well into the nineteenth century. The inhumane treatment of animals has generally been associated with the lower classes. Harriet Ritvo (1987) points out that during the nineteenth century the treatment of animals was considered to be an index of the extent to which a person had managed to control his or her lower urges (1987:132).

3 We do not mean to suggest that there is nothing teachers can do to intervene in the circulation and reproduction of sexism and racism. We believe that the anti-bias curricula that have the most chance of succeeding are those that begin by acknowledging the students' prior knowledge and experience with racial and gender distinctions in the larger society. For sophisticated approaches to this problem, see Deborah Britzman (1991), Bronwyn Davies (1989) and Gemma Moss (1989).

References

BAKHTIN, M. (1968) *Rabelais and His World*, Trans. ISWOLSKY, H., Cambridge, MA: MIT Press.

BAKHTIN, M. (1981) *Discourse in the Novel*, Austin, TX: University of Texas Press.

BARTHES, R. (1975) *The Pleasure of the Text*, New York: Hill and Wang.

BRITZMAN, D. (1991) Decentering discourses in teacher education: Or, the unleashing of unpopular things, *Journal of Education*, **173** (3), 60–80.

BUCKINGHAM, D. (Ed.) (1990) *Watching Media Learning: Making Sense of Media Education*, London: Falmer Press.

BUCKINGHAM, D. and SEFTON-GREEN, J. (1994) *Cultural Studies Goes to School: Reading and Teaching Popular Media*, London: Taylor and Francis.

BUCKINGHAM, D., GRAHAME, J. and SEFTON-GREEN, J. (1995) *Making Media: Practical Production in Media Education*, London: English and Media Centre.

D'AMATO, J. (1988) Acting: Hawaiian children's resistance to teachers, *The Elementary School Journal*, **88** (5), 529–43.

DAVIES, B. (1989) *Frogs and Snails and Feminist Tales: Preschool Children and Gender*, Sydney New South Wales: Allen and Unwin.

DYSON, A. (1993) *Social Worlds of Children Learning to Write in an Urban Primary School*, New York: Teachers College Press.

FISKE, J. (1989) *Understanding Popular Culture*, London: Unwin Hyman.

KING, N. (1979) Play: The kindergartners' perspective, *The Elementary School Journal*, **80**, 81–7.

KING, N. (1992) The impact of context on the play of young children, in KESSLER, S. and SWADENER, B. (Eds) *Reconceptualizing the Early Childhood Curriculum: Beginning the Dialogue*, New York: Teacher's College Press.

LURIE, A. (1990) *Don't Tell the Grown-ups: Subversive Children's Literature*, Boston, MA: Little, Brown.

McLAREN, P. (1986) *Schooling as a Ritual Performance: Towards a Political Economy of Educational Symbols and Gestures*, London: Routledge and Kegan Paul.

MOSS, G. (1989) *Un/popular Fictions*, London: Virago.

NEWKIRK, T. (1992) *Listening In: Children Talk about Books (and Other Things)*, Portsmouth: Heinemann.

RITVO, H. (1987) *The Animal Estate: The English and Other Creatures in the Victorian Age*, Cambridge: Harvard University Press.

ROMERO, M. (1989) Work and Play in the Nursery School, *Educational Policy*, **3** (4), 401–19.

RUSSO, M. (1986) Female grotesques: Carnival and theory, in DE LAURETIS, T. (Ed.) *Feminist Studies/Critical Studies*, Bloomington, IN: Indiana University Press.

SEDGWICK, E. (1997) *Gary Fisher in Your Pocket*, Durham, NC: Duke University Press.

STAM, R. (1989) *Subversive Pleasures: Bakhtin, Cultural Criticism, and Film*, Baltimore, MD: The Johns Hopkins University Press.

TURNER, V. (1977) Frame, flow and reflection: Ritual and drama as public liminality, in BENAMOU, M. and CARAMELLO, C. (Eds) *Performance in Postmodern Culture*, Madison, WI: Coda.

WALKERDINE, V. (1990) Sex, power, and pedagogy, in *Schoolgirl Fictions*, London: Verso.

WILLIS, P. (1981) *Learning to Labor*, New York: Columbia University Press.

Chapter 4

Pedagogy, Parody and Political Correctness

David Buckingham

Anyone who has spent time observing children's play will recognize the significance of parody and imitation. Even very young children will engage in parodies of their parents, teachers and peers – and, inevitably, of the media that surround them. Pre-schoolers can produce telling parodies of advertisements or of the news, complete with self-consciously fake smiles or imaginary microphones; and of course, scenarios drawn from cartoons and action–adventure series feature regularly in their play. Acting out *Baywatch* in the bath or swimming pool, setting traps in the house for burglars as in *Home Alone*, or leaping around the living room in the guise of Power Rangers are all (at least in my experience) common elements in childhood games.

Nevertheless, this phenomenon often generates considerable anxiety, particularly when it relates to adult concerns about the negative effects of the media – for example, about gender stereotyping, about the influence of other cultures or (most frequently) about 'violence'. Such behaviour is frequently taken as evidence of the mesmeric power of the media, their ability to colonize and ultimately to destroy children's imagination (see, for example, Carlsson-Paige and Levin, 1990). Imitation of this kind is seen to reflect children's inability to make clear distinctions between fantasy and reality; and this is seen in turn to give rise to some very problematic consequences, most obviously in apparent instances of copycat violence. While commonsense wisdom about child-rearing consistently emphasizes the developmental benefits of play, the boundary between play and real life is one that seems to be in constant need of reinforcement and policing.

Imitation and Deconstruction in Media Education

It is perhaps not surprising that such forms of parody and imitation should recur later in life, when children and adults have the opportunity to produce their own media texts. A definitive study of the domestic uses of video camcorders has yet to be undertaken; but I would suspect that parodies of well-known movies or TV shows are far from uncommon here.[1] When it comes to more formal educational contexts, parody and imitation seem almost impossible to avoid. While they are sometimes explicitly invited by teachers (as we shall see), they are almost a guaranteed element in most groups' initial uses of media technology, and particularly of portable video. Students will readily take on the role of the game show host, the news interviewer, or the disc jockey – let alone a whole range of fictional personae – already seemingly fluent in their conventional style and mode of address. Such behaviour is not confined to performers; students can often very easily mimic the visual style of pop videos, investigative documentaries or advertisements, with a minimum of instruction or guidance.

Again, this phenomenon has been surrounded with a considerable amount of anxiety. Of course, there are positive accounts of what is taking place here, albeit ones which raise their own problems. Advocates of a vocational approach to media education would doubtless see this imitation of mainstream media forms as an essential process whereby students acquire technical skills and learn the language of the media. Likewise, arguments for media production work in other areas of the curriculum have pointed to the ways in which using genres such as news and documentary can encourage students to develop greater facility in standard English (cf. Buckingham, 1987; and Lorac and Weiss, 1981).

Yet among critical media educators, the dominant response here has been one of hostility and suspicion. Students' use of dominant media forms is often perceived as merely a process of ideological reproduction. Perhaps the classic statement of this view can be found in Len Masterman's book *Teaching About Television*, published in 1980. Compared with the comprehensive range of strategies for critical analysis contained there, the book's chapter on practical work is very much the shortest, and much of it is extraordinarily negative. What happens, Masterman asks, when you give students video cameras?

> In my experience an endless wilderness of dreary third-rate imitative 'pop'-shows, embarrassing video dramas, and derivative documentaries courageously condemning war or poverty, much of it condoned by teachers to whom technique is all and the medium the only message (Masterman, 1980:140).

What is quite striking about this quote now, over 15 years later, is its reliance on precisely the kind of Leavisite critical criteria that the rest of the book sought to challenge (cf. Leavis and Thompson, 1933). Students' work is condemned as 'imitative', 'derivative' and 'third-rate', in exactly the same terms that one might find Leavis condemning a novel that had failed to gain entry to the Great Tradition. There is also a remarkable contempt for students' perspectives here, particularly in the sarcastic use of expressions like 'courageously condemning'.

Similar arguments can be found in other work of this period (see Collins, 1976; Ferguson, 1981); and to a large extent, this suspicion of students' uses of dominant media forms came to be institutionalized in the examination syllabuses which emerged in the decade that followed (Stafford, 1990). For these writers, practical production was only acceptable in the form of 'deconstruction' or 'code-breaking exercises'. Here is Ferguson's account:

> one concentrates on making brief, often modest media artefacts which are designed to highlight a form of construction usually accepted unquestioningly as the norm. One is here encouraging students to manipulate televisual or filmic language for a *specific purpose*. Not to express oneself, but to manufacture a meaning through the conscious manipulation of production techniques and norms (Ferguson, 1981:46).

In so far as such activities were to result in complete texts, these were to be rigorously confined to 'oppositional' forms (for example, those of anti-realism) which would directly challenge and subvert the norms of professional media practice (Collins, 1976).

This general stance towards practical work can partly be explained in terms of contemporary curriculum politics. In attempting to put Media Studies on the map, such writers were bound to make claims for its status and uniqueness as a subject discipline. In the accounts from which I have quoted, distinctions are implicitly and explicitly drawn between Media Studies and other curriculum areas, such as Art and English, which are condemned for their reliance on liberal progressivist notions of creativity. The general emphasis on the importance of theory and critical analysis, and the concomitant neglect or denigration of practical work, reflect an attempt to define Media Studies as a serious, difficult *academic* subject – albeit a claim that is made in highly traditional terms.

Yet at the same time, these arguments seem to be based on a deep-seated fear of imitation – a belief that if students imitate dominant forms, they will somehow inevitably and invisibly imbibe the ideologies those forms are seen to contain. Making your own version of a pop music show, for example, is just reinforcing sexism and consumerism and the mindless vacuity which these writers seem to detect in such programmes (and here the ghost of Leavis definitely is standing over their shoulders). What is offered here – and in many accounts of media education more broadly – is a notion of learning that is rigidly intellectual and rationalistic. It is about 'construction' and 'conscious manipulation' – or, in Ferguson's terms, about 'cognitive *rather than* experiential development' (Ferguson, 1981:53, my emphasis).

The Problem of Pleasure

Clearly, there are several difficulties with this approach. In terms of media theory, it seems to be based on a kind of formalism, and indeed on a rather simplistic notion of ideological effects – and in this respect, it obviously reflects the dominant tendencies of its time. Fifteen years on, it is reasonable to ask whether it still makes sense to talk in terms of a singular 'dominant professional practice' with a singular set of 'norms', or to conceive of media forms in such binary terms as 'dominant' and 'oppositional'. Furthermore, such arguments can only be sustained by virtue of their neglect of audiences – and in this instance, of learners also. 'Dominant' forms do not necessarily produce 'dominant' readings; and they can clearly be used to invite 'oppositional' ones. To oppose the 'cognitive' and the 'experiential' in this way is obviously highly problematic; and to imply that 'ideology' will be overcome simply through the application of conscious rationality is little more than wishful thinking.

These theoretical assumptions have been significantly questioned by more recent work in the field, and in particular by the detailed analysis of classroom practice (see Alvarado and Boyd-Barrett, 1992; Buckingham, 1990; Buckingham and Sefton-Green, 1994; Buckingham, Grahame and Sefton-Green, 1995). As such research has shown, it is very rare for students simply to imitate 'dominant' media practice. There is almost always an element of parody, a knowing distance – and hence a critical potential – in the ways in which students use mainstream forms and genres. Yet even slavish imitation is never simply unthinking; it must involve a conscious and active understanding of the forms and conventions which are being used.

As subsequent critics have argued, the rationalistic approach to media education which is embodied in deconstruction exercises seems to offer little place for *pleasure* or *play*. Of course, even to utter such words is to risk the accusation of being a hopeless liberal – or at least it would have been 15 years ago. These days, at least in academic circles, one is more likely to encounter a fashionable celebration of such things, as though they were necessarily and inherently subversive of the 'dominant ideology'. Pleasure, it would seem, is not about confirming or reproducing dominant power-relationships and values; on the contrary, it involves a form of liberation from such constraints. Play, likewise, is seen as a situation in which rules can be broken and more powerful identities assumed, if only on the level of fantasy.

This emphasis is, on one level, a necessary corrective to earlier approaches, not least because it appears to recognize a significant aspect of students' experience. It is largely because of the potential enjoyment that seems to be offered by practical work that students opt for Media Studies courses in the first place. While I would not want to underestimate the considerable pleasures of analysis, the pleasure of practical work and the degree of motivation and enthusiasm that students bring to it is a significant reason for the continuing success of media education. It is also a reason why practical work has continued to feature quite prominently in Media Studies syllabuses, despite the kinds of criticisms outlined above.

Yet on the other hand, pleasure is not innocent of power. Play-acting, dressing up, 'having a laugh', making a fool of yourself, wandering freely around parts of the school that are normally off limits – these are often, for the students, the most important elements of the process. And while these pleasures can be gained irrespective of the context, they also carry a particular resonance in the highly regulated environment of the school. In this respect, practical work often seems to challenge or transgress the established power relations between teachers and students. Yet this transgression is not necessarily a form of liberation, or one which brings about more egalitarian relationships in general. On the contrary, as we shall see, it can often reinforce existing inequalities – albeit in ambiguous and sometimes contradictory ways.

Thus, while I would challenge the rationalistic emphasis of earlier approaches to media education, it seems to me to be inadequate simply to assert the 'progressive' potential of pleasure and play. On a theoretical level, such arguments appear to essentialize and to reinforce the very oppositions they set out to challenge – oppositions between reason and emotion, between ideology and pleasure, between critical theory and cultural practice. On a practical level, they would seem to provide little basis for devising effective classroom strategies, or for evaluating students' *learning*. As I shall indicate, the pleasure and play that are entailed in media production provide a complex and uneasy mixture of opportunities and problems.

Contemporary Compromises: Simulations and the Impossible Text

While the arguments of earlier media educators may now appear somewhat fundamentalist, the anxieties they reflect are nevertheless apparent in a good deal of contemporary classroom practice in the field. Practical work is still implicitly defined in many syllabuses as an adjunct of 'theory', or simply as an opportunity to demonstrate predetermined theoretical principles. This is reflected in two dominant tendencies in current practice: the use of simulations and the approach which I shall term the '*impossible text*'.

Of course, most media production work in classrooms is simulated, in the sense that it rarely approximates to the conditions of professional practice. Yet the explicit use of simulations, in which students are invited to take on the roles of real media producers, has become the dominant model for production in most contemporary media classrooms (for good examples of such activities, see Grahame, 1994). As in the case of the first piece of work I shall discuss below, students are typically provided with a brief which requires them to work within specific – albeit imaginary – institutional or economic constraints, and/or to target a particular audience.

In some respects, simulation could be seen as a kind of compromise between the theoretically over-determined approach of 'deconstruction exercises' and the more open-ended, 'creative' approach of progressivism. Nevertheless, it remains a comparatively *conceptual* technique, in the sense that creative self-expression (whatever one might conceive that to mean) is ultimately subordinated to the consideration of abstract theoretical issues. The key moment in such simulations is the 'debriefing', in which students are required to make explicit the reasons for their choices, and to analyze their potential consequences, for example, in terms of audience responses (see Buckingham *et al.*, 1995, Chapter 8). The use of simulation thus invites a direct analytical comparison with 'dominant' practice – not so much in terms of the 'professional' quality of the finished product (or the lack of it), but in terms of the formal, generic and representational aspects of the text. As I shall argue, the difficulties and limitations of 'debriefing' – whether in written or spoken form – can prove particularly problematic. Yet it is clear that the central aims of such activities – and the terms by which they are largely assessed – are essentially defined in terms of theoretical or conceptual understanding.

In many instances, however, the requirements of media simulations are in themselves highly contradictory. Anxieties about 'political correctness' – or about the dangers of what used to be called 'ideological reproduction' – often seem to lead to a recipe for the 'impossible text'. This is the text which is simultaneously 'dominant' *and* 'oppositional'. Thus, students can be required to encode 'oppositional' content within a 'dominant' form; or (less frequently) 'dominant' content within an 'oppositional' form. Thus, in my experience, media teachers routinely ask older students to produce 'alternative' soap operas or 'non-sexist' teenage magazines or even 'anti-realist' advertisements, when they have rarely had a chance to explore the possibilities of the technology, or indeed to gain some experience with the dominant forms they are supposedly expected to be moving beyond. If not impossible, such assignments are at least unrealistic, not only in terms of what can be achieved with the technology but also in terms of the internal contradictions of the tasks themselves.

A Place for Parody?

In different ways, both these approaches seem to walk an awkward line between imitation and a more self-conscious or 'critical' form of production practice. Of course, imitation is often seen as a necessary and important stage in children's learning, for example in the case of language acquisition. Yet in this context, imitation is clearly seen as insufficient in itself; and in many instances, *parody* seems to serve as a useful way of negotiating the contradictory demands of the situation. It allows one to use 'dominant' forms while simultaneously disavowing any commitment to them.

Of course, parody necessarily entails imitation; although imitation does not have to be parodic. Yet when it comes to discussions of popular culture, this distinction is also highly pejorative. Imitation is seen here as an essentially unthinking process, in which particular behaviours, values and ideologies are simply reproduced – and thereby reinforced. Parody, on the other hand, is generally seen to be a matter of conscious deliberation. While parody does not (as we shall see) necessarily involve a rejection of that which it parodies, it must involve a form of critical distance from it – however affectionate it may be.

In practice, however, the distinction between imitation and parody may be very difficult to sustain. This issue is a recurrent theme in literary discussions of parody (for example, Hutcheon, 1985; Rose, 1979). Is parody a matter of the author's intention, or does it not also depend on the judgment of the reader? If the reader does not recognize the signals of the parodic intention, or the difference between the two 'text-worlds' of the original and the parody, what consequences does this have? How far can we trust what the author says about the work – since the claim to parody can obviously function as a *post hoc* rationalization or justification? To what extent does parody necessarily reproduce the ideologies and pleasures of the original, while at the same time appearing to undermine them? And how can we weigh these two sides of parody in the balance?

As these discussions make clear, ambiguity is essential to parody. On the one hand, parody clearly does possess a critical potential. According to Rose (1979), parody relies on 'the effect of comic discrepancy between the original and its "imitation"'. In the process, it often serves to expose the constructed nature of the original, and to highlight generic conventions, for example through inversion. It is, in this sense, a form of *meta-fiction*, which provides an implicit critique of the truth-status of artistic representations. In the contemporary context, parody has become central to the wider challenge to the concept of representation, and a crucial dimension of new forms of self-reflexive cultural practice (Hutcheon, 1985). Yet at the same time as it demythologizes, parody can also release or reinforce repressed wishes or fears, in the same way as Freud suggests is the case with jokes. Parody unmasks the fantasy, but it also perpetuates it; it is simultaneously destructive and reconstructive (Rose, 1979).

These difficulties and ambiguities are perhaps even more acute in the context of teaching and learning about popular culture. As I have noted, rationales for media education typically place a central emphasis on the need to develop conscious deliberation and critical distance. Yet there are significant difficulties in identifying evidence of these, particularly in the context of students' production work. How can we distinguish here between the self-conscious use and manipulation of media conventions and the 'mindless' imitation of them? To what extent is parody (or the appearance of parody) in itself an indication of a 'critical' perspective? Is there not a danger that we will 'read in' a parodic intention where none exists – or fail to detect one where it does? To what extent can we take students' claims about such things at face value? If students argue that their own work is a critical deconstruction of dominant media forms – and hence perhaps in our terms 'politically correct' – do we necessarily have to believe them? And if not, on what grounds can we challenge them?

In the account which follows, I offer a brief analysis of two pieces of students' work which illustrate the potential and the problems of the two strategies outlined above. My intention here is not to offer a vindication of the 'creativity' or 'pleasures' of these students' work. On the contrary, I have chosen these particular examples because of the dilemmas they pose, both in terms of how we as teachers might read and evaluate them, and in terms of what we think the students might have learnt. Both seem to me to raise fundamental questions about the aims and methods of media education, and in particular about its *politics*.

As I shall indicate, parody may have a significant potential here. It can offer a safe space in which difficult tensions and conflicts can be explored, and in which new and challenging insights can be generated. It can function as a critical mode in its own right, which provides access to the parts that more closed forms of analysis cannot reach. Yet as I have implied, parody can be read in very contradictory ways, both by its authors and by its readers. And if parody offers a freedom, it is a freedom in which nobody can be held to account for what they say. As a pedagogic strategy, parody therefore raises significant problems; it is ultimately, I shall argue, insufficient in itself.

Ideological Dilemmas: The Case of *Flat Broke*

The first piece I want to consider here was produced by a group of Year 10 boys in a selective, predominantly middle-class, North London secondary school, as part of their GCSE Media Studies/English coursework.[2] The class was given a brief which required them to produce a short trailer for an imaginary new series to be transmitted on the children's cable channel Nickelodeon. The class worked in four groups, each of which was given a brief relating to a different genre (documentary, game show, literary adaptation and situation comedy). The new series was expected to build upon the appeal of existing programmes in the genre, but also to offer something distinctively new.

One significant dimension to this project, which I will not be able to discuss in detail here, was that it included elements of audience research. The students were required to target their programme at a younger age group (Year 7), and to conduct focus group discussions with children in this group both at the initial stage of devising ideas and once the trailer had been completed. Our intention here was partly to assist the students in their written self-evaluations: testing their ideas against a 'real' audience might, we hoped, make the process of debriefing and self-evaluation less of an abstract requirement on our part, and might make it easier for the students to reflect back on the choices they had made.

I want to focus here on one group whose work was generally agreed by the other students to be the most successful production in the class. It was also the one which proved to be particularly problematic for us as teachers. This group of six boys produced a trailer for a situation comedy entitled *Flat Broke*, about a group of four contrasting individuals who shared a flat. A storyboard of the video is included on pages 71–2. One boy, Jamie, described the initial idea as follows:

[Male voice-over:]
Where would you
expect the following
four people to live?

*Emma talking with boy
in bedroom. She walks
to the bed, he follows.
They sit on the bed.
She pulls a machine
gun from under the
pillow and points it at
him, saying 'you've go
three seconds'. He
exits hurriedly.*

Name: Dino
Papadopolou
Occupation: part-time
helper in kebab shop.
Likes: jewellery, easy
women, Mercedes and
Cyprus. Dislikes: gays,
feminists, English
people and fish and
chips.

*Dino enters room.
Girls' screams are
heard. Dino exits,
smiling. The door
closes to reveal the
sign: 'Girls' Changing
Room'.*

Name: Leonard White.
Occupation:
entertainer. Likes:
men, flowers, rubber
trousers and wrestling.
Dislikes: nothing.

Name: Emma Frazer.
Occupation:
suffragette. Likes: long
skirts and non-sexist
men. Dislikes: bimbos,
short skirts and
washing up.

*Two boys are in bed.
There is a knock at the
door. Boy 1: 'Do you
want to answer that?'
Boy 2: 'Yeah, I'll get it'.
He exits to open the
door, than returns
hurriedly.*

Figure 4.1 *Flat Broke*

Boy 2: 'It's Leonard!' In fright, they strap themselves into their beds. Leonard enters, flapping his wrists. Leonard: 'Are there any boys here? Oooh, I like it!' He kneels at the bed of Boy 2, only to discover that he is strapped in. Leonard [weeping]: 'Oh no!'

The four characters emerge from their bedrooms onto the landing of the flat. They look at each other, scream and rush back to their rooms.

Name: Lisa, last name unknown. Occupation: none. Borrows money to pay her rent. Likes, men, short skirts, tight tops, expensive jewellery, men who will buy her expensive jewallery. Dislikes: feminists, Greeks, men with no money.

Unfortunately, under these circumstances, they live together.

Kitchen. Dino and Emma are arguing. Emma: 'You pervert!' Dino: 'It's not my fault you're frigid!' Emma picks up a glass of water and throws it at him.

Lisa is walking along the street. She turns her heed to look at a man and calls out 'allo, darling'. Not looking where she is going, she walks into a lamp-post and falls to the ground.

Join them in *Flat Broke*, weekdays at five.

Under normal circumstances, as far away as possible.

[Group voice-over, American accents:] Only on Nickelodeon!

Figure 4.1 *Continued*

Our idea . . . was to have a series based around a flat with four different people that didn't get on. This idea was similar to *The Young
Ones*. The four people would be: a feminist, a tart, a sexist rude
Greek, and a gay. The gay would keep making passes at the Greek
and become very unpopular. The Greek would be very sexist, think
a lot of himself, and not get on at all with anyone. The tart would go
out looking for men with the gay, and not get on with the feminist.
And lastly the feminist would be anti-social and unfriendly. We
thought this was a very good, bizarre mix of people, and would be
very popular . . .

Flat Broke was in fact one of the three ideas the students were asked to
develop and to present to their focus group, although the choice between them
was never in doubt. There was too much invested in the production of *Flat
Broke*, both personally and in the social context of school, for it to be rejected
in favour of something safer.

In terms of personal investments, what is interesting even from this brief
summary is how it positions the different characters. It is worth noting here
that Nicky, who was the originator of the idea and the prime mover in the
group, is second-generation Greek Cypriot/British himself, and eventually
played the part of 'the Greek' in the video. Significantly, while the Greek is
defined as 'sexist', he is also 'fancied' both by the gay character and by the
feminist – which, while it may simply reflect a degree of vanity, also seems to
suggest that both these 'deviant' characters can be recuperated into a form of
normality.

This group clearly had to negotiate some difficulties in presenting their
ideas to us and to the rest of the class. One key issue which was raised early on
(both by us as teachers and by other students in the class) was that of its
appropriateness for its target audience. In his debriefing, Ian subsequently
wrote:

At one stage we thought we would reject *Flat Broke*. This is because
we thought that children's parents would not allow them to watch it
as it has a gay and a bimbo (as Nicky said, 'a bimbo who wears tight
tops and short leather skirts') and I did not think that my parents
would have let me watch it when I was eleven. However, we thought
that if we toned it down and concentrated on making it funny without
involving the gay all the time, then it would be more acceptable.

It is significant here that it is the gay character who is seen as most problematic
from the point of view of parents – although he is also the most interesting and
problematic character for the group as well. Indeed, the programme was
repeatedly referred to by other students in the class as 'the gay one'.

Nicky, by contrast, was much more forthright, significantly dismissing the
concerns raised by his teacher as those of 'the censors', and arguing that

parents would be much more 'open-minded'. Nevertheless, the dismissal of this objection was also supported by the responses of the Year 7 focus group. As Jamie subsequently wrote:

> The only question hanging over this wonderful idea was whether it would be suitable for a 5 o'clock slot on tele. Anyway, after lengthy group discussions, we decided that as long as we kept it clean, it would be okay. The focus group's opinion was also pleasing. They all said they could watch it and all thought they'd be allowed to watch it.

However, the most significant problem the group had to negotiate here was an ideological one – and our objections on the grounds of appropriateness largely reflected these more covert concerns. Even in initially presenting the idea to the whole class, Nicky hesitated when it came to the 'tart'. The word 'slag' was also used here, although eventually the group had recourse to the (perhaps less overtly objectionable) term 'bimbo'. At the same time, the terminology varied according to the context. In less guarded moments, the 'gay' was occasionally termed the 'queer' – and not, it might be added, in response to the advent of 'queer politics', which has yet to make much impression on North London adolescents.

Yet these difficulties with terminology were only a part of the ideological policing to which the students felt themselves to be subject. The question of the programme's stance towards the characters – all of whom could be seen to represent 'minorities', albeit of different kinds – was raised consistently, both by us as teachers and by other students. While the group occasionally sought to ignore such concerns, they generally confronted them directly, by insisting on the even-handed nature of the humour. When we sought reassurance that the programme was not just about laughing at the gay character, for example, Nicky responded by saying that it was about laughing at *all* the characters.

Similar objections were raised in the focus group discussion. One girl argued, 'Greek people could think it was racist' and 'gay people might think it was against them', but her objections were laughed off. Jonathan insisted:

> it's going to be laughing at the whole cast, not just the gay. There's the feminist and . . . It's like it's from all extremes of society.

Interestingly however, the focus group's suggestion of including a 'posh' character was also dismissed, on the grounds that this would not be as funny or as 'perfect' as their own characters. This is important because, as it stands, all the characters are in some way deviant: the norm is not being satirized, only the margins, and to introduce a 'posh' character might undermine this.

Quite where the programme might be positioned in terms of debates about stereotyping is hard to identify, however. For the boys themselves, the boundary between using (and even parodying) stereotypes and simply reproducing them was not always clear. In their written debriefing, four of the six in fact used the word 'stereotype' in describing the aims of the programme – although significantly Nicky was one of the ones who did not. Jonathan, for example, notes the objections of the focus group, but argues that parents would be unlikely to worry about a programme featuring 'such exaggerated stereotypes'. Even Daniel, who disagreed with this latter point, argues that the programme will attract a 'cult following' because of its 'outrageous stereotypes'. Even where the word 'stereotype' or 'caricature' is not used, there is a sense in which the programme is seen to be playing with conventional expectations, and is consciously 'over the top' and parodic. Thus Nicky, with characteristic modesty, described the responses of the focus group as follows: 'They thought it was funny, bold, outrageous, rebellious and a dozen other things apart from offensive.'

Quite who is being outraged and rebelled against here, and with what effect, is of course the key question. However self-conscious the stereotypes in the programme may be, they are undeniably offensive: a gay child-molester, a violent, man-hating feminist, a lecherous 'ethnic minority' and an intellectually challenged nymphomaniac can hardly be counted as politically correct representations. On one level, it is tempting to dismiss them simply as evidence of the insecurities and delusions of male adolescence – although it is worth remarking how such delusions and insecurities seem to feature so frequently both in mainstream and in so-called 'alternative' comedy.

Yet the 'outrageous' nature of the production also needs to be set in context. For the people who are being outraged and rebelled against here are obviously us as teachers and the wider institution of the school. (It is perhaps notable here that the feminist character is given the surname of the (male) class teacher.) In a sense, the students saw the project as an opportunity to speak the unspeakable – to unleash the 'unpopular' and subversive things that are normally restrained by the institution of the school (cf. Britzman, 1991).

This is not to offer an apologia for the work that was produced by this group, or to attempt to reclaim it in terms of some simple-minded notion of resistance. The leaders of this group – and particularly Nicky – were classic adolescent homophobics, and to this extent they can hardly be seen as untypical of heterosexual adolescent boys in general. This is most apparent in Daniel's written account of the production, where he notes bluntly, 'we were all similar people in the way we were boys who hated gays and so the opinion for taking the mick out of gays was unanimous.' My parting memory, as the students left the classroom at the end of the concluding lesson of the project, is of Nicky sticking a label on Daniel's back saying, 'I'm a queer – shaft me!' While it is possible to deal with this kind of behaviour as an infringement of discipline (as we did in this case), quite how one responds to the ideological dimension of the students' work in the context of an examined course of study is more problematic.

One of the most significant difficulties here, as I have implied, is that the students were able to co-opt the arguments that one might use to challenge them. In his written account, David even describes Dino, the Greek character, as 'homophobic' – thus implicitly distancing himself from this affliction – while Daniel suggests that a 'liberal' station like Nickelodeon would be unlikely to show a series that is so 'politically incorrect' (his words). The fact that the programme is targeted at a young audience also allows some room for manoeuvre: in his written account, Jonathan suggests, 'although it's aimed at children, it's worth a look for any adults who can put up with the slightly immature jokes.'

Yet the fact that the activity was a *simulation* is particularly relevant here. The students were not being required to produce a 'real' programme; nor, despite our use of the audience research dimension, were they addressing a 'real' audience. On the contrary, by incorporating some highly specific constraints into the project brief, we were seeking to bring about some more abstract or conceptual understandings of the relationships between media institutions and their audiences. Yet this approach has potentially ambiguous consequences. By virtue of being placed in the role of *fictional* producers, the students can effectively disclaim the suggestion that the programme represents their own views. In fact, our brief did not require the students to produce a politically correct situation comedy (which might serve as a good example of an impossible text); nor did it imply that what they produced would be taken as evidence of their own personal beliefs. In effect, the ambiguous nature of the production – as simultaneously fictional and real – enables the students to have their cake and eat it. Given that we had established these parameters in the first place, we were hardly in a position to complain about the consequences.

To what extent did this group learn anything from their encounter with the 'real' audience? When it came to the final focus group discussions, some of the students appeared to rethink their approach in the light of the younger students' criticisms. Some quite constructive comments were made here, for example about the need to sustain the series by introducing additional characters. Yet Nicky seemed unable to accept even these comparatively neutral critical comments, or the reactions of his peers and eventually walked out. In fact, the sole ideological objection made by the younger students in this group was one which Nicky was in an ideal position to counter: when one boy dared to suggest that Greek people might be offended by the programme, Nicky responded by pointing out that the boy was not Greek himself – and thus, by implication, that he had no right to make a judgment on the matter.

While the reasons for Nicky's defensiveness are obviously hard to identify, two possibilities are relevant here. The first follows directly from the last point, which is to do with his perception of his 'ethnic' identity. Nicky certainly took the lead in the group in defining the negative qualities of his character as distinctively Greek. The character's lechery, his liking for kebabs and his macho, 'medallion man' persona were seen as inseparable from his Greek nationalism and his tendency to 'babble on' in Greek. In creating this character, Nicky both inhabits this persona and distances himself from it: it represents a form of ethnic disavowal that only he is in a position to make.

The second point here relates to the issue of assessment. Nicky's behaviour in both focus group discussions, and in subsequently describing these, suggests that (like many others in the class) he perceived them partly as a form of assessment. It was important to gain the endorsement of the focus group because this would serve as a vindication of his ideas, and hence serve him well in the final assessment. Admitting to self-doubt, on the other hand, was a good way of losing marks.

While not all the students were as defensive or impervious to criticism as Nicky, this group was certainly the one that was most dismissive of the focus group discussions. On the other hand, however, they were very well aware of their audience – and in a sense were more aware of the *actual* 'real audience' of peers and teachers, rather than the somewhat hypothetical 'real audience' we had created for them. As I have implied, the whole production could be seen as a very knowing move in a debate about representation, and a conscious subversion of the 'official' approaches of teachers, which are reinforced by the disciplinary structures of the school – although this is not in any sense to imply that it is therefore politically radical. The tortuous negotiations that had to be gone through in order for this act of transgression to be committed do in fact reflect a considerable degree of awareness of the potential audience, and of the politics of representation – even if this was more explicit in some cases than others (the price of Nicky's defensiveness is that he was one of the least willing or able to articulate this in his writing). In terms of assessment, this creates an interesting dilemma: however much we might wish to mark this work down on ideological grounds, we cannot really do so on the basis that it shows little awareness of the conceptual issues contained in the syllabus.

Reading Parody: *Slutmopolitan*

The second piece of work I want to look at here is one that raises similar contradictions and dilemmas. *Slutmopolitan* is a systematic parody of the woman's magazine *Cosmopolitan* produced by four working-class girls in Year 13 of another North London school, as part of their A-level Media Studies coursework.[3] The criteria for the Advanced Production Module, for which this project was produced, require that the work should be based on an explicit consideration of an aspect of Media Studies theory. Students are thus expected to 'translate' their theoretical understanding of Media Studies into texts that are both formally and politically radical. The implicit model here would appear to be that of the political avant-garde – for example, the work of the British independent film and video movement of the 1970s and early 1980s, with its emphasis on self-reflexivity, formal experimentation and direct opposition to the pleasures of popular culture. It is this model which, in a sense, provides a way out of the dilemmas of the 'impossible text' – although, for these students, parody certainly seemed to offer another.

Following a unit of work on issues of realism and 'positive images', the students were required to produce a video or series of images, that engaged with the representation of 'hidden' minorities or groups and simultaneously worked against the dominant conventions of realism. The work the students devised was quite varied, although in some ways *Slutmopolitan* appears to be most at odds with these lofty theoretical aims. The magazine comprises 16 pages in full colour. There is a front cover, which is basically a photograph of a cleavage adorned with an anti-nuclear pendant; an advert for Tina's Tights comprising a shot of legs clad in 'tarty' fishnets; and a back cover which takes the form of a full page advert for Flake, in traditional fellatio style. Inside, there are a number of problem pages, including Dear Doreen, who deals with 'the dreaded broken nail'; Clare's Clever Cookery Page describes how to cook frozen peas, illustrated by a model in 'suggestive' poses; and Deirdre's Do-it-Yourself explains the complexities of changing a light bulb. In addition, there is a comics page entitled 25 Ways to Keep your Man, letters, beauty and horoscope pages. The magazine includes original photography and has a high degree of professional finish in terms of graphics, typography and general design.

On one level, *Slutmopolitan* appears to be a parodic deconstruction of a dominant (and perhaps 'realist') form, in which issues of gender representation are very much the central concern – and in this sense, it does address the theoretical aims of the teaching. Yet, as is perhaps obvious, the pleasures of *Slutmo* seem to derive their energy not from theoretical critique but from the display of the body, a rude and vigorous sense of humour, and above all from the sense of a shared joke.

There is a theory behind *Slutmo*, but it emerged *during* the process of production and (as we shall see) with considerable contradictions. The following piece of dialogue, which took place in the classroom one day, suggests a resistance to academic theory on a number of levels:

Teacher: So you're criticizing the representation of femininity in women's magazines?
Clare: We just want to have a laugh.

The over-serious media teacher is clearly being satirized here, in the best time-honoured tradition. But a number of further implications seem to be present in this exchange. We have the problematic situation of the male teacher explaining feminism to the female student – motivated, perhaps, by a fear that her work might not be as 'politically correct' as he (and indeed the examiner) would like it to be. We have the student resisting the theoretical (and ideological) appropriation of her work, through an emphasis on fun and 'having a laugh', thereby opposing the teacher's insistence on serious, academic discourse. 'Having a laugh', not taking things seriously, very effectively provides a kind of ambiguity, a space for play, in which meanings cannot be fixed once and for all.

For this reason, the project poses significant dilemmas in terms of inter-pretation and evaluation. If it is to be evaluated according to the examination criteria, we should pay attention to the textual strategies by which *Slutmo* critiques the dominant ideology of women's magazines (although precisely what that dominant ideology might be remains a complex question). On one level, this kind of critique was one with which the girls themselves were already very familiar, and they may not have felt the need to draw an elaborate academic map to show us that they knew their way around. Yet while this was explicit from their written accounts, it is something that has to be inferred from its encoded and implicit form in the product itself.

In fact, it is by no means clear that all the parody in the magazine works in this way, nor that all the authors agreed about what was being parodied – or indeed, that they even saw parody as being the point of their work. Thus, one of the girls argued that the anti-nuclear pendant pictured on the front cover showed that its wearer, the eponymous slut, would be too stupid to realize its significance. On the other hand, another pointed out that the parody was directed against the social stereotyping of sluts (whatever that word might mean within the language of patriarchal society – as she herself pointed out), because it demonstrated independence of thought and action.

As this implies, it was often far from clear who was the butt of the joke – the conventional media representation of the 'slut' or simply real 'sluts' them-selves. Of course, this reflects the essential ambiguity of parody. As I have noted, parody raises awkward questions of intent and explicitness. Parody only becomes parodic, it is assumed, if it is conscious and deliberate: otherwise it is imitation and could be criticized for merely reproducing what it seeks to mock. Yet this raises the question of whether parody is necessarily critical – or whether it is perhaps an intermediate stage in the development of a truly critical awareness. To what extent, for example, is it possible to mock some-thing without understanding why? Or to imitate without understanding?

In fact, it became clear that this project was working in several different directions, both from the point of view of its creators and of ourselves as teachers – and indeed that this ambiguity was partly the point of it all. By sanctioning opportunities to enact 'sluttish' behaviour, the project enabled the girls to display their sexuality (or a construction of their sexuality) in a semi-public forum. The resulting material could be seen as, on one level, hopelessly 'sexist' – or at least as permitting the possibility of a sexist reading. This certainly accounted for some of the interest in the work among the boys who saw it – and indeed, for condemnation among some of the teachers to whom we have shown it. On this basis, the girls could be seen to have actively colluded in a process of self-objectification.

On the other hand, this overt display of sexuality could also be seen as subversive – at least in the context of the girls' positioning as children within the power-relations of the school. From this perspective, *Slutmo* could be seen as an example of what Bakhtin (1968) calls the *carnivalesque*, subverting the respectable through a form of bodily transgression. Indeed, from a post-modern feminist perspective, *Slutmo* could be seen as a kind of celebration and a deconstruction of the masquerade of femininity. From this position, gender comes to be seen not just as a form of behaviour or a personal attribute but in itself as a form of parody. As Judith Butler (1990) argues, gender is a continual 'performance' parodying 'the very notion *of* an individual'. It functions as a way of exposing identity as fabricated and possessing no 'depth or inner substance':

> Gender is the repeated stylisation of the body, a set of repeated acts within a highly rigid regulatory frame that congeal over time to produce the appearance of substance, of a natural sort of being.

Page after page of *Slutmo* rehearses precisely this kind of stylized regulation and policing of the female body, as we are shown eye make-up, hair care, nails and laddered stockings, all formulaically laid out and ritualized. The women depicted in the magazine are thus undergoing the process of congealing Butler describes; and the project of *Slutmo* parodies the surface structures of femininity to expose the constructed nature of gender itself.

Nevertheless, this still leaves an uncomfortable gap between my reading of the project and the interpretations of its authors. Even the most explicitly 'feminist' of the authors – and this is a label I suspect they would all have refused – would not have conceptualized the politics of their project in this way. On one level, there is a sense in which the parodic dimension I have identified implicitly positions its target as other people; yet it simultaneously permits the girls to *become* those other people, or at least to recognize (and indulge) the 'otherness' in themselves. In becoming 'sluts', the girls also announce that they are not.

This kind of ambiguity was particularly apparent in the case of one of the girls, Zerrin, whose emotive written account of the project seemed quite at odds with our dryly theoretical agenda. It shows very clearly the futility of attempting to divorce theoretical analysis from the personal aspects of the work:

> . . . the most original idea was to undermine the other women's magazines, we didn't want to aim for the 'working girl' image and definitely not for the 'housewife and Mummy' look so we decided on having the whole magazine based on the idea of being a slut, who's so outrageous you couldn't believe your eyes. This meant we'd be mocking the other magazines with a 'Tarty' theme with the magazine aimed at the women whose skirt is never short enough, who's worried about her nails breaking and whose dress sense could have been thrown off the back of a lorry instead of just dropped, her lipstick was the cheapest thing going apart from herself that is, and most of all if she looked hot enough for the men?

For this to work as a group we had to think hard of examples of what is slutty/Tarty, it wasn't that hard since being girls, it was easy to think of things that we would never do or wear, we thought of things like ESSEX girls, such as SHARON and TRACY[4] which was really stereotypical. Also images of white stilettos and black fishnet tights were head off the list also bright coloured clothes with childish play-like jewellery, such as plastic earrings, yellow beads, plastic rings etc.

Its always been easy thinking of slutty things since there's so many things that are considered so-called 'Slutty'. Its even worse to think of why these stereotypical views and ideas are slutty anyway . . . How does anyone know if the way I dress is slutty or not? I expect these views come from old values and expectations of women being 'virgin' who's clean, respectable (listens to parents) and generally does what is seen proper to do. Now young lady/woman in traditional views would be seen as a respectable lady who's willing to keep her legs firmly shut until she gets married to the man of her dreams!!!? Also she must love children, cleaning, sewing, cooking and brilliant lover to husband! She must not spend money like there's no tomorrow seeing as she has to make sure there's food to be eaten, also no unnecessary leaving of the house. Then the final thing is she should dress appropriately, a long skirt, shirt, hair back, basically no make-up and no bright pink lipstick . . .

So its easy just think in the completely opposite of these views and you'll have everything to know about sluts/tarts and how to be a slut, that is. So a slut is a woman who can't control her urges, who pastes make-up on, who flirts, who goes out, who drinks, smokes, buys outrageous clothes, with no dress sense, long nails, short skirts, big earrings, fishnet tights, and white stilettos . . .

The tensions here are obvious enough. If one wants to, it is easy to relate the expectations of Zerrin's traditional Muslim home to the pent-up feelings of this outburst. The compulsive repetitions (there are even more in her original account), the lavish itemizing of 'white stilettos' and the detailed descriptions of clashing colours were unsettling for us as male researchers and teachers. Yet before becoming consumed by voyeuristic angst, it is worth considering that this may be part of the object of the exercise from Zerrin's point of view. In other words, the piece is as self-consciously *resistant* as it is expressive; and, as the male readers to whom it is immediately addressed, we are being deliberately implicated in its exploration of sexual identity.

The project clearly allows Zerrin to negotiate her sexuality, and to make connections between media consumption and what she perceives as personal freedom. What is less clear is what she thinks *Slutmo* is aiming to do. The sheer enjoyment Zerrin has derived from being allowed to explore 'sluttishness', and the pleasure she seems to have gained from simulating oral sex in an imitation

Flake advertisement is only implicitly measured here against the respectable educational discourse. This leads to considerable intellectual confusion. It is not clear whether 'sluts' really do or do not exist, whether they are powerful or powerless, or whether the alternatives to being a slut are actually preferable. Neither is it clear whether the magazine is satirizing 'sluts' themselves or the people who are critical of them, and who have constructed the stereotype in the first place. Unlike Madonna (the unspoken presence here), Zerrin can't explicitly acknowledge the 'slut' in herself and is therefore unable to explain how the magazine uses the slut figure in its satirical message – although, as with Madonna, it is the fundamental ambiguity of the process that is essential if it is to serve the functions that it does.

Broadly speaking, I would argue that the experience of this project gave Zerrin an opportunity to explore issues of gender and sexuality on both a personal and a wider social level. Yet what is puzzling is the extent to which the project 'empowers' Zerrin – whatever we might take that to mean (cf. Ellsworth, 1989). What is even more difficult to ascertain is the kind of *learning* that might be going on here, and the relation of that learning to any kind of political consciousness. If Zerrin can't disentangle the levels of parody explicitly in her writing, what can one claim for the educational value of the activity? Of course, this question raises a secondary one: the educational value *for whom*? Zerrin, as a 17-year-old girl from a Turkish family, and her ageing, middle-class, male Media Studies teachers inevitably have different agendas to explore. One can obviously value the way the project gives Zerrin opportunities to explore these issues – although its value for her depends largely on its status as a piece of creative work rather than the attempt to generate a distanced, rational account in the accompanying writing.

There are, then, very real possibilities that can be offered by this kind of work. What Zerrin is attempting to do here is something rather more complex than simply 'finding a voice'. If anything, what she finds is a set of multiple, conflicting voices, in which the positions that are available to her are far from stable or fixed (cf. Orner, 1992). The confusions of her written account reflect the difficulty, but also the honesty, of her attempt to view herself, especially facets of her gender and sexuality, as somehow 'other'. Rather than opting for the safety of rationalistic critique, Zerrin leaps into the pleasures of positioning herself in other people's categories of gender. Yet working on the project also allows her a comparatively safe space in which she can play with the range of gender positions that are available to her and reflect upon their contradictory possibilities and consequences.

Conclusion: Beyond Political Correctness

The two pieces of work I have analysed here cannot be seen simply as instances of students' 'creative self-expression'. On the contrary, they came about through a process of negotiation between the students' perspectives and our own requirements and expectations as teachers. Both positively and negatively – in terms of what they say and what they do not say – they bear the marks of the social and institutional contexts in which they were produced.

Our requirements were, on one level, *theoretical* – and, at least outwardly, quite neutral. Both these projects were intended to raise theoretical questions which relate directly to the key concepts on the Media Studies syllabus. In the case of the sitcom project, these themes were primarily those of *audience* and *genre*. In devising their trailers, the students were expected to negotiate a difficult series of demands. On the one hand, they were expected to be original; but on the other, they were required to devise a programme that built on the strengths of existing examples of the genre. They were also expected to target a specific audience, and to take account of what they could find out about that audience, as well as what others (notably adults) would see as appropriate for them. In the case of *Slutmopolitan*, these themes were broadly those of *realism* and *representation*. Here again, the students were negotiating contradictory demands: they chose to use a popular form, but they were caught between the implicit requirement to subvert it (through anti-realism) and the impulse to celebrate it. While they were not always explicitly articulated, the project raised complex questions about the relationships between representation and subjectivity.

On another level, however, our requirements were also *political*. We ourselves were only occasionally explicit about this dimension of the situation, not least because of our own ambiguous feelings about it. Yet the students were clearly well-acquainted with a whole range of constraints on their speech and behaviour – constraints which they knew to be enforced through disciplinary processes of different kinds, ranging from the allocation of grades to overt forms of punishment by teachers. To some extent, these were the traditional moral constraints of schooling, in which students are positioned as 'children' in a system which is controlled by adults. The overtly sexual display of the girls who produced *Slutmopolitan* could be read, on one level, as a conscious and flagrant violation of these constraints – albeit one with ambiguous consequences.

Yet in both cases, there were further constraints which I have intermittently referred to here as *political correctness* – which seemed to apply despite the fact that these were very different kinds of schools. Again, these constraints were partly enforced through the disciplinary apparatus of the school – which, for example, caused considerable difficulties for the sitcom group in terms of the language they used to describe their work, at least in the more public context of whole class discussion. Yet they can also be traced to the more apparently academic requirements of the examination syllabus, which required the students to make explicit, and to distance themselves from, the potentially objectionable elements of their productions. In both cases, this occasioned a certain degree of anxiety for us as teachers. Thus, it was permissible for the boys to include all manner of 'stereotypes' in their production, as long as they clearly labelled them as such; while the girls could produce images which could be read as 'sexist', as long as they claimed that they were in fact critical deconstructions of the dominant objectification of the female body. In both cases, the notion of parody seemed to serve as a useful means of *post hoc* justification: it allowed the students to have their cake and eat it too.

As I have implied, this process is partly a matter of learning the rules of a particular genre of discourse – in this case, the discourse of 'critical analysis' (see Buckingham, 1993). Learning Media Studies, like learning any other school subject, is partly a matter of socializing oneself into a particular discourse community: one's membership of that community is displayed through one's employment of a particular terminology – in this case, for example, of terms like *representation*, *stereotype* and *genre*. Membership of this community implies a certain distance from those who are not members – in this case, those whose inferior powers of critical analysis render them vulnerable to the ideological effects of the media, to which members themselves have of course become immune. The discourse of Media Studies is thus, unavoidably, a discourse of political correctness; and, I would argue, carries an ineradicable taint of self-righteousness.

The students responded to these requirements partly by 'playing the game', but also by consciously subverting its rules – and it is in this sense that their work can be read as a form of negotiation. On one level, the pleasures which were afforded by these activities were extremely positive, or at least comparatively innocuous. As I have implied, much of the pleasure in both cases depended upon the collaborative nature of the activity: sharing your work with peers, 'having a laugh', dressing up and enjoying in-jokes, are absolutely central to what is taking place. Yet at the same time, there is a sense in which both projects reflect a kind of subversion or transgression of the rules of serious educational endeavour. In different ways, the simulated situation of the first project and the parodic dimension of the second seemed to allow a sanctioned space for play, in which it became possible to speak the unspeakable, to flirt with what was clearly recognized as taboo. Most of these students already knew the politically correct things they were expected to do and say: much of the pleasure here came from the fact that they could do and say precisely the opposite, without any necessary commitment, but also without fear of reprisal.

As I have shown, the political *consequences* of this situation are far from straightforward: pleasures which may be 'subversive' in some respects may be distinctly less so in others. Yet, I would question the view that either project simply reproduces dominant values – or indeed, simply opposes them. The ambiguous space which is made available by parody permits the students a degree of open-ended exploration, in which positions and fantasies can be tried on for size. While the *products themselves* can indeed be read in a variety of ways – from 'dominant' to 'oppositional' – what seems to have been going on for their authors was rather less straightforward.

Yet it is this ambiguity that also makes these productions difficult to evaluate – and, for us as teachers, to assess. Thus, many of these students were able to produce the required critical discourse in their written work, although it is hard to avoid the conclusion that much of this was a form of *post hoc* self-justification. This was particularly the case for the middle-class boys in the first school, for whom academic writing posed comparatively few problems. On the other hand, such requirements clearly discriminate against a student like Zerrin, whose writing cannot do justice to the complexity of the experience – or even help her to sort out the confusions which it entailed. Indeed, I would argue that in both cases, the requirements for written assessment were only able to capture a very limited dimension of what took place. A great deal of what might have been significant for these students – and indeed, a great deal of what they might have *learnt* – simply exceeded our means of gaining access to it.

It is not my intention merely to celebrate this – as, perhaps, a partial victory of 'pleasure' over the narrow constraints of academic discourse; although equally, it is hard to see what alternatives one might devise. Simply policing students behaviour in order to ensure that they produce politically correct texts is, I would argue, a futile activity that will only be counter-productive. Yet it is not enough simply to retreat from the difficulties of such work – on the grounds, perhaps, that so much of what goes on in such situations will remain forever 'unknowable' (Ellsworth, 1989).

In undertaking critical analysis of the media in classrooms, it is comparatively easy for teachers to retain ideological control. As I have shown in other research, such activities often become an exercise in 'guessing what's in teacher's mind' (Buckingham, Fraser and Mayman, 1990). It is not difficult to socialize students into rehearsing the correct anti-sexist, anti-racist lines – although whether that actually makes any difference to what they think is another question. But with practical work, we are no longer holding the reins. If we want to enable students to explore the theoretical issues in a genuinely open-ended way – rather than simply using practical work to demonstrate our own agenda – we have to acknowledge the possibility that they will not arrive at the correct positions that we might like them to occupy. This may be particularly true in situations where students appear to imitate and parody so-called 'dominant' forms. As I have implied, imitation may in fact be a necessary part of all language learning; and parody may offer substantial critical insights in its own right. To try to replace this by an insistence on some form of 'oppositional practice' or 'deconstruction' is simply to set up another model to be imitated.

Notes

1 One indication of this form of popular media literacy would be the current UK television series *Hotshots*, in which viewers contribute their parodies and remakes of advertisements and programmes.

David Buckingham

2 For a fuller account of this research, see Buckingham, Grahame and Sefton-Green (1995). Thanks to Pete Fraser for his collaboration on this work; and to the Gulbenkian Foundation for their funding of the project.
3 For a fuller account of this research, see Buckingham and Sefton-Green (1994). Thanks to Julian Sefton-Green for his collaboration on this project, and for his analysis of the dynamics of *Slutmo*.
4 'Essex girls' were effectively invented by the British popular press in 1992, as a local variant of the 'bimbo/slut' stereotype. 'Sharon and Tracy' may be a reference to the characters in BBC series *Birds of a Feather*: while they come from Essex, they don't really fit the image Zerrin is describing here. Alternatively, these names are often used disparaginly as identikit white working-class names: perhaps this is how Zerrin is using them here.

References

ALVARADO, M. and BOYD-BARRETT, O. (Eds) (1992) *Media Education: An Introduction*, London: British Film Institute and The Open University Press.
BAKHTIN, M. (1968) *Rabelais and his World*, Cambridge, MA: MIT Press.
BRITZMAN, D. (1991) Decentering discourses in teacher education: Or, the unleashing of unpopular things, *Journal of Education*, **173** (3), 60–80.
BUCKINGHAM, D. (1987) *Unit 27: Media Education* (EH207 *Communication and Education*), Milton Keynes: Open University Press.
BUCKINGHAM, D. (Ed.) (1990) *Watching Media Learning: Making Sense of Media Education*, London: Falmer Press.
BUCKINGHAM, D. (1993) Going critical: The limits of media literacy, *Australian Journal of Education*, **37** (2), 142–52.
BUCKINGHAM, D. and SEFTON-GREEN, J. (1994) *Cultural Studies Goes to School: Reading and Teaching Popular Media*, London: Taylor and Francis.
BUCKINGHAM, D., FRASER, P. and MAYMAN, N. (1990) Stepping into the void: Beginning classroom research in media education, in BUCKINGHAM, D. (Ed.) *Watching Media Learning, Making Sense of Media Education*, London: Falmer Press, 19–59.
BUCKINGHAM, D., GRAHAME, J. and SEFTON-GREEN, J. (1995) *Making Media: Practical Production in Media Education*, London: English and Media Centre.
BUTLER, J. (1990) *Gender Trouble: Feminism and the Subversion of Identity*, London: Routledge
CARLSSON-PAIGE, N. and LEVIN, D. (1990) *Who's Calling the Shots? How to Respond Effectively to Children's Fascination with War Play and War Toys*, Santa Cruz, CA: New Society.
COLLINS, R. (1976) Media studies: Alternative or oppositional practice, in WHITTY, G. and YOUNG, M. (Eds) *Explorations in the Politics of School Knowledge*, Driffield: Nafferton.

ELLSWORTH, E. (1989) Why doesn't this feel empowering? Working through the repressive myths of critical pedagogy, *Harvard Educational Review*, **59** (3), 297–324.

FERGUSON, B. (1981) Practical work and pedagogy, *Screen Education*, **38**, 42–55.

GRAHAME, J. (Ed.) (1994) *Production Practices*, London: The English and Media Centre.

HUTCHEON, L. (1985) *A Theory of Parody*, London: Methuen.

LORAC, C. and WEISS, M. (1981) *Communication and Social Skills*, Exeter: Wheaton.

LEAVIS, F. R. and THOMPSON, D. (1933) *Culture and Environment*, London: Chatto and Windus.

MASTERMAN, L. (1980) *Teaching About Television*, London: Macmillan.

ORNER, M. (1992) Interrupting the calls for student voice in 'liberatory' education: A feminist poststructuralist perspective, in LUKE, C. and GORE, J. (Eds) *Feminisms and Critical Pedagogy*, New York: Routledge.

ROSE, M. A. (1979) *Parody/Meta-Fiction: An Analysis of Parody as a Critical Mirror to the Writing and Reception of Fiction*, London: Croom Helm.

STAFFORD, R. (1990) Rethinking creativity: Extended practical projects in GCSE Media Studies, in BUCKINGHAM, D. (Ed.) *Watching Media Learning*, London: Falmer Press.

Chapter 5

Dealing with Feeling: Why Girl Number Twenty Still Doesn't Answer

Sue Turnbull

One of the more poignant aspects of re-reading Judith Williamson's memorable 1981/2 *Screen Education* essay 'How does Girl Number Twenty understand ideology?' is the sad realization that whatever Girl Number Twenty did understand about ideology (and it was probably quite a lot) she certainly wasn't going to tell Williamson – for reasons which this essay will attempt to investigate. The original Girl Number Twenty was Sissy Jupe in Charles Dickens' novel, *Hard Times*, an extract from which Williamson uses to preface this account of her own teaching experience. Asked to define a horse by the tyrannical rationalist, Mr Gradgrind, Sissy Jupe, who 'knows' horses from her experience in the circus where she lives, is silent while the creepy Bitzer does his stuff, parrotting off an encyclopaedic definition of the gramnivorous quadruped in question. Williamson's quotation of this fictional moment is clearly intended to resonate with the classroom experience she goes on to describe. And it does. Asked to consider the 'Representation of women in the media: myth, convention and code' in a second year Graphics Option, the three girls in her class sit in embarrassed silence while one of the more numerous boys, Mark, does his number on the romantic comics supposedly directed to a predominantly female market (I say supposedly, because my best friend's brother used to steal ours but would never admit he read them). Williamson is deeply troubled by this unintended outcome of her attempt to empower the girls through an analysis of the kinds of popular culture which she believes hold them in thrall to patriarchy through the workings of ideology.

Williamson's own Girl Twenty would appear to be Astrid (although I understand how her fictional exemplar works as a powerful metaphor for the other teaching situations she describes):

> My worst problem is Astrid. She looks, actually, very like the blonde
> heroines of the comic strip, her self image is clearly bound to the
> things we seem to be attacking. She sits at the front of the class and
> says, literally, nothing. She may file her nails, or just stare: I'm really
> worried about her. I offer to teach her with the other girls, but she
> doesn't particularly want to (Williamson, 1981/2:82).

As if to explain this refusal, Williamson adds in a footnote: 'Astrid is a good example of someone who could *not* learn about sexism "analytically", as Alvarado suggests, precisely because it was so bound up with her own experience' (Williamson, 1981/2:82). For Williamson, Astrid represents the problem of what to do with personal knowledge in the classroom. The reference to Alvarado involves an earlier article on 'progressive pedagogy' in *Screen Education* in which, according to Williamson, he refused to take this problem seriously. But it is a problem which nags and to which she returns some five years later, asking plaintively, 'Is there anyone here from a classroom?' (Williamson, 1985). This time the problem is cast more clearly as the unbreachable divide separating the subjective experience of teachers and students in the classroom and the rhetoric of a 'progressive pedagogy' which never addresses the specifics of classroom interaction. Once again Williamson asks how the proponents of what has since come to be called critical pedagogy would actually go about teaching students who are racist, sexist or otherwise unwilling (like Astrid) to embrace the enlightenment offered them by their well meaning teachers.

Williamson is worried about Astrid, as am I, though I suspect for different reasons. I've seen Astrid at work in innumerable secondary school classrooms in England, the US and Australia, and I've met her in other accounts of classroom practice, like Williamson's, where she always figures as a trope of passive resistance. I too have wondered about Astrid. What does Astrid know? Why won't she speak up? Although I think Williamson is on the right lines when she suggests that Astrid's silence may be an effect of the ways in which her self-image is bound up in the 'things we seem to be attacking', I think Williamson's analysis stops short of realizing how all our selves are bound up in expressions of taste, so that what any of us can say about our media preferences depends on the communicative context in which such an utterance takes place. Astrid is no fool. She knows that to admit to any pleasure in the teen comics under attack is to risk the ridicule of her peers and the disapproval of her teacher. While the other two girls in her class subsequently strive to obtain the teacher's approval by embracing the topic of their weight and the tyranny of slenderness, Astrid's tactic is silence. Astrid seeks nobody's approval in this context but her own.

But Astrid is not Williamson's only worry. There is also her first year Media and Communications class who have adopted the mass culture critique of the Frankfurt School developed by the radical left during the seventies (one legacy of which we might take to be the critical pedagogy movement of the eighties) in order to cheerfully dump on the cultural dopes who watch soap operas (women again?) and read the tabloid press. Although Williamson does not expand on this point, it is obvious that this is the place where left meets right, where cultural dopism is associated with the objects of low culture as opposed to the culturally valued objects of the elite (of which, ironically, *Hard Times* itself might be a good example – though Dickens, a great populist, would probably hoot at the thought of being thus elevated by the passage of time). Like Astrid, but more like Mark, these first year students were also unwilling to risk themselves and their pleasures in the classroom, preferring to ridicule the taste of others in a discourse of disapproval learned from their teachers and those everyday encounters with talk about the media (often in the media themselves) in which the disapproval of specific genres, texts and popular tastes circulate as a regime of truth.[1]

Finally we learn of Williamson's third year photography class who valiantly plodded in the wake of their mentor through the thickets of Freud, Marx, Saussure, Althusser and even Stuart Hall, only to find themselves unable to take photographs, immobilized by theory:

> And after two year's careful work – you know the kind of thing, as if it were a moral principle that they should understand semiotics, and ideological apparatuses – I found myself saying things like – 'Don't think too hard, just get out and do *something*' (Williamson, 1981/2:86).

Williamson is right to be worried. As a progressive and radical teacher committed to enlightening and empowering her students, she is faced with the realization that what she has achieved may be anything but.[2] To her credit, Williamson acknowledges this but can't think of a way out of the impasse, so strongly is she committed to an ideology of progressivism. With the benefit of hindsight, and not wishing to condescend to the past, Williamson's blind spot (her ideological commitment to empowerment through teacherly intervention) constitutes the black hole into which the laudable intentions of critical pedagogy have been sucked over the intervening years. This is true even though Williamson has the prescience to ask the all important questions of Alvarado – and this is my version not hers: 'So if pedagogy does not depend on personal experience, then on what does it depend? What am I to do about Astrid and Mark?'

Reading Carmen Luke and Jennifer Gore's collection of essays concerned with feminisms and critical pedagogy published some 14 years later, we find a depressingly similar scenario (Luke and Gore, 1992). This time the progressive theorists are Henry Giroux and Peter McLaren:[3] the self-critical and perturbed teacher is Elizabeth Ellsworth who asks from the classroom, 'Why doesn't this feel empowering?' There would seem to be a particular pattern here: male theorists make abstract pronouncements about the emancipatory possibilities of critical pedagogy while women teachers confront the limitations of this Utopian rhetoric in the messy reality of schools, universities and classrooms.[4] This is not to deny the existence of women theorists (Williamson and Ellsworth are both struggling more or less successfully to theorize their own experience); or the existence of male teachers who have also struggled to implement critical pedagogy in their own teaching practice; or the work of Buckingham and Sefton-Green (1994) who have attempted to bridge the chasm between theory and practice and to reflect critically on their classroom teaching. Indeed, Giroux (1994) himself has more recently attempted to describe how theory and practice come together as he 'gently exercis[es] my own authority' as the teacher of a graduate education and cultural studies class; a description which leaves this reader cold since it just sounds too good to be true. Apparently Giroux has only to deconstruct his own authoritative position as teacher, present his students with the appropriate readings in orientalism, difference, multiculturalism, postcolonialism, race, feminism, nationalism and the politics of speaking for Others; and ask them to write about how such theory intersects with their own experience of the world, in order to achieve instant success. Students willingly present their thoughts to the rest of the class in the safe space created by teacherly fiat. There are no Astrids here. Ironically, Giroux would appear to see no contradiction between the theory he advocates and the practice he embraces in speaking on behalf of his students about the unmitigated success of this exemplary exercise in liberatory pedagogy for them.

Meanwhile, back in the less than exemplary (but much more familiar) classrooms described above, Williamson draws attention to a whole set of issues which I want to explore in more detail with reference to another group of students and a different classroom context. Although Giroux may believe that he has solved the problem of how to teach in an emancipatory way, there are some of us still struggling with what often appear to be insurmountable problems when dealing with our own messy realities. In order to address these problems, I want to repose and expand Williamson's initial question, 'What does Girl Number Twenty understand about ideology?' to include the additional question 'and why isn't she telling us?' and describe my own attempts to find an answer to both.

An Australian Context

In 1987 I spent one year as a participant observer at a girls' secondary school in the inner suburbs of the large Australian city where I now live. The research I undertook then was motivated by that combination of altruism and self-interest which would appear to characterize most professional careers in academia. I was doing a Ph.D. but I was also trying to find the answers to a whole set of questions which I had been asking since I left Britain and secondary school teaching at a moment when I felt discouraged and disappointed, not only with the political climate, but also with the kind of teaching in which I was engaged. As a product of a grammar school education (they made us read *Hard Times* in the lower fifth), an elite university course in English Literature (which took us up to 1890 but no further), I myself had embraced the ideals of 'critical pedagogy' when I encountered them in my own teacher education course during the early seventies. Like Williamson, I strode into the classroom buoyed up by visions of empowerment but slunk out dismayed by my failure to make any difference where I thought it really mattered. At the moment when I began my research, I was pretty much in the same place as Williamson. I'd worked out that something was going on with the Astrids of this world which I didn't fully comprehend (as a woman I thought I had a better chance of understanding Astrid than Mark – though of late I've been thinking more about Mark)[5] and chose an all-girls school precisely because I had learned, like Williamson, that the presence of boys in the class often silenced the girls.

Because I was not required to teach, I was afforded the luxury of time to think about the kinds of teaching I observed and the nature of the social context in which this took place. But this was not my primary interest: my quarry was Astrid and I was merely using the school as a means to flush her out into the open. I wanted to find out how the media figured in her life, her pleasures, her fantasies. I was determined she'd talk to me since Astrid was the object of my intellectual desire and will to power through knowledge. As a consequence, I ended up with 22 very different Astrids (aged 16–17 from 11 different ethnic backgrounds) in a school where the students from non-English speaking backgrounds were in the majority (60 per cent–40 per cent), and where most of the teachers were women of Anglo-Celtic origin, like me. In the early stages of my research, I simply watched and listened as the girls in the Year 11 media class talked to their teacher, each other and me, the rather ambiguous figure understood to be writing 'a book' about them. I listened in the staffroom and at the Friday afternoon pub sessions down the road as the teachers talked about the girls, their expectations, their media preferences and all of the above in the relation to themselves as teachers. I became acutely aware of the discourses of disapproval circulating in the staff room about the girls' media preferences and tastes: romance, soap opera, male pop stars, fashion, etc. As far as I could tell, these discourses appeared to derive from:

- a leftish critique of mass culture in conjunction with the conservatism of a high culture position;[6]
- a popular feminism rejecting the objectifications of women in the media and the tyranny of slenderness (even though many of the teachers were themselves on diets) which was manifest in constant criticism of the girls for what was regarded as an excessive interest in hairstyles and appearance;
- a fairly broad interpretation of feminism, generally expressed in the teachers' shared belief that the girls should set their sights on academic success and a career rather than on short term social acceptance and early marriage.

I began to realize that the girls were well aware of these discourses of disapproval, so that what they could say about themselves and their media preferences was always framed in such a way as to take account of how their pronouncements might be received by an interlocutor. In other words, the girls understood the expression of media preferences to have profound consequences for what I shall call, following Romano Harré (1993), the conduct of their social and moral careers.[7] What they could say about the media to their teachers, their parents or each other therefore depended on their prediction of how such a pronouncement might be received and their willingness to seek the approval or risk the disapproval of their addressee.

This was brought home to me most effectively during the interviews which I conducted with each girl towards the end of the year. By this time, I had collected a diverse set of miscellaneous data including: questionnaires about their media habits, their answers to questions about family life and collages they had made about their favourite stars. But most importantly, I had simply been in the classroom experiencing the same lessons, going on the occasional school trip to a local TV station, and generally being around. However, as the interviews proceeded, I realized how limited my understanding of their lives could be, since what each girl chose to reveal about herself and her media preferences depended on how she constructed me, an Anglo-Celtic older woman who might or might not disapprove of her media practices (like her teachers), and what kinds of approval (if any) she desired from me.

On *Not* Reading the Romance

Because Williamson's starting point is Astrid and how to empower her through a revelation of the false promises contained within the ideology of girls' romantic comics, I too will focus on romance as an issue. But I want to present the larger picture. I want to discuss how romance figured in relation to a whole set of related discourses, including those concerned with sexuality, marriage and domestic responsibility which the girls encountered at school and at home. I want to demonstrate the contradictory nature of these different discourses and how the girls attempted to negotiate them in the conduct of their moral careers.

For example, I have already suggested that a discourse of disapproval about romance circulated among teachers in the staff room. The librarian complained to me that the girls were 'addicted' to romantic novels and that she fully intended to remove these from the library if only she could persuade the girls to read something else. That the girls were aware of the low esteem in which romance novels were held by the staff became apparent in the interviews when six out of the 12 girls who said they read romance suggested that this was something they 'used to do' but had grown out of. One of these girls, Portia, the second daughter of Portugese migrants, was only too willing to condemn romance on the basis of its perceived lack of realism:

> *Portia*: I used to read a lot of romances and things like that – but now
>   I hardly read at all – I'm not interested in reading romances any
>   more – they are all just a big fantasy.
> *Sue*: So what would a typical romance story be?

> *Portia*: Oh – love at first sight – they head off into the sunset – make
> love and then they get married – and it's all crap – it's all crap – and
> I used to think of that last year – two years ago – I'd think I'd love
> that to happen to me – it's nothing like that – and the movies are
> all crap as well – it's all crap – if you've ever been in that position.
> *Sue*: Of having a boyfriend?
> *Portia*: It's not like that at all.

At this particular moment in the school year, Portia had a boyfriend: a relationship which was causing a great deal of conflict at home, especially with her
father who thought that at 16 she was too young. To be fair, Portia, her father
and her mother seemed to be at loggerheads about everything and her accounts of life at home were dismal in the extreme. However, what her comments here reveal is that whatever her commitment to romance might have
been, her direct experience of relationships (that of herself and her boyfriend,
and indeed, that of her mother and father as reported by her) has enabled her
to 'see through' notions of romantic love as presented in such genres.

But I'm not entirely convinced that Portia had completely foresworn the
pleasures of the romantic fiction she was so eager to ridicule, since she was
regularly to be found reading love stories in popular magazines under the table
in class. What should we make of this behaviour in the light of her disavowal?
Is it possible that Portia can take pleasure in romantic stories without necessarily being committed to their status as truth? Is it possible that she enjoyed
the stories precisely because of their formulaic quality, their aesthetic properties as a popular genre? Could it be that reading romance under the table was
simply a tactic to avoid engaging in the lesson? Could it be that the appeal of
romance fiction is the fact that it addresses her as a sexualized adult in a
classroom environment where she is conventionally treated like a child? Or
could it be that she expects me to disapprove of romance reading and seeks my
approval through disavowing her own pleasure?

It might be noted that the issue of erotic fantasies and their potentially
subversive nature (especially when one is supposed to be doing something
else) are seldom raised in relation to the reading of romantic fiction. Barbara
Creed's essay on 'The woman's romance as sexual fantasy' (1984) is therefore
a valuable exception to this rule, exploring as it does the erotic charge in such
texts which present the male as the sexual object of a desiring female gaze.
However, the more usual assumption is that an attachment to such popular
forms is always accompanied by a commitment to the 'false' ideology of
romance which they propose.[8] Such texts are thus constructed as agents in the
oppression of women under patriarchy. Whatever the truth of the matter in
the case of Portia, the above exchange clearly reveals: a) her understanding
that romantic fiction is a specific genre with specific formulae; b) that life is not
like that; c) that this is what I (an adult who supposedly shares the same taste
culture as her teachers) would probably want to hear.

I want to go further here and raise the possibility that for *all* the girls in the classroom their real-life experience and their reading of romance produced challenging contradictions. Furthermore, I want to suggest that the girls were acutely aware of these contradictions and well able to express them (although unable to resolve them) even though the forms of this critique differed greatly from the kinds of critical discourse favoured by academics and teachers. It is here we hit on a crucial issue for Williamson and for other teachers. Is the girls' understanding of these contradictions and their ability to work through them diminished or inadequate because of their lack of the conventional critical discourse couched in terms of ideology and power? Or are their own creative and idiosyncratic forms of communication sufficient for their purposes? In order to demonstrate what I mean, I would like to cite one particular set of classroom experiences, and their implications.

A Different Kind of Knowledge

From early February until June (halfway through the academic year), every-one in Year 11 Media was aware of the presence of Amanda, a pregnant Anglo-Celtic student whose baby was born in July. Amanda subsequently returned to school to finish her Year 11, and on several occasions brought in her baby, over whom the teachers fussed and gushed. The reactions of Amanda's teachers (who appeared to accept and even congratulate Amanda for managing the birth of her baby and returning to school), and the reactions of her parents (who supported her and encouraged her to keep the baby which her mother, a registered child minder, was willing to care for during the day), appeared puzzling for many of the non-Anglo girls. For them, an unmarried pregnancy would appear to be the worst fate they could imagine for them-selves in terms of their moral careers and the reaction of their families. At about the same time Amanda left to have her baby, as part of a class video production exercise five Macedonian girls[9] wrote the script for a radio play vividly portraying (and parodying) how they imagined their own families would deal with such an event. *Wogs at Home* (a title borrowed from the then current comedy stage show entitled *Wogs at Work*, which originally appropri-ated the racial slur 'wog' for strategic political purposes) constructed a grimly humorous version of the imagined reactions of a stereotypical Macedonian family to the pregnancy of their daughter (this extract comes from the closing moments of the play):[10]

> *Bozna* [the grandmother]: You Australian people stupid. No sex before marriage. You prostitute if sex. You two times prostitute if pregnant.
> *Trayan* [the grandfather]: Lele, my poor family name – oohhh—
> *Zvezda* [mother]: Lele, my daughter make for me sick. You only 20 years old. You too young for sex. Very young.
> *Dragi* [father]: Get out – if anybody hear you have baby – me kill

myself. This way you better go and me tell people you get hit by
aeroplane going to Macedonia – go.
Yadranka [daughter]: But –
Zvezda: Go, Go. No come home. Go, no come home.
Everyone: Lele Australia.

It is interesting to note that the grandmother addresses her criticism of the
grandaughter in terms of 'you Australian people' and that the climax of
the piece is structured in terms of what appears to be a general lament about
the pernicious influence of Australia. For this stereotypical migrant family,
Australia seems to stand for whatever threatens their traditional values: in
this case 'proper' codes of sexual conduct for girls. And so, by succumbing
to the cultural influence of Australia, the daughter of the house has brought
such shame on the family that her father and mother would rather reject
her than have the disgrace made public. Becoming sexually active would
therefore seem to be a particularly hazardous move for the daughters of
migrants who cling to traditional forms of courtship which enable them to
control their daughter's sexuality. In a way, the elders of this Macedonian
family are right, because it is within an Australian classroom that their daughters have encountered Amanda and other sexually active girls like her. It is
in the Australian media (which are also British and American)[11] that the girls
are encountering representations of active female sexuality. For example, in
those same magazines which they read for the romantic fiction under the
tables or in the playgrounds at break and at lunch time, all the girls were being
confronted with many different kinds of messages addressing them as sexually
active adults, including advice on sexually transmitted diseases, positions
for better sex, etc. These articles they read avidly, often collectively, while
discussing their opinions on many aspects of the information and pictures
presented.

I want to argue that *Wogs at Home* is a clear example of how the Macedonian girls understand the force of contradictory sexual codes of behaviour
which they are attempting to negotiate in the conduct of their own moral
careers. Moreover, the play demonstrates their understanding of the potential
consequences (in terms of a worst case scenario) of breaking with what is
constructed as their parents' traditional and 'old-fashioned' ways ('old-
fashioned' being a term used by almost all of them in interviews with me as
the best way of characterizing their parents' attitudes and expectations). *Wogs
at Home* reveals the girls' understanding of how ideology operates in the
context of their own lives, but most importantly, it reveals that this knowledge
has not necessarily been obtained as a consequence of teacherly intervention
in terms of lessons on ideology. In other words, this form of knowledge is
neither a *knowing that* (of facts or theoretical principles) nor a *knowing how* (a
knowledge of technique) but a *knowing from*, or as Shotter (1990) terms it,
'knowing of the third kind'.[12] This kind of knowing is a form of practical
knowledge:

it is knowledge of a *moral* kind, for it depends upon the judgements of others as to whether its expression or its use is ethically proper or not – one cannot just have it or express it on one's own, or wholly within oneself. It is the kind of knowledge one has *only from within a social situation* . . . and which thus takes into account (and is accountable to) the others in the social situation . . . (Shotter, 1993:7).

To be fair to Williamson, she recognizes the significance of this kind of knowledge, the sort of personal experience which Alvarado would exclude from the classroom but which she found she couldn't ignore, particularly when it might be a valuable teaching tool:

So I would say that students learn best to see the 'invisible', ideology, when it becomes in their own interest to – when they are actually caught in a contradiction, believing things which are directly hindering their own well being or wishes, or which conflict with a change in experience (Williamson, 1981/2:85).

However, while Williamson fears that once you make students aware of ideology, the effect is often 'traumatic', even 'terrifying', and for her photography students, sadly 'immobilising', I want to suggest that the trauma, the fear and the immobility may be an effect of the contradictions themselves, and I want to suggest how these contradictions are produced by considering the case of Leah, one of the most quiet and reserved girls in the classroom I observed – my own Astrid.

Living the Contradictions

The eldest of six children (four girls and two boys), Leah was an academically gifted student whose parents had migrated to Australia from Lebanon when she was a toddler. From her account, it would appear that her parents worked and socialized only with other Lebanese families and expected their children to do likewise. Leah and her brothers and sisters were therefore being brought up in what Leah predictably characterized as traditional and 'old-fashioned' ways, and contact with 'Australia' was limited as far as possible. They were never allowed out unchaperoned and if Leah was needed at home, her domestic duties always took precedence over her schooling:

There is a lot expected of my family – of the girls in my family especially – they [her parents] don't like to be shamed in any way – you know – they want to be respected in the community – they're high up on respect – they love it you know. If you do anything that is shameful – God help you. So we've been – like we are not allowed to

go out very often. Occasionally we go to a supermarket – but I always
have to have someone with me. You know – I can never go by myself
or with friends. Cinema – like I asked my Dad if I can go to the
cinema with a couple of friends the other day – and he wouldn't let
me. We are very restricted – they won't let us go anywhere in case –
they are mainly worried in case somebody sees us and starts spread-
ing rumours – you know – the whole thing in Lebanon is you don't
have boyfriends and things like that – they do in some parts of
Lebanon – but where we lived – the village and all that – they're still
very old fashioned – and there's no boyfriend – there's no going out.
If a guy is sort of interested in you – he comes over and talks to your
parents about you – that's why they are very strict on reputations – so
they don't allow you to go out in case somebody spreads a rumour
about you and that rumour spreads so your reputation sort of falls in
the community.

Here, Leah provides us with an account of the politics of reputation and the
strict codes of sexual conduct operative in migrant families from rural areas
which mirror those inferred by the Macedonian girls in their play.[13] Leah was
experiencing the force of these moral codes in very immediate ways since her
parents had recently endeavoured to introduce her to one potential suitor,
whom she had rejected, apparently without experiencing any negative consequences. It is in relation to this experience that she was able to articulate how
she was attempting to negotiate the contradiction between the romantic ideology of being 'in love' with the traditional ideology of making a 'good
marriage'. So far, Leah's parents appeared to be going along with her desire
to choose a husband towards whom she could at least feel romantically
inclined.

Leah was only too well aware of other contradictions emerging from her
contact with different social and moral expectations about how she should
conduct herself and imagine her future. Another aspect of this was the pressure she was feeling from her teachers to think about a career and independence, in direct contradiction to her parents' expectations. 'They [the teachers]
pressure you a lot into – girls shouldn't be stuck at home – and I don't
really blame them. I think that way too – and if I had my way I'd do it.'
Leah admitted that she herself aspired to a career as a pharmacist and wanted
to go to university like her two uncles who both had Masters degrees in
Engineering:

I'd love a career – but I'm not too sure yet – I haven't really discussed
it with my parents – and they'll probably say to me, 'What's the point
– you know – you have to be married and you have to have children
eventually and you are going to stop the career and come home and
work in the house and be a housewife' – you know – sort of thing –
and they might stop me from actually going to university.

Leah needed no help in identifying the source of the contradiction:

> The thing is, we've been brought up in Australia – if we'd been brought up in Lebanon – we'd probably have different ideas – different views – on a lot of things – but we are brought up here and so we are seeing two different types of cultures and we're comparing our lives to other people's.

But what was she to do? How was she to negotiate these different sets of expectations? For all the girls from non-English speaking backgrounds, the problem was not that of identifying conflicting ideologies about women and their social role which they encountered at home, at school and in the media. The problem was that of dealing with their affective ties to their families and the moral expectations that they be 'good girls'.

It is here that the media figured in another interesting way, as offering an alternative set of possibilities for the conduct of family life. In a discussion of the then current American sitcom, *The Cosby Show*, Leah made some telling comments in this regard, suggesting that the Cosby parents gave their children support and freedom to pursue their own careers while providing them with a solid moral framework:

> *Leah*: I like my relationship with my parents – I think they have a very good relationship – they understand – it's just they have rules – like *The Cosby Show* parents my parents have rules and you have to abide by them – if you don't – you know – you suffer the consequences . . .
>
> *Sue*: But are they very protective?
>
> *Leah*: Yes very – sometimes you can say over-protective – and one thing I really like is . . . that no matter how old the parents get – they [Lebanese families] always have their children with them [she provides a detailed example of a cousin looking after his aged mother].
>
> *Sue*: And so it's very important to look after your family – you look after your parents – children have that responsibility.
>
> *Leah*: Family is the main thing.

And it is with Leah's assertion 'family is the main thing' that we come to her insurmountable stumbling block. It should therefore come as no surprise to learn that she did not complete her final year of school and so did not go to University, but left school to become a beautician, a move which we can only hope went some way to satisfying her own interest in pharmacy as well as her parents' notion of a suitable time filler for a daughter waiting to get married.

So what are the implications of Leah's story and self-presentation for a radical-pedagogy which seeks to bring about social change through teacherly intervention in schools? What could such a pedagogy accomplish for Leah?

She already knows that the future projected for her by her parents is not inevitable. She knows she could choose an alternative path, but at what cost? She loves her family and is committed to them. She can see that the family values of care and responsibility which they espouse are not all bad. Should she reject these (as encouraged by her teachers) in pursuit of her own interests envisaged as a career and freedom from the kinds of control exterted by the family? What are the moral and emotional dimensions of her dilemma? I have to admit that I am not sure what the rhetoric of empowerment in the discourse of critical pedagogy would really mean for Leah. Is it empowering to reject one's family and their values? Is it empowering to choose a university course and a career over marriage and children? What is at stake here?

I believe that the stakes are very high and that we should be very careful in assuming we know the answers to these questions. So, while critical thinkers like Giroux and hooks remain committed to education as the practice of freedom obtained via a transformative pedagogy which can only result in the inevitable empowerment of their students, I'm not convinced that this would be as easy or as straightforward as they make out. I believe that our students face all kinds of problems and issues in the negotiation of their lives and futures which we can only guess at – and that we should leave such negotiation up to them while remaining committed to a vision of society in which everyone has the same democratic opportunities for happiness and self-fulfilment. If this is so, then what should we be teaching in the media classroom?

I want to argue that as teachers we should be extremely wary of using media teaching as a platform to advance our own political and moral positions, assuming that these alone are valid and viable. In the postcolonial context of the present when everything and everybody's social and moral position would appear to be in a state of flux – a state of flux brought about at least in part by the very media we are asked to condemn – social change would seem inevitable without our seeking to bring it about any more rapidly. Instead of imposing our own interpretations of the media on our students, we should be aware of how racial, cultural, class and gender differences shape all our experiences of the media, so that it is quite impossible to assume we know what the political and emotional significance of a media text might be for anyone else. For example, if commitment to the ideology of romantic fiction signifies for Leah a gesture of independence in relation to her parents and their expectations that she marry a person chosen by them, then what right have we to condemn and dismiss it, especially when she already knows the status of romance as fiction and text?

Rather than being intent on teaching our students *what* to think about the media, I believe we should be intent on teaching them *how* to think. In other words, rather than being intent on working towards agreed upon answers, I think we should be intent on devising the significant *questions* we should all be asking about the role of the media in our lives. It is in this regard that I can envisage a much more constructive role for theory in the classroom: 'other people's theories' should only ever be introduced as a set of explanatory possibilities which may or may not fit our own or our students' experience of the text. In this way, theory may then fulfil the 'healing function' ascribed to it by bell hooks (1994) who argues that learning about other people's attempts to deal with their own experience can help soothe the pain produced by the difficult social and historical circumstances in which we find ourselves.

But exactly how should such personal experience be addressed in the classroom? Should we be asking our students to reveal all as we ask them to talk about their media practices? Asked to describe the role of the media (in the context of an interview with me). Leah responded:

> Media – in my life? I think it plays a big part – I don't know where I would be if there was no television – or videos – to tell you the truth. I'm sort of addicted to TV and it's a way of seeing the outside world – 'cos I know I'll never see it – I never go out – so TV is a way of seeing it – and knowing and learning about life – so it plays a big part in my life.

It is possible that Leah's construction of the role of the media in her life and her whole self-presentation as torn between two cultures is simply what she thought I, an older Anglo-Celtic woman with an interest in the media, would want to hear. It is also possible that this version of herself has become a way of accounting for (and justifying to herself) the gap between her lived reality and the alternatives which she can imagine but cannot, or will not, bring about. But should we be asking Leah (and Astrid) to lay themselves and their lives on the line in this way within the media classroom? What is at risk in students revealing intimate details about themselves and their media preferences in a social context and at an age when other people's opinions may have considerable impact on, and consequences for, their self-esteem?

It has been demonstrated time and again that the well-intentioned teacher bent on radical pedagogy often produces silence rather than critical reflection, particularly when asking students to bring their personal experience into the classroom. Sandra Taylor's (1989) life history project with sixteen Year 9 students, half of whom were from non-English speaking backgrounds, marks yet another doomed attempt to empower girls by asking them to critically reflect on family photographs as a way of deconstructing their own cultural and social space. What Taylor appears to have overlooked is how these teenage girls might *feel* about their families and 'daggy' family photos at an age when they may well be trying to define themselves as separate from, while still emotionally attached to and financially dependent on, their families. So even though Taylor simply wants to use the photos to get to somewhere else, what has again been overlooked is the emotional or affective dimension of the girls' relationships to the photos, their families and themselves. What is significant about this failed endeavour for media teachers is the fact that a particular media form, the family photograph, is being used as a means, not of teaching about the media, but as a means of teaching a moral and political lesson: a lesson the students reject.

It is interesting to speculate what would have happened if Taylor had tried a different strategy; if she had asked the girls to engage in a form of practical work which asked them to create an image of *themselves* in the past, present and the future using a variety of already existing or especially created media forms. If she had asked them, in other words, to devise an original articulation of themselves in and through the media. This task could then have led to the kinds of open-ended exploration of self and media which characterize a progressive rather than a radical form of pedagogy: a pedagogy which allows the students to explore the contradictions in their own experience of specific social contexts and the media, rather than seeking to overlay a template of critical theory imported from other times and other places.[14] For example, the teacher involved could have asked *why* the girls involved saw themselves and their futures in particular ways, what the use of media images rendered imaginable and unimaginable, and to explore the premises underlying these projections. In this way, the teacher asks students to articulate and explore their knowledge of the third kind in order to move from this *knowing from* to a *knowing why*.

But would the outcome necessarily be empowering? Does knowing why the world is the way it is (or should not be) a necessary component of empowerment? Surely the most critical and overlooked factor for the migrant girls in Taylor's study and my own is the question of literacy, in that high levels of accredited literacy still lead to more and better academic qualifications, hence more freedom of choice about jobs, a potentially greater degree of economic power and thus more control over the direction of one's life. Empowerment is thus inextricably linked to questions of cultural literacy.

This brings us back to what Williamson and Taylor want from their respective Astrids and why Astrid won't come to the party. Astrid fears that to satisfy these teachers she is going to have to deny her pleasure in the media text and assume a pose of critical self-consciousness which mimics the cultural literacy espoused, advocated and ultimately rewarded by her teachers. In other words, she will have to assess her media attachments and her life from their point of view. Astrid suspects that the aesthetic pleasures involving both mind and body which she derives from the texts in question will be rendered ridiculous, while the aesthetic pleasures of the teachers in *their* preferred texts will not be put in question. Astrid knows that in the hierarchy of tastes underpinned by the hierarchy of status and power in the classroom, her pleasures count for very little. She therefore has little incentive and no desire to risk exposing them to negative critical scrutiny. In so refusing, Astrid earns the animosity of her teachers, fails the course, leaves school early and ends up with even fewer choices about herself and her life than she might have had. No wonder Astrid is a worry. She marks the site where well-intentioned critical pedagogy and well-intentioned feminism collide in a crash course to nowhere.

Is it possible to avoid this dead-end? Can we succeed where so many others have failed? I believe we can (or I wouldn't still be a teacher), but that it will demand much more of us as media educators than espousing the appropriate rhetoric. I believe that we have to look hard at our assumptions about the purpose of media education and how this might practically improve the life choices of our students. In other words, I think we have to consider how media education might play a role in the development of less prescriptive forms of cultural literacy which will lead to accreditation and hence participation in a changing work force on more equal terms. In order to achieve this, we must reconsider the nature of our students' affective relationship with the media text under scrutiny and its cultural role in their lives and consider how that knowledge might be valued and evaluated. We must also acknowledge that Astrid's complex moral career as a student, daughter and young women negotiating relationships outside the home, is also crucial to her engagement with the media, affecting not only what she can say, but also what she can do about it. In this way, like us all, Astrid is caught between desire and duty, thought and action. Once we recognize this experience as our own, then maybe we can work together with our students towards articulating and understanding the contradictions we experience differently and in common.

I therefore believe that the valuable new forms of cultural literacy which can be enabled through media education will only become a reality when we as teachers learn to listen as well as well as to talk. In other words, if we ask Astrid to tell us about the nature of her engagement with the media we must not assume we already know all the answers. If we can do all this, and if we are really interested in listening to what Girl Number Twenty has to say, then maybe, just maybe, she will finally speak up and join in a conversation which has so far been about her rather than with her. Maybe then we will find out what Girl Number Twenty knows about ideology – and we don't.

Notes

1 I have dealt with these issues in more detail elsewhere. See Sue Turnbull (1993b).
2 An anxiety also voiced by Jennifer Gore (1992) with reference to her own teacher education programme.
3 Giroux and McLaren have been prolific writers on the topic of critical pedagogy. The essay specifically referred to by Ellsworth is: Henry A. Giroux and Peter McLaren (1986), 'Teacher education and the politics of engagement: The case for democratic schooling'.
4 Here I am echoing the critique voiced by Allan Luke in his introduction to David Buckingham and Julian Sefton-Green (1994).
5 As has Jane Gallop (1994) in her essay 'The teachers' breasts' which interrogates the construction of the male student as problem.

6 Indeed the kinds of negative discourses about the media voiced by teachers in Pete Fraser's (1990) study of teacher's talk.

7 Harré suggests that our social lives are organized around the perceived imperative to avoid contempt and to seek the respect of those whose opinions we value. I have discussed the implications of this principle in more depth elsewhere (Turnbull, 1993a).

8 I believe this to be the case even in a detailed study such as that of Janice Radway (1984). Although Radway gestures towards the subversive potential of such texts, she nevertheless concludes with dire warnings about their potentially reactionary implications.

9 In 1987, these girls chose to define themselves as Macedonian, a designation I readily accepted, being at that time very naive about its political dimensions. Two other girls defined themselves as Yugoslavian.

10 The appropriation by the oppressed of the terms of abuse used by the oppressors is a well known political strategy. We might think of the use of the term *black* by black Americans in the black power movement – or even the current use of the term *nigger* within black American populations. It might be noted, however, that the only people who may call themselves *wogs* with impunity are other 'wogs', and the use of this term by others may still be offensive. This was demonstrated most recently (January 1996) in Australia when a right-wing politician created a furore by describing the citizenship ceremony (during which migrants swear allegiance to Australia) as a 'de-wogging' experience. What distinguished the cast of *Wogs Out of Work*, and the girls in this study, is their status as second generation migrants with ambivalent feelings about their culture of origin and the culture in which they find themselves labelled as 'wogs'. This is a complex issue and one which deserves a more detailed consideration than there is space for here.

11 It should be noted that Australian Broadcasting Authority is responsible for maintaining quotas so that Australian made programmes make up at least half of the viewing time available. This quota is high compared with past years when the majority of television programs shown on the Australian screen were imported.

12 There is much more to be said about Williamson's construction of ideology as always 'invisible' and Shotter's concept of ideology as visible through lived experience than is possible here. It might be noted that to Shotter's concept of 'knowing from' we might need to add a fourth kind of knowing, a 'knowing why' which helps us cope or even challenge the consquences. This may well be the 'healing function' of theory suggested by bell hooks and referred to later in this essay.

13 There is a considerable literature on this topic in Australia, good examples of which include: Bottomley (1979); Strintzos (1984); Bottomley et al. (1991).

14 See Buckingham and Sefton-Green (1994:184–210) for the description of

just such an exercise and an elaboration of these concepts of progressive and radical pedagogy.

References

BOTTOMLEY, G. (1979) *After the Odyssey: A Study of Greek Australians*, Brisbane, Queensland: University of Queensland Press.

BOTTOMLEY, G., DE LEPERVANCHE, M. and MARTIN, J. (1991) *Intersexions: Gender/Class/Culture/Ethnicity*, Sydney, New South Wales: Allen and Unwin.

BUCKINGHAM, D. and SEFTON-GREEN, J. (1994) *Cultural Studies Goes to School*, London: Taylor and Francis.

CREED, B. (1984) The woman's romance as sexual fantasy: Mills and Boon, in *All Her Labours*, **2**, Published Proceedings of the Women and Labour Conference, Sydney, New South Wales: Hale and Ironmonger.

FRASER, P. (1990) How do teachers and students talk about television?, in BUCKINGHAM, D. (Ed.) *Watching Media Learning: Making Sense of Media Education*, London: Falmer Press.

GALLOP, J. (1994) The teacher's breasts, in MATTHEWS, J. (Ed.) *Jane Gallop Seminar Papers*, Canberra, New South Wales: Humanities Research Centre.

GIROUX, H. and McLAREN, P. (1986) Teacher education and the politics of engagement: The case for democratic schooling, *Harvard Educational Review*, **56**, 213–38.

GIROUX, H. (1994) *Disturbing Pleasures: Learning Popular Culture*, London: Routledge.

GORE, J. (1992) What can we do for you! What *can* 'we' do for 'you'? Struggling over empowerment in critical and feminist pedagogy, in LUKE, C. and GORE, J. (Eds) *Feminisms and Critical Pedagogy*, New York: Routledge.

HARRE, R. (1993) *Social Being*, 2nd edition, Oxford: Blackwell.

HOOKS, B. (1994) *Teaching to Transgress: Education as the Practice of Freedom*, London: Routledge.

LUKE, C. and GORE, J. (Eds) (1992) *Feminisms and Critical Pedagogy*, New York: Routledge.

RADWAY, J. (1984) *Reading The Romance: Women, Patriarchy and Popular Literature*, Chapel Hill, NC: University of North Carolina Press.

SHOTTER, J. (1990) *Knowing of the Third Kind*, Utrecht: ISOR, 1990.

SHOTTER, J. (1993) *Cultural Politics of Everyday Life*, Toronto, Canada: University of Toronto Press.

STRINTZOS, M. (1984) To be Greek is to be good, in JOHNSON, L. and TYLER, D. (Eds) *Cultural Politics*, Melbourne Working Papers, **5**, Sociology Research Group in Cultural and Educational Studies, Victoria: University of Melbourne.

TAYLOR, S. (1989) Empowering girls and women: The challenge of the gender-inclusive curriculum, *Curriculum Studies*, **21** (5), 441–56.

TURNBULL, S. (1993a) The media: moral lessons and moral careers, *Australian Journal of Education*, **37** (2), 153–68.

TURNBULL, S. (1993b) Accounting for taste: The moral and aesthetic dimension of media practices, in YATES, L. (Ed.) *Feminism and Education: Melbourne Studies in Education*, Melbourne, Victoria: La Trobe University Press, 95–106.

WILLIAMSON, J. (1981/2) How does Girl Number Twenty understand ideology?, *Screen Education*, **40**, 80–7.

WILLIAMSON, J. (1985) Is there anyone here from a classroom?, *Screen*, **26** (1), 90–5.

Chapter 6

Provocations for a Media Education in Small Letters

Robert Morgan

Over the past decade media education has made significant inroads into secondary schooling in Ontario, Canada. Previously a marginal presence in the attention of individual teachers to newspapers and films, it was officially endorsed in the 1987 *English Curriculum Guideline: Intermediate and Senior Divisions* (Ministry of Education, 1987), becoming a required part of the work of English departments. Each school, however, was left on its own to decide what curricular form this would take, so long as they met the stipulation that 'media shall be included as a category of study for one-third of scheduled classroom time in one mandatory English credit at each of the Intermediate and Senior Divisions levels' (1987:9). By 1995, 73 per cent of the respondents surveyed in our research indicated that a distinct media course existed apart from media units taught within regular English courses.[1] In practice, this stand-alone credit represented widely divergent versions of media education depending on the individual teacher's interest in or anxiety about teaching in this area, their media-biographic experience, prior educational background, available resources and departmental support (cf. Coghill, 1993). A majority of teachers had no media-related course work as undergraduates, and 90 per cent indicated that they had received no training in the area during pre-service at a faculty of education.

The first stages of standardized practice and curricula came about in several ways. In 1989 the Ministry of Education published a *Resource Guide for Media Literacy* with suggested topics and framing key concepts. Soon afterwards several commercial textbooks were published in anticipation of teacher demand. These have subsequently met with mixed success. On the one hand they supplied teachers, some of whom clearly felt that media literacy was thrust upon them, with an elaborated curriculum. On the other hand, many teachers found they dated quickly in terms of topics, references and conceptual approach. The group which lobbied for the Ministry initiative and subsequently drafted the *Resource Guide* was the Association for Media Literacy (AML). A group of approximately 25 Toronto teachers pre-1987, they experienced exponential growth following state endorsement of media literacy, comprising by their own estimate some 1100 members in 1992 (Duncan, 1993:15).

The executive of the AML has been instrumental in shaping Ontario media education discourse in several ways apart from the *Resource Guide*: teaching 'additional qualification' evening and summer courses for practising teachers, publishing a regular newsletter, *Mediacy*, sponsoring periodic workshops and two international conferences. They credit the 'Ontario achievement' with 'catalyz[ing] activities in other provinces' (Duncan, 1993:15), and functioning as 'a leader in media education not only in Canada but across North America' (Pungente, 1993:60). On the other hand, critics have been correspondingly harsh, characterizing the AML's approach as 'scapegoat sociology' (Dornan, 1994). A well known liberal-left Canadian writer has described it as offering merely redundant knowledge, a procrustean explication of what most students intuitively know about the media 'with instincts honed on the electromagnetic spectrum since birth' (Salutin, 1994).

My intention in what follows is neither an unqualified endorsement nor a wholesale condemnation of the media literacy movement. Clearly this group has been responsible for kick-starting media education in the province, and a great deal of innovative media teaching traces its roots to their initiatives. Rather, based on three years of listening to media teachers describe their work, I offer several suggestions for reformulating current conceptions of media teaching, broaching four sets of issues. First, I argue that, particularly in the Ontario context, we need to rethink questions of access, constituency and the structural effects which have resulted from the positioning of media literacy within English departments. This empirical question of who is (and, crucially, who *is not*) a student in secondary media courses is related to another more discursive-theoretical one: who is the imagined subject of media literacy as this figure emerges from the discourse of practising teachers? Here I raise questions about media literacy's pastoral orientation, its goal of critical autonomy and largely repressive stance towards media pleasures. A third focus examines teacher discourses from another angle: how are 'media' typically constituted in media literacy classrooms? Here I argue for both a rebalancing of textual critique with a sense of polyvalent media practices (for which the text is often only an accessory), and, briefly, for more locally-oriented forms of classroom production. The pervasive textualism of media literacy has largely obscured the category of experience and its correlates (memory, the quotidian, fantasy, fear and desire) in understanding the nature of media learning.[2] I also note in passing the problems of a professed constructivist approach which many teachers take to be the iconoclastic edge of media study. This move away from formalist, unidirectional, text-centric models and towards a view of adolescents actively involved in ambivalent, heterodox, situated relationships with media has been advocated in cultural studies writing for some time (Buckingham 1990, 1993a; McRobbie, 1992). My particular contribution to this initiative is to suggest that conceptions of dialogism (Bakhtin, 1981), performativity (Butler, 1993), and the quotidian nature of media experience (Silverstone, 1994) might help us break with the current pantextualism of media teaching. Consistent with the notion of dialogism, I end by endorsing versions of classroom media production which are responsive to local communities and their dilemmas.

Not Shakespeare: Issues of Access and Constituency

Over two decades ago, Murdock and Phelps conducted a survey in England on teacher and student attitudes to media and media education. Their discussion of its results in *Mass Media and the Secondary School* (1973) makes for relevant reading, providing a commentary on issues that continue to haunt us. One of their findings was that early forms of media education were largely restricted to working-class students and to so-called 'low-ability bands' within secondary schooling. This was the case in spite of the fact that their research indicated that academic students were just as 'deeply involved in . . . the mass media' and thus it seemed logical for 'media based teaching' to become 'an integral part' of all secondary school programmes (1973:140).

Current patterns of who is and who is not likely to take media education in Ontario secondary schools confirm many of Murdock and Phelps' apprehensions. Seventy-three per cent of dedicated, stand-alone media courses in Ontario are aimed at 'general' or 'basic level' (i.e., non-academic) students in their final two years of high school. There are several reasons for the emergence of this pattern. Decisive is the historical conjunction, three years prior to the 1987 underwriting of media literacy, of new provincial standards requiring that all students obtain five credits in English for secondary graduation. In this context, English departments designed a number of 'fifth credit' courses for non-university-bound students. Indeed, when we asked teachers to rank the reasons students might have for selecting the media course, over 70 per cent indicated its status as a 'fifth credit' was the primary consideration.

Another aspect of this trend emerges from our interviews with 40 media teachers. One of the questions we asked them was to describe their aims in teaching the media option, and to follow this up by relating their sense of student expectations in selecting the course. The gap between their objectives and student motives was predictably very wide. Below are typical teacher responses to the question, 'What do you think are the most common reasons students have for taking the media course?':

> *Janice*: [T]heir motive is to get an English credit . . . so we basically are blackmailing them into taking the course. I wish we weren't.
> *Victoria*: [They] are just taking it because they really believe it's an easy credit; they just think it will be easier than studying Shakespeare or novels.
> *Carmen*: They have to get another credit so why not take something different . . . they're tired of regular English: a novel, a play, some

poetry, some essays, some short stories . . . they want something different.

John: They expect to get an English credit out of this. That's one of their expectations, and they seem to think that because it's a media course they're not going to have to do a lot of reading, and they're definitely not going to have to do Shakespeare!

Carlos: To get a credit. It's their fifth English credit for the general level and that's one of the motivations, OK?

Interviewer: Is that a problem, do you think, the fact that it is the fifth credit?

Carlos: Yeah, I think it, uh, it attracts a lot of the kinds of students who, uh, you know, which I got this semester.

Crucial to understanding teachers' and students' experience of media education in Ontario, then, is its paradoxical location: media literacy both is and is not English. The fact that media study is not novels, not lots of reading and essay writing is its initial defining characteristic for many students. Compared to academic English with the inevitable Shakespearean tragedy at the senior level, media literacy has a reputation as 'an easy credit' – a representation circulated not just by students, but also by many guidance and English teachers – a point frequently noted by media teachers even when, as was almost always the case, they disputed its validity. That media literacy offers a respite from the conventional content of English usually meant it outdrew other options like 'business English' or scaled down, 'general level' literature-based courses intended for these students.

Yet students also found its reputed difference deceptive, since many teachers felt Ministry requirements for English applied with equal force to their media teaching. For example, one teacher spoke of 'teasing [the general level student] with equipment and movies and sound and camera and yet . . . still sneak in reading and writing.' In many schools, media units within English courses are simply a continuation of thematic study utilizing media in a transparent manner. This may be due to both teachers' lack of training in the area and (a suggestion that frequently emerged in interviews) active teacher resistance:

Mario: [T]here is a media component, as stated by Ministry policy, in each English course in the school. However, the problem is this. Number one, you've got great resistance by many English teachers – mainly because English teachers are pushed to the wall. They came here to teach literature, and all of a sudden, they've got to be experts on media, they've got to be experts on every social programme that comes along . . . [They are] getting less and less time to teach literature . . . Second, English teachers have not been trained as media teachers, and many of them feel very uncomfortable with it, OK? And many particularly, when they start zooming in a lot of machinery . . . I mean there's a lot of people that are just machine-phobic. And I don't see why they shouldn't be.

For a variety of reasons, then, media study in Ontario has been marginalized as a 'fifth credit' for 'general level' students. When we asked teachers directly if this was a fair observation and reflected the situation in their school, a majority agreed this was the case. In turn, this positioning affects academically-oriented students' potential interest in the media option, course content and faculty perceptions of the value and status of media education. One teacher noted how over time the students taking his course had changed and his materials had 'become more conservative': 'What happened, for two years the advanced level worked really well and I got full classes. But the advanced level students, for some reason, and maybe it was the year that the general were put in there, that it became unpopular . . .' Or, as an English Head euphemistically put it, there is a 'different orientation' to the media course since it is 'geared to a slightly different kind of teaching, a slightly different kind of student, perhaps who has slightly different kinds of interests.' In the multiracial multi-ethnic context of metropolitan high schools in contemporary Canada this difference is inevitably a classed and raced one. Marginalized social groups consistently shunted into 'general level' streams are the most likely candidates for the media option in their final semester.

Placing Subjects

It is not only the *students* who are perceived as different, however. The fact that the media course is 'a course disconnected from other courses' (Galbo, 1992:47) can mean the designated media teacher experiences a contradictory mix of collegial approval and misunderstanding. One facet of this is suggested by survey results indicating that while 46 per cent of teachers reported a high level of general support for media literacy within their department, 84 per cent checked low to moderate levels of understanding when asked to rate colleagues' knowledge of their particular work. While English teachers typically comprehend each others' labour even if they focus on different texts or grades (sharing a common background in literary reading and criticism), the media teacher is very likely to be on his or her own in developing a corner of the curriculum, engaging new conceptual tools like 'ideology', acquiring rudimentary skills in media production and negotiating a fundamentally different relationship to students' prior knowledge and cultural lives. The following excerpts from teacher interviews illustrate how even the most confident and effective practitioners have difficulty operating in this context:

Interviewer: To what extent is there consensus about the aims and value of media education amongst the teachers in your department?

Karen: (laughter) Um, no consensus! No comment! (laughter) I mean when I started talking with them about what I was doing, the teachers were going 'but look at what we have to do in the curriculum!' And I learned, OK, I'm going to shut up, I'm going to do it, and I'm not going to say what I'm doing. And I know my kids are going to get a whole lot more out of it because they're not falling asleep and they're not skipping classes.

Interviewer: So, are there tensions or differences within the department over the presence and value of media education?

Karen: No, because I keep my mouth shut.

Interviewer: So you don't tell them. So, do these beliefs and attitudes affect your teaching in any way?

Karen: No, I keep smiling, and they keep going 'yes, yes, yes.' And I keep, I make sure I cover what needs to be covered, like the appeals and claims, and things like that so I won't . . . Oh, it's terrible. It's the most boring stuff! Um, but I don't cause the shit to fly, so to speak . . . making sure the key concepts are being taught – which they think are key, and then I go off.

Interviewer: So, do you think this affects you though?

Karen: No, I work around things. I think you have to anyway, in any position that you have. It doesn't bother me. You just work around it and you, I mean, I'm doing it because I believe that the way I teach is a very good way. I think there're other ways of teaching that are very good, but this is the best way that I can teach given my background and so I feel that it's fine and that I will be ripping the students off and I would be torn into two if I had to teach the way that they taught. So I figure, this is a compromise that's fine for me.

*   *   *   *   *

Interviewer: How would you characterize the relationship between English and media education?

Chantal: I find the umbrella under English kind of problematic because I find it very restrictive. When I was offered this Grade 12 combination advanced/general media literacy course, the Head mentioned I should teach a Shakespeare, and I told him to bugger off! Because I didn't think that would be included in my mandate for teaching media. 'But you could show Romeo and Juliet!' Well, this is what he said. Wouldn't that be fun! He ran off after. I really blew up at him because I was very mad about that, because Shakespeare gets in everywhere. This is a media course, there are so many other areas that I could teach and so much I could cover I didn't want to waste time teaching Shakespeare in a media class. Not that Shakespeare is a waste of time, but you know what I mean. And just because it was under this English thing, he figured that because they were getting an English credit – also, I have to agree, because it was a Grade 12 English credit, theoretically they could go from there into an OAC [Ontario Academic Credit], it's advanced, so they could take it and go into the OAC, and not have a Grade 12 Shakespeare, as if they didn't already have [Shakespeare in] 9, 10 and 11! So I was kind of mad about that one. And I immediately requested that the new course be quoted as an EMD [English Media] and not an EMG [English Media General] – so its not both, it's actually quoted as an EMD. It's a media code, a separate code within our Board, at least.

Interviewer: Is it still an English credit?

Chantal: Yeah. But I wanted at least that much autonomy on paper, saying it was a Media coding course, so I don't have to teach the English stuff.

Interviewer: So what are the effects of media education being located within English?

Chantal: Um, there's a problem which I've had all the way through teaching media literacy in that I get some of the lower level students in my class because I get some of the students whose guidance counsellors think, because we don't do novels or literature, that it's going to be an easy course. But I've also had them dump ESL students in my class who have never watched television in their lives, and they don't know what we are talking about. So there's been a problem with the cultural rift . . . I requested also when I started this Grade 12 course, also that the kids have an advanced level of English or the Grade 11 media literacy course so they have some background. And they've almost completely ignored that. There are maybe five out of 30 who have that background, and three of them were in my class last year and failed. They are taking it again. So that's been really frustrating. It's like, 'So you need an extra English credit? Here, have this one.'

Interviewer: So . . . your courses aren't building on each other? They're just assuming because it's English anyone can take it?

Chantal: Yeah, exactly.

* * * * *

Interviewer: To what extent is there consensus about the aims and value of media education amongst the teachers in your department?

> *Andrew*: I would think that it is very low because it's utterly remote from most people's experiences – most people have no access to the media courses, no experience with them, no inkling really of what goes on in these classrooms, which is itself a problem.
>
> *Interviewer*: Are there any tensions within the department over the presence and value of media education?
>
> *Andrew*: Uh, to a degree, yeah. Because some of us, as I say, have much more commitment to the need for alternative forms of communication [than print] and particularly for greatly expanded resources to let students work in the media. And, yeah, that creates some tension, sure.

*   *   *   *   *

> *Interviewer*: What are the effects of media education being located within English?
>
> *Andrew*: Well, I think that like a number of other what you could call fifth English credit courses, that there's a certain ghettoization of this course. I don't think that there's necessarily a great commitment to the need for um, for example, electronic media, to let the students communicate in, um, other forms than writing. Obviously there's an enormous print bias, and I'm not sure what the solution is. I think a solution is really having more integration but really that means what goes on in media class should have a bigger impact on other English courses rather than the other way around, 'cause it's been my experience in this school and elsewhere that, um, generally that media component in mainstream English courses is very much lip service . . . it's something that gets tacked on as a requirement of the course that you deal with at the end of the term. And certainly in this school I can say that there's an enormous print literacy bias, overwhelming print literacy bias, and I think that it's an effect of that, to the extent that other media are dealt with in other English classes, it's necessarily lip service.

All of these teachers experience and react to what Andrew accurately describes as the 'ghettoization' of media courses in different ways. Karen, who works in an area of high unemployment with students officially designated as 'at-risk' (of dropping out of school), has decided not to confront tensions between her topical issues, production-oriented media teaching, and the text-based, rationalistic evaluation of the appeals and claims of advertising advocated by colleagues. Yet, in identifying primarily with the students and choosing to 'work around things' she finds irrelevant in the department's interpretation of the English guidelines, she experiences a high degree of alienation from her coworkers, which in turn has led to repeated efforts to find a teaching job elsewhere.

In contrast to Karen's resolution to keep her 'mouth shut', Chantal is dramatically outspoken about her vision of media education. This confidence comes partly from her extensive background in the area, having taught media since it was first mandated, shortly after entering teaching. Upon graduation from university, she worked for a while as a professional photographer. While a teacher, she has taken all the additional qualification media literacy courses offered by the Ministry, becoming a media specialist, enrolled in a practical television workshop to learn 'how to use the camera equipment and the switcher and the sound board, stuff like that . . .', and studied media theory at the postgraduate level. This background, and a good relationship with a normally 'very supportive Head', enables her to openly reject what she regards as patently absurd demands upon her course. Nevertheless, she finds herself caught in a dilemma: if her media class is to include academic students for whom this will be their only fourth year English credit, it will be disfigured in some way by traditional English demands – hence the pressure to include Shakespeare. On the other hand, its renomination as an EMD course does nothing to alter its marginal status for guidance teachers and 'academic' students. Chantal must continuously reclaim what she understands as different and valuable about media education in the face of this structural positioning. The EMD label exacts a toll in the end: media's status as non-intellectual knowledge, an extra English credit for 'lower level students' is confirmed by the kind of students she discovers have been referred to the course. Galbo's (1992) observation that media courses exist disconnected from other courses applies here, even to her own portfolio of media courses, since she cannot assume any continuity or cumulative knowledge in the students she gets.

Andrew also directly addresses his differences from his colleagues, distancing himself from the 'knee-jerk response to . . . what they perceive as the negative impact of media in terms of reading and writing skills'. His desire for greater integration between English and media is evident in his attempt to reform 'the blackboard course' he 'inherited' when he assumed his position. His teaching emphasizes production and analysis across a wide variety of media including print, the latter 'the overwhelming . . . bias' of his associates. Yet his greatest contribution to media pedagogy may lie in his effort to break away from the average/academic student dichotomy crippling most media literacy programmes in Ontario:

> *Interviewer:* One criticism of media education's current location within English notes the way in which its status as fifth English credit can function to restrict media education to general level students. Any comment?
>
> *Andrew:* [C]ertainly it's marginalized or it's, um, ghettoized; as I

said, there certainly was a reputation of the fifth English credit when I first came in. The first couple of years I had the course, quite frankly, I was really getting the dregs – I was getting the students who were pure and simple looking for an English credit. I was not getting academically strong or committed students, you know, with few exceptions, but for the most part I was getting people who plain and simple were looking for a fifth English credit; they took it because they thought it would be the easiest . . . [I]t was very much on the margin. I don't think most people in the English department – and we have maybe 17, 18 people here, had an inkling what went on in the media class. Most people would actively resist teaching it because they said, 'I know nothing about media.' In other words it was being perceived purely in terms of knowledge and it was knowledge overwhelmingly that was being crammed down their throats with the course, most of which had no relevance to their own lives. And it's taken me two to three years to really shed that, to make the course flexible enough, uh, that I think it can have some relevance for the students' lives and that I think it can attract, um, the more motivated, interested students. Uh, and I think the more that happens the more that will get rid of that marginalization, but still you know, it, uh, is very much some-thing that is on the fringe of the English department . . .

Andrew's working premise – greater integration of English and media along a continuum of technologies – is gestured to in his insight that 'what goes on in media class should have a bigger impact on other English courses rather than the other way around.' This view is consistent with current reconceptualizations of the field along the lines of multimodal literacy (New London Group, 1995); modes of information (Poster, 1995); cultural mapping (Collins, 1995); and differant technologies (Green, 1995) – all of which call 'for an educational apparatus that includes video and television' (Ulmer, 1989:xi), alongside print and emergent, hybrid forms of signifying practice. All of the teachers quoted above are frustrated by either the level of support for, or the misapprehension of, media education in their host department. For Andrew, the marginalization of his media course is paralleled by the lip-service, 'add-on' positioning of media units within colleagues' English courses – the first unit sacrificed under time pressure. It also correlates with a poverty of technical resources for his media work, the difficulty he has convincing the department to invest in media equipment, in other words an indirect, systemic form of resistance to media education. Relevant here is Murdock and Phelps' (1973) observation that '[w]ithout a substantial increase in funds many of the more adventurous media-based creative work called for . . . cannot be put into prac-tice.' Fifty-five per cent of the teachers surveyed complained of inadequate resources for hands-on production work. It is not surprising in this context that the standard modes of the English classroom (writing folders, oral presentations, written tests) are imported intact into media classrooms as familiar, inexpensive modes of production and evaluation.

There is another sharp irony here: distinctions between high and low culture – which media theory explicitly sets out to undo – have largely been renewed by the structural placement of media literacy in Ontario. Academic students read canonic literary texts like *Romeo and Juliet*; those perceived as average students 'read' mundane media texts like *Married with Children*; both write essays. Yet, as Murdock and Phelps (1973) argued long ago, divisions between an academic literary education and a general-level, hands-on media education reproduce in displaced form class divisions, and tensions between school culture and that of everyday life (1973:148). For these writers, media education ultimately has to mount challenges to some of the inherited assumptions and organizational structures of traditional schooling: segregation by supposed 'ability groups' centred on different kinds of cultural capital; the fragmentation of curricular subjects, each parcelling out discrete, unrelated knowledges. Indeed, their claim that we cannot 'introduce media-based activities without a corresponding change in the formal organization' of schooling as a whole could well have been written with Ontario's current version of media literacy in mind.

Missionary Positions, Prophylactics, Consensual Relations

> There is no reason why *media* teachers should be competent [on moral questions] any more than math teachers should. We can only look forward to the day when the teaching of politics and ethics through *media* lessons will seem as odd as the teaching of history through algebra does (Hunter, 1995) (emphasis added).

In the quotation above, I have taken the liberty of substituting the word *media* for *English* – Hunter's own theme. His work carefully illustrates how English teaching is the modern descendant of missionary work, the place in the curriculum most likely to replicate a secular form of pastoral care. I don't think any of us want to give up the relationship between media and values, or between English and politics; after all, we have just got to the point where we can talk about them in the same breath. Yet, viewed from Hunter's perspective, there are striking similarities between Protestantism as a 'religion of the book' and the way we employ media texts as occasions for personal/social growth, exercises in which students discover themselves in apparently open-ended, but nonetheless carefully guided readings of frequently teacher-selected texts. But if you bridle at a description of media teachers as 'preachers of culture', then listen to a sample of responses from our survey to the linked questions A) 'How do you define the aims of media education?' and B) 'What difference should media education make for the students who take it?'

A1) To make students aware of the different media, their influences, power, the dangers, and the effects of each. B1) They should know how to deconstruct the messages delivered by the various media and be less vulnerable to manipulation. They should be critical thinkers about the media.

A2) To have students develop a healthy scepticism and critical outlook on the various media, especially how information is manipulated and packaged; to empower them. B2) To be able to understand what the media are doing and be able to deconstruct it.

A3) To help students become more aware, more critical with respect to mass media. B3) They should question media more critically; be more aware of how media products are constructed.

A4) To educate all students about the power of the media. B4) They should be aware of the influence media exerts on them. They should see how our culture and values are shaped by the media and respond accordingly.

A5) To make the student more aware of the influences and choices in the media; to expose their bias and assumptions; to make intelligent choices regarding the impact of the media on oneself. B5) Their wariness of media and its impact should be remarkably heightened.

A6) To offer intellectual self defence for students, a critique of consumer society and a challenge to stereotypes (race and gender). B6) These goals are largely reached according to student self-reporting.

A7) Media are to be deconstructed as text. B7) To provide students with the ability to discriminate and judge the media and their messages; to protect themselves against manipulation; to enjoy the artistry and creativity of thoughtful media presentations.

Not all answers spoke in terms of counteracting media manipulation. Several made reference to 'appreciation,' 'aesthetic' response and media production. I have also not included statements couched in terms of disease imagery (the media as 'unhealthy,' students as 'addicted', 'hooked'). Rather, the answers above are representative, providing a sense of the tone and framework within which most teachers appear to work. The language here is worth noting in detail. Media are the active force in the relationship: the media *do* – they construct, act upon, manipulate, seduce, influence identity, shape culture – exert power in short; students, on the other hand, are *done to* – acted upon, manipulated by, exposed or vulnerable to – are victims in essence. The implicit assumptions are fairly behaviouristic: that adolescents are overwhelmingly passive in relation to media; second, that effects flow only in one direction, from media institutions outwards; third, media effects are 'massive', overwhelmingly negative, and directly absorbed; fourth, that teachers can counteract media influence by 'empowering' students and turning them into 'sceptical media consumers'. This process involves learning to adopt the rational discourse modelled by teachers, one that secures discriminating taste, 'critical autonomy' and 'distance' in future media interactions. As one teacher remarked, 'Hopefully, they will think before flipping a switch on an electronic medium' once they have taken a media literacy course. In contrast to English, where the goal is to provoke a greater interest in books and reading, it seems the desired effect of media literacy is *less* frequent media use, and a 'resistant', 'self-defensive' posture if one does succumb. Note also the pastoral attitude overtly surfaces in the notion of students' confessional self-monitoring of their media practices in B6, and in a state of 'heightened' 'wariness' to media sins in B5. That such views are widely held is confirmed by another respondent:

> I have found overall, 1) a negative portrayal of the media [in media workshops and provided materials]; 2) a constant implication that the media are involved in a conspiracy. Some of the workshops sound like Robert Ludlum novels; 3) a lack of knowledge about practical restrictions facing media [institutions] . . .

The concept of deconstruction that figures prominently in several answers (B1, B2, B3, A7) directly echoes the primary key concept in the *Resource Guide*: 'all media are constructions' (Ministry of Education, 1989:8). This widely endorsed axiom can obscure as much as it reveals. To the extent that analysis remains at the level of a structural parsing of contents, the *performative* aspects of media are underplayed. This approach neglects the fact that media texts are experienced as active social processes, such as watching television with others, and are constituted differently depending on the interpretive community in which they are activated. This form of textual constructivism thus has a tendency to discount the illocutionary force of media practices – a move evident in A7 for example. I revisit this issue of the textualization of media experience in the final section of this chapter. For now, I want to stress how the notion that all media are constructed comfortably dovetails with conspiracy theory. Thus, references in teachers' comments to the compositional nature of media regularly occurred in conjunction with the discourse of manipulation:

> *Jenny:* The general one [aim] of course is that I simply want them to be able to be critical thinkers about the media. I mean critical in the sense they understand that media is a series of constructions and how that's put together . . . And it's going to keep them from being duped in some way.

*   *   *   *   *

> *Anna:* Well, I would say that the aims of media education are to create in the minds of our students, questioners, critical thinkers, not just taking everything that they see for granted . . . [I]t's waking

them up to understanding the connections and how media is constructed and just how much of a part of our daily lives it is and how it can affect us sometimes without noticing it . . . I would like to see it as a relationship where they are able to meet the media on their terms and they are not controlled by it.

Deconstruction in this context appears simply to involve exposing strategies of manipulation. The anatomizing of media texts somehow provides an antidote, results in a transition from an unconscious to a conscious state (being 'duped' and 'waking up'), a change from indiscriminate bodily pleasures and emotional responses to rationality ('critical thinkers'). A related premise is that if something is constructed, it is consciously designed, marked by a singular will and intention. What remains unexplored in this version of constructionism are the collective, impersonal dimensions of media production, as well as the dynamics of media appropriation.

The polarity in Anna's final sentence – either students control the media or are controlled by it – introduces a dichotomy at work in some of the remarks cited: critical autonomy versus passive pleasure. Murdock and Phelps (1973) noted that becoming an English teacher seemed to require students to 'cut away or suppress large areas of personal experience' by supplanting their 'involvement with popular culture' with a commitment to high culture and a 'critical' discourse on 'Mass Culture'. Instead, the authors recommended that media education might usefully start from another premise: students' and teachers' media interests and pleasures. Teachers in particular should attempt 'to understand their own experience[s] of popular culture' if they really expect to engage in 'a constructive dialogue' with students about the media. The basic questions to ask in such an approach are to do with what is of value in our media choices and preoccupations, and what is the basis of that value (1973:148–9). For the most part, teachers have overlooked their question: 'not what are the mass media doing to adolescents, but what are adolescents doing with the media' (1973:141).

As in the classrooms Murdock and Phelps examined, the responses above indicate an overemphasis on 'deleting, criticizing and inhibiting' media use, while at the same time teachers neglect the fact that most students already actively 'mak[e] judgements and discriminations' about popular culture, 'selecting . . . and rejecting' what they encounter. In contrast, the *Resource Guide* suggests that it is principally the learning of 'media-literacy techniques' which 'enables students to establish and maintain the kind of critical distance on their culture that makes possible critical autonomy: the ability to decode, encode, and evaluate the symbol systems that dominate their world' (Ministry of Education, 1989:10). Indeed, code-cracking is the order of the day in most media classrooms. This approach both confirms a long history of suspicion regarding the media within education (Lusted, 1985), and reinforces the view that the important meanings are the 'hidden' ones.

This conception of 'critical distance' is a problematic one for postmodern educators. Collins suggests that the idea of critical distance which underpins most teachers' self-definitions and course objectives is a conception which 'grows ever less compelling':

> [W]hat does 'distance' mean in information cultures defined not just by new technologies of access and storage which completely alter who is a collector and what is collected, but also by shifting taste cartographies which reflect profound changes in the nature of cultural authority and what it's supposed to accomplish? Distance remains a vital category in determining professional identity, yet in the early nineties it seems necessary to ask . . . distanced from whom, by which mechanisms, for what purpose? (Collins, 1995:218).

Beyond Deconstruction

What comes after the idea of critical distance? Collins' approach implies that criticism always comes from somewhere, from specific discourses and interpretive protocols grounded in particular forms of social existence and economies of value. He also challenges the distinction between *critical* and *average* viewers, since contemporary life undercuts secure notions of 'critical authority . . . chang[ing] forever what can and cannot be said, about whom, from what position, and in which cultural model we envision as we write and teach' (Collins, 1989:279). Once we realize that the fiction of an Archimedean interpretive *'outside'*, fundamentally distinct from the cultural processes analyzed, has collapsed, Collins invites us to develop more *'partial'*, *self-conscious*, *'inside/outside'* versions of media pedagogy. In contrast to the goal of producing 'critically autonomous', 'sceptical media consumers', teachers and students would explore the dynamics of media practices they are implicated in and which are central to their communities. Such a pedagogy is thus *partial* in that it enacts self-conscious, situated, contingent responses to media, while resisting the lure of 'imagined consensus' and 'imagined mastery . . . over the cultural terrain' (1995:212). It is also *dialogic* in that it 'coordinates and exposes' divergent discourses about the media to each other, so that what might be gained is a 'coming to know one's own language as it is perceived by someone else's language' (Bakhtin, 1981:365).

This perspective thus begins by acknowledging the individual, ambivalent, contradictory and shifting practices of media use, rather than attempting to suppress them through the assignation of stable, inherent textual meanings. It recognizes that the discursively constituted meanings we make from the media change from one context to another, because our discourses are 'washed by heteroglot waves from all sides' (Bakhtin in Pearce, 1994:65). In media-rich environments, the media themselves are active contributors to discursive hybridization, an essential aspect of the negotiation of subjectivity-in-culture. This dialogic notion of media teaching as the mutual exposure/

illumination of media languages, unlike 'empowering' versions of media literacy, does not require the displacement of student media experience with the rational discourse of teachers. On the contrary, it aspires to a self-reflexive understanding of the grounds of different appropriations and 'conflicting taste cartographies' in relation to the media, especially those in which we are personally invested.

We need, therefore, to find a pathway between a host of polarities pervasive within media pedagogy: critical versus duped, autonomous versus controlled, rational versus emotive, active versus passive. Silverstone's notion of 'transitional objects' offers one such route (discussed in my final section), and Bakhtin's concept of objectification another. The latter explores the 'concealed and overt dialogues' which occur in any use of cultural signs (Pearce, 1994:37). Bakhtin is interested in situations in which someone employs the words of another, but reaccentuates these signs to their own purposes (Bakhtin, 1986:79). This process of establishing one's meaning by inhabiting another's discourse with a 'sideways glance' (Bakhtin in Dentith, 1995) passes through a phase of *objectification*:

> The importance of struggling with another's discourse, its influence in the history of the individual's coming to . . . consciousness, is enormous. One's own discourse, and one's own voice, although born of another or dynamically stimulated by another, will sooner or later begin to liberate themselves from the authority of another's discourse (Bakhtin, 1981:348).

This conception bypasses Anna's view of adolescents either controlled by or controlling the media since it views all discourse as hybridized, containing both unconscious, inherited elements, and intentional, performative aspects at the same time. Beyond the commonplace view that students simply assimilate or compulsively reiterate media-provided signs, Bakhtin draws our attention to processes of displacement in any appropriation: complex repetitions, forms of ventriloquism, stylization, irony and pastiche (Pearce, 1994:97). As Pearce remarks, he points to 'the perpetual negotiation of sameness and difference . . . [in] our relationship to a language which simultaneously is, and is not, our own' (1994:98).

It is time, then, to give ideological deprogramming a rest (cf. Buckingham, 1986). A teacher in our study who described himself as 'very production-oriented' remarked that his colleagues employed 'the prophylactic system – you know, teach them to deconstruct, [makes the sign of the cross as though in front of a vampire], deconstruct and protect yourself.' He is right to the extent that media teachers currently work with a drastically simplified version of the concept of ideology, lending it an 'ascribed unity and omniscience', 'homogeneity' and 'stasis' when applied to a specific media practice (Mercer, 1986:54). Instead of searching for either global political meanings or individual significance in media artefacts, Mercer suggests an examination of the 'spirals of pleasure and power': 'the modes of pleasure, the modes of persuasion, the [types of] consent operative within a given cultural form' (1986:55). A pedagogy of 'complicit pleasures' thus explores 'processes of consensualisation' rather than of 'direct ideological capture' (1986:58). It posits unstable identifications, multiple points of resistance and negotiation (1986:57), rather than the victimology we now have.

In this way, media teaching might get beyond inoculatory approaches and move towards a more nuanced understanding of, for example, the way ads can be both ideologically odious capitalist creations and forms of positive desire at one and the same time (cf. Nava and Nava, 1990). Advertising, the favourite genre of media teachers, is also the 'site of cultural contradictions of the myths of general desire' (Wicke, 1988:17); that is, it cannibalizes other discourses in general circulation – discourses in which even educators have their investments.

Similarly, Mission (1995) has written of the complex pleasures involved in our relationships with popular media: pleasures of closure, of coherence, of multiple identifications, and the exhilaration of identity-in-process. In an article on computer games, Buckingham (1993b) cautions teachers about the limits of critique, the fact that a relentless criticism is likely to miss the dynamics of solidarity, belonging and group formation usually at stake in the sharing of any media practice. In a sub-section entitled 'the place of pleasure', he argues that to understand the sources of enjoyment and value attached to computer games, a teacher might best approach the area '[a]s an outsider . . . with a sense of a mystery to be solved: what do children see in these games, and why on earth do they like them?' Unfortunately, this is a stance too few teachers currently adopt. Andrew, for instance, was one of the few teachers we interviewed who allowed students to set the curricular agenda, apart from independent study units where this was typical:

Andrew: [T]he latter part of the year is largely determined by ideas which they come up with themselves in their media logs. They really have to set the agenda for the last part of the year.

To conclude, I am not suggesting that we completely turn away from critical classroom discourses on the media in favour of some naive celebratory stance. Rather, my argument is with the version of deconstruction now dominant in media literacy classrooms in Ontario. If one of the advantages of studying media is that 'learners can come to see themselves as part of the object of study, part of the culture in which their own identities and subjectivities, their own choices are at stake' (Lusted, 1987:121), then what is the underlying message of current approaches? Where in them is there room for the hybrid, transitional, emergent states to which Bakhtin's work offers access? What happens to questions of ambivalent, conflicted, ironic, sampled, environmental and non-semantic uses of media in this framework? Why are versions of media education currently found within the subject of English unlikely, as Barthes would put it, to fully enter the 'kitchen of meaning' (Barthes, 1988:158)?

Pantextualism or Performativity?

Understanding the social life of signs entails for Barthes that 'meaning [is] never analyzed in an isolated fashion', but sought across a range of intricated social practices (1988:159). In principle, media educators subscribe to this approach, described in Anglo-American contexts as a 'key concepts' (Masterman, 1985), 'aspects of media education' (Bazalgette, 1992), or British Film Institute model (Bowker, 1991). Yet the working categories here – media technologies, institutions, representations, audiences, languages and genres – are usually taught in a fragmented, layer-cake fashion, and the reigning pedagogical method in most classrooms remains that of textual decoding. Hart and Benson (1995) found that, of the teachers they observed, even 'the most dedicated to the need for Media Education . . . brought with them to the study of media texts habits learned from teaching Literature' (1995:20). Similarly, many of the teachers we interviewed saw media as 'a vehicle . . . [a] source to draw out the ideas from', which was 'no different' from other aspects of English. The *Resource Guide* secures this compact between media teaching and textual critique. Teachers are informed that their 'task is to expose the complexities of media texts', unearthing the 'value systems . . . attitudes, interpretations, and conclusions already built in'. The aim is to foster 'an awareness of the broad range of social and political effects stemming from the media' (Ministry of Education, 1989:8–10).

I have described the problems of this textual fixation of media literacy in greater depth elsewhere (Morgan, 1996). Three aspects of this orientation are worth noting in particular in order to contrast it with the quotidian or everyday life approach I wish to argue for here. First, in focusing on immanent textual meanings and forms of universalist interpretation, text-centric models fail to problematize the 'will to interpretation' of media teaching itself (Nelson, 1986:3). Lost is a self-reflexive awareness of classroom language games and interpretive discourses (Mohanty, 1986). The point here is that classroom discourse never simply lays bare the truth at the heart of media texts. Instead it is constitutive of what counts as 'the text', the particular interests and conceptual categories which govern meaning making, and thus the preferred 'meaning-effects' students are likely to take away from the classroom.

Second, the form of textuality most frequently on trial in media literacy classrooms is the 'deceitful' media text (Mellor and Patterson, 1994:51). The polarities of truth versus bias, reality versus fantasy, media manipulation versus critical reason, provide the framework for classroom activity. The amalgam of media, biography and social desire (Moffat, 1995; Walkerdine

1990), the media's role in the formation of cultural memory (Lipsitz, 1990), their intrication with everyday concerns (Silverstone, 1994) are largely eclipsed.

Finally, media experiences are more than simply 'texts'. Any pedagogical text is a unit cut out of a larger social practice. The nomination 'media text' is thus a fiction, a construal of autonomy and closure not evident in daily experience. The multimodal, grounded nature of media experience disappears when complex media events are converted solely into matters of language and textuality. Relevant, then, is the question: why has English been so hospitable to media education if not precisely because it turns everything into texts? Bennett claims we risk merely providing 'a new set of objects' for English 'to latch on to' (1993:227), a reinvigoration of 'formalist analysis with critique' over a wider moral 'terrain which [now] encompasses the popular...' (1993:228).

In contrast, a quotidian approach recaptures the processural, communal dimensions of media experience. It posits a 'dialogic engagement' (Saenz, 1992:42) between everyday concerns, as the horizon of significance and intelligibility and commercial media processes. In an important sense, what count as textual dynamics are constituted by the regional situations a text enters into, 'the specific semantic of the everyday' in which it is embedded (Ang, 1994:374). The result of this dialogic encounter is a hybrid discourse, 'half-ours and half-someone else's' (Bakhtin, 1981:345).

Fiske contends that, unlike that of text, the concept of discourse cannot be abstracted from its conditions of circulation:

> Discourse is the continuous process of making sense and of circulating it socially . . . [D]iscourse is both a noun and a verb, it is ever on the move. At times it becomes visible or audible, in a text, or a speech, or a conversation. These public moments are all that the discourse analyst has to work on, but their availability does not necessarily equate with their importance (Fiske, 1994:3,6).

While texts are the 'nouns' of discursive activity, he shifts attention to the verbing of culture: 'culture as the constant circulation and recirculation of discursive currents' (1994:7). Quotidian discursive work occurs at the level of 'struggles to disarticulate and rearticulate' media representations with our prior concerns and forms of knowledge (1994:7). Everyday life consists of numerous such acts of grounded discursive realignment. Media texts are the high profile surface of discursive activity, frequently masking the less visible micro-discursive activities of local communities, each with their 'moral economies' of interpretation (Silverstone, 1994:45). From a quotidian perspective, texts are therefore the 'in-between' of cultural processes, a single moment of discursive activity.

Bakhtin's concept of *utterance* offers another way of exploring texts as the 'in-between' points of discursive practices. By 'utterance' he denotes any sign set as a speech act shaped by the presence of embedded 'dialogic partners' (Holquist, 1986:63). What this opens up for media educators is a space to raise issues, not just about the social relations embedded within texts, but the contexts in which texts are performative and performed.

> [A]n utterance is defined not only by its relation to the object [of reference] and to the speaking subject–author . . . but – for us most important of all – by its direct relation to other utterances within the limits of a given sphere of communication. It does not *actually* exist outside this relationship (only as a *text*) (Bakhtin, 1986:123).

Only by attending to this discursive force field within which texts are activated do they become more than 'de-originated utterances' (Jameson, 1975:214). Restored to their status as utterance, texts are by definition incomplete, and meaning is a property which exists *in between* discursive practices rather than as a quality of texts *per se*. Only a fraction of the dramas of meaning at work in discursive exchanges are touched by decoding models: they examine signification only as text.

Reconstituted as speech acts, texts are partial responses within macro-social question-and-answer structures (Jameson, 1987). Jameson suggests that once we

> pose the text as an active reaction in a specific historical situation, it is no longer autonomous. And if the text is an answer, a solution, a reaction, it is a form of praxis; it can no longer be grasped passively, it must be seen as an active intervention in a concrete situation . . . (1987:19).

Yet texts not only perform, they are *performed* by those who appropriate them. 'Performativity' is the 'process of repetition' of provided discourses which simultaneously enables a 'deconstituting possibility' (Butler, 1993:10), modes of supplementation/displacement in the act of reiteration. Performative uses of media are 'citational practices' drawing upon provided cultural signs but resignifying them to 'address the local politics of "home"' (Walcott, 1995:62).

This approach regards media practices as more indeterminate and ambiguous than ideology critique does, by acknowledging the *double-voicing* of media experience, the way in which 'a discourse and a counter-discourse . . . instead of following one after the other and being uttered by two different mouths, are superimposed one on the other and merge into a *single* utterance issuing from a *single* mouth' (Bakhtin in Dentith, 1995:164). In short, media texts are not the message. Media users are part of the content, provided semiotic materials reconstituted through embodied reworkings. Double-voicing also applies to media teaching; teachers reanimate texts in terms of both personal preoccupations and professional language games. Media teaching is itself performative.

Silverstone provides the fullest justification for this everyday life approach:

> It is significant because in the everyday our lives become meaningful, and without those meanings and without understanding those meanings and properly locating them in social space, we . . . will miss the dynamics of the social, and fail to comprehend its politics (1994:164).

Like Bakhtin, he advocates 'a more processural . . . [and] provisional form of thinking' (1994:161) about media as 'transitional objects' (1994:164). Media experience is seen as the site of a number of overlapping tensions: imposed meanings and created meanings, mass-produced commodities and private recodings, control and decontrol. It is 'precisely through [their] constant juxtaposition' (1994:167) that media narratives and 'the lived narratives of daily life' gain their significance. Similarly, Gillespie explores 'how TV is . . . assimilated into the social formation and how that social formation is read back into the text' (1995:60). The priority of a quotidian over a textualist framework for these authors derives from the fact that media texts remain inert until

> [t]hey enter a social space, a moral economy, that will use them to help define its own identity and integrity . . . [I]t is in this process of bringing things and meanings home that . . . our own domesticity is produced and sustained (Silverstone, 1994:175).

This idea of 'bringing things home' for multicultural media classrooms leads to my final provocation. It involves extending the quotidian perspective to include the dialectics of difference and community, to forms of teaching 'in the contact zone' (Bizzell, 1994). This means acknowledging in any classroom 'all the relevant struggles that are going on there' so that '[v]irtually every student has the experience of seeing the world described' with their media experience in it (1994:167). The aim is not to do justice to the interpretation of media texts, but to media experiences that matter to students, to forms of production that might make a difference to local communities.

Once again, Murdock and Phelps (1973) are ahead of us in asserting that media pedagogy is not simply a 'school subject', since dealing with popular media inevitably means addressing everyday experience, local contexts and public issues. They therefore end their report by stating that media assignments 'should be produced with a real audience or public in mind . . . the school, or, even better, the local neighbourhood' (1973:143). The notion that media education is a dialogue with and a taking 'back into the streets' of discussions which originate there constitutes a challenge to contemporary media educators to breach the divisions, not only between school subjects, but between formal education, everyday life and public culture. Media education might thus imply a form of publicly responsive discursive production rather than a 'one-size fits all' curriculum with standard genres and set topics.

I have argued here for the adoption of concepts like utterance, performativity and the quotidian in order to reclaim what most students already know: that media in everyday life are experienced as processes of making and remaking rather than merely as 'texts' for decipherment. Going beyond textualism and radical critique means shifting our attention to the *verbing* of media experience instead of the *noun* of text, to active subjects-in-culture rather than inert meanings-in-texts. It also suggests that we should retire current professional self-definitions and romantic narratives that locate media teachers as heroic warriors rescuing Critical Reason, Authentic Expression and Truth from a debased Mass Media.

In contrast, a less dramatic version of media education, one cast 'in small letters' (Canclini, 1993), would explore in open-ended fashion the liminal transactions that occur in the space between everyday concerns and provided media commodities. It would examine such mundane interactions in order to discover what is vitally new and important about *these* media appropriations by *this* group in *these* specific social situations. It would focus on the innovations and micro-displacements accomplished by everyday uses, local discourses and communal values – including of course the practices of the media classroom itself. It is time, in other words, to move away from de-contextualized 'models of media education that work anywhere' (Strategies, 1989), and to devise approaches that situate media representations within the lifeworlds in which they are taken up and lived.

Notes

1 Excerpts and statistics in this chapter come from both a random sample of 100 responses to a questionnaire mailed to secondary schools in Ontario, and interviews with 40 media teachers conducted between 1992 and 1995 by graduate students and myself. Special thanks to James Fowlie for his help with the preparation and analysis of the questionnaire. Generous support for this project was provided by the Social Science and Humanities Research Council of Canada.
2 I am indebted to conversations with Sandra Moffatt for developing a fuller sense of the past, present and future dimensions of any media experience along these lines.

References

ANG, I. (1994) Understanding television audiencehood, in NEWCOMB, H. (Ed.) *Television, The Critical View*, 5th edition, New York and Oxford: Oxford University Press, 367–86.

BAKHTIN, M. (1981) The dialogic imagination: Four essays by M. M. Bakhtin, in HOLQUIST, M. (Ed.) Austin, TX: University of Texas Press.

BAKHTIN, M. (1986) Speech genres and other late essays, in EMERSON, C. and HOLQUIST, M. (Eds) Trans. V. W. McGee, Austin, TX: University of Texas Press.

BARTHES, R. (1988) *The Semiotic Challenge*, Trans. R. Howard, New York: Hill and Wang, 157–9.

BAZALGETTE, C. (1992) Key aspects of media education, in ALVARADO, M. and BOYD-BARRETT, O. (Eds) *Media Education*, London: British Film Institute, 189–219.

BENNETT, T. (1993) Being in the true of cultural studies, *Southern Review*, **26** (2), 217–38.

BIZZELL, P. (1994) Contact zones and English studies, *College English*, **56** (2), 163–9.

BOWKER, J. (Ed.) (1991) *Secondary Media Education: A Curriculum Statement*, London: British Film Institute.

BUCKINGHAM, D. (1986) Against demystification, *Screen*, **27** (5), 80–95.

BUCKINGHAM, D. (Ed.) (1990) *Watching Media Learning: Making Seuse of Media Education*, London: Falmer Press.

BUCKINGHAM, D. (1993a) *Children Talking Television: The Making of Television Literacy*, London: Falmer Press.

BUCKINGHAM, D. (1993b) Just playing games, *The English and Media Magazine*, **28**, Summer, 21–5.

BUTLER, J. (1993) *Bodies That Matter*, New York and London: Routledge.

CANCLINI, N. (1993) Conclusion: Toward a popular culture in small letters, in CANCLINI, N. *Transforming Modernity: Popular Culture in Mexico*, Austin, TX: University of Texas Press.

COGHILL, J. (1993) Exploring media implementation in Ontario: A perspective on the experiences of two media literacy teachers, *English Quarterly*, **25** (2–3), 20–6.

COLLINS, J. (1989) Watching ourselves watch television, or who's your agent?, *Cultural Studies*, **3** (3), 261–81.

COLLINS, J. (1995) *Architectures of Excess: Cultural Life in the Information Age*, New York and London: Routledge.

DENTITH, S. (1995) *Bakhtinian Thought*, London and New York: Routledge.

DORNAN, C. (1994) Scapegoat sociology: Ontario students getting opposite of education about mass media, *Ottawa Citizen*, 18 April, A7.

DUNCAN, B. (1993) Surviving education's desert storms: Adventures in media literacy, *English Quarterly*, **25** (2–3), 14–18.

FISKE, J. (1994) *Media Matters: Everyday Culture and Political Change*, Minneapolis, MN: University of Minnesota Press.

GALBO, J. (1992) Teaching the media in schools, *Borderlines*, **26**, 43–7.

GILLESPIE, M. (1995) *Television, Ethnicity and Cultural Change*, London: Routledge.

GREEN, B. (1995) Differant technologies: On English teaching, technocultural change and post-educational politics, lecture at Ontario Institute for Studies in Education, 2nd August.

HART, A. and BENSON, A. (1995) Researching media education in English classrooms in the UK, presentation at the Congreso Internacional de Pedagoxia da Imaxe, Coruna, Spain, 3–8 July.

HOLQUIST, M. (1986) Answering as authoring: Mikhail Bakhtin's translinguistics, in MORRISON, G. (Ed.) *Bakhtin: Essays and Dialogues on His Work*, Chicago, IL: University of Chicago Press, 59–71.

HUNTER, I. (1995) After English: Towards a less critical literacy, unpublished manuscript, Geelong, Victoria: Deakin University.

JAMESON, F. (1975) The ideology of the text, *Salmagundi*, **31**, 204–46.

JAMESON, F. (1987) The state of the subject, *Critical Quarterly*, **29** (4), 16–25.

LIPSITZ, G. (1990) *Time Passages*, Minneapolis, MN: University of Minnesota Press.

LUSTED, D. (1985) A history of suspicion: Educational attitudes to television, in LUSTED, D. and DRUMMOND, P. (Eds) *TV and Schooling*, London: British Film Institute, 11–18.

LUSTED, D. (1987) English teaching and media education: Culture and curriculum, in GREEN, M. (Ed.) *English and Cultural Studies: Broadening the Curriculum*, London: John Murray, 118–28.

MCROBBIE, A. (1992) Post-marxism and cultural studies: A post-script, in GROSSBERG, L., NELSON, C. and TREICHLER, P. (Eds) *Cultural Studies*, New York and London: Routledge, 719–30.

MASTERMAN, L. (1985) *Teaching the Media*, London: Comedia.

MELLOR, B. and PATTERSON, A. (1994) Producing readings: Freedom versus normativity, *English in Australia*, **109**, Sept., 42–56.

MERCER, C. (1986) Complicit pleasures, in BENNETT, T., MERCER, C. and WOOLLACOTT, J. (Eds) *Popular Culture and Social Relations*, Milton Keynes: Open University Press, 50–68.

MINISTRY OF EDUCATION, ONTARIO (1987) *English Curriculum Guideline: Intermediate and Senior Divisions*, Toronto: Queen's Printer.

MINISTRY OF EDUCATION, ONTARIO (1989) *Resource Guide: Media Literacy*, Toronto: Queen's Printer.

MISSION, R. (1995) Every newsagent has them: Teaching popular teenage magazines, unpublished manuscript, Toronto: OISE.

MOFFAT, S. (1995) Learning to imagine: Uncovering affective investments in female representations, unpublished article, Toronto: OISE.

MOHANTY, S. (1986) Radical teaching, radical theory: The ambiguous politics of meaning, in NELSON, C. (Ed.) *Theory in the Classroom*, Urbana, IL: University of Illinois Press, 147–76.

MORGAN, R. (1996) Pantextualism, everyday life and media education, *Continuum*, **9** (2), 14–34.

MURDOCK, G. and PHELPS, G. (1973) *Mass Media and the Secondary School*, Basingstoke and London: Macmillan Education Ltd.

NAVA, M. and NAVA, O. (1990) Discriminating or duped: Young people as consumers of advertising/art, *Magazine of Cultural Studies*, **1** (1), 15–21.

NEW LONDON GROUP (1995) A pedagogy of multiliteracies: Designing social futures, unpublished manuscript, International Federation of Teachers of English Conference, New York, July.

PEARCE, L. (1994) *Reading Dialogics*, London: Edward Arnold.

POSTER, M. (1995) *The Second Media Age*, Cambridge: Polity Press.

PUNGENTE, J. (1993) The second spring: Media education in Canada's secondary schools, *Canadian Journal of Educational Communication*, **22**, 47–60.

SAENZ, M. (1992) Television viewing as a cultural practice, *Journal of Communication Inquiry*, **16** (2), 37–51.

SALUTIN, R. (1994) Teenage student media-literates, *Globe and Mail*, Toronto, 4 February, C1.

SILVERSTONE, R. (1994) *Television and Everyday Life*, London: Routledge.

STRATEGIES FOR MEDIA LITERACY (1989) International models of media education that work anywhere, handout at AML Thinktank Conference, Canada: Trent University.

ULMER, G. (1989) *Teletheory*, New York: Routledge.

WALCOTT, R. (1995) Performing the postmodern: Black Atlantic rap and identity in North America, unpublished PhD thesis, Ontario Institute for Studies in Education.

WALKERDINE, V. (1990) Video replay, in ALVARADO, M. and THOMPSON, J. (Eds) *The Media Reader*, London: British Film Institute, 339–57.

WICKE, J. (1988) *Advertising Fictions*, New York: Columbia University Press.

Chapter 7

Beyond Classroom Culture

Chris Richards

This chapter will examine three interrelated sets of questions. First of all, what versions of cultural credibility and competence do teachers represent to their students? Second, to what extent is the *classroom* still appropriately regarded as the privileged place for significant learning? Do other settings, such as studios, imply different and more productive relationships between teachers and students? Third, what other kind of educational arrangements might allow a more constructive and more flexible process of learning for students and teachers alike? Are forms of education which decentre the classroom – as in some kinds of media practical work – productive because they do not depend upon stable and distinct teacher and student identities?

The following account is informed by a series of case studies[1] involving a group of 15–16-year-old students at a Hackney (East London) comprehensive school and a group of 16–17-year-old students at a selective school in Edmonton (North London). Here, I want to focus specifically upon *teachers'* accounts of their experiences in teaching Media Studies, with particular reference to popular music.

Over the past 30 years, and particularly through the seventies and eighties, the prevailing approach to teaching about the media has been one which emphasized the need to protect or arm students against their ideological power. In such a context, teaching about pop music has occupied a particularly awkward position: if pop music could be challenged in much the same way as advertising, such ideological critique inevitably encountered the more obvious commitments to such music among the 'adolescents' for whom most Media Studies courses were intended. Pop music was thus an uncomfortably contradictory object of study and, more often than not, did not figure prominently among what media teachers felt should be their concern. My research has developed out of this perception of the unsettling consequences of engaging with pop music in teaching Media Studies. Furthermore, I have argued for teaching this area of popular culture in terms which do not conform to notions of Media Studies as ideological inoculation.[2]

A Popular Curriculum?

In his book *Common Culture*, Paul Willis (1990) argues a convincing case against the elitism of traditional views of the arts and of a culture defined exclusively around them. The marginality of such arts to the majority of young people seems undeniable. He argues:

> Most young people's lives are not involved with the arts and yet are actually full of expressions, signs and symbols through which individuals and groups seek creatively to establish their presence, identity and meaning. Young people are all the time expressing or attempting to express something about their actual or potential *cultural significance* (1990:1).

> In conditions of late modernization and the widespread crisis of cultural values they [expressions, signs and symbols] can be crucial to the creation and sustenance of individual and group identities, even to cultural survival of identity itself (1990:2).

Willis regards these 'expressions, signs and symbols' as virtually ignored by the formal school curriculum which, he suggests, continues to privilege an official culture in which a majority do not find the resources to sustain desirable self-identities. In the process of my research, it has been possible to respond in two particular ways to the evident pessimism of Willis's view of formal education. One has involved re-emphasizing the fact that it is in schools that much of what constitutes the informal culture of children and young people is formed and sustained – just because that is where they spend so much time together. The second has been to argue that the school curriculum, if resisted and ignored, is also in practice renegotiated in terms which students find more acceptable, and not simply in conformity with the prescriptions of educational policy from above. The development of media education, and the inclusion of popular music within it, can be understood, in part, in this context.

Indeed, making curricular space for the diversity of music cultures, while responding to the interest of some students, is also a refusal of some influential neo-conservative accounts of 'culture'. For example, Roger Scruton's idea of culture is, in Richard Johnson's words (CCCS Education Group II):

> thought of as a homogeneous way of life or tradition, not as a sphere of difference, relationship, or power. No recognition is given to the real diversity of social orientations and cultures within a given nation-state or people. Yet a selective version of a national culture is installed as an absolute condition for any social identity at all. The borrowing, mixing and fusion of elements from different cultural systems, a commonplace everyday practice in societies like contem-

porary Britain, is unthinkable within this framework, or is seen only as a kind of cultural misrule that will produce 'nothing more than a void'. So the 'choices' are between hermetically sealed national cultures of an incompatible kind, or between a national culture and no culture at all (1990:71).

It could be argued that, in opposition to such new Right formulations, the classroom study of popular music aspires to preserve and extend elements of a 'progressive' English teaching, making curricular space for the cultures of students and reviving efforts to render official definitions of knowledge problematic. At the level of public debate around educational policy, such a strategy should still be regarded as a worthwhile intervention in the politics of culture. But such a politics of culture is sustained at a high level of generality and, as Richard Johnson's challenge to Roger Scruton illustrates, frequently invokes very broad notions of *cultural identity* as the main focus of competing claims. Often, of course, 'cultural identity' substitutes for more explicit reference to 'race' and nationality. By contrast, my own concern in this chapter is to use a more focused engagement with the practice of media teaching as a way of engaging with these broader arguments around educational policies and the versions of cultural identity they favour. In effect, I am posing such questions from within the everyday context in which teachers and students negotiate classroom time and what to do with it.

So, I want to acknowledge that this 'progressive' argument is still vulnerable to considerable, and justifiable, scepticism at the level of actual practice in schools. If, as Willis suggests, the most 'vital' elements of youth identities are effectively made elsewhere, 'space' in the school curriculum may be of less importance for young people themselves than for teachers anxious to 'know' their students. In earlier research Willis (1977) has argued that working-class schools are not places in which it is easy for teachers to secure productive *working* relationships with many of those unwilling to be there. In such schools, I and many others have found that to offer popular culture as an object of study does not simply, or automatically, produce a radical transformation of the social relations which can make teaching and learning so difficult.[3]

Elsewhere,[4] I have argued that one purpose of media education should be to encourage the *social self-understanding* of those currently positioned as 'children' in the education system. A part of what I have intended that phrase to imply has been the need for students to have access to the means of reflecting upon their location in complex, and changing, social and cultural relations. Such reflection might include being able to recognize what they already know as constitutive of a cultural competence beyond the existing priorities of the school curriculum. But I have also intended 'social self-understanding' to imply the capacity to become more reflexively conscious of how they construct their own cultural routes through 'adolescence' into adulthood.[5] In both respects, my emphasis has been not on empowerment, but upon the ways in which limited, though already constituted, forms of cultural agency might be engaged, if often critically, from within the school context.[6]

However, other arguments, beyond the issue of curriculum contents, need to be explored. I want to address the question of how productive the routines of the classroom might be in the facilitation of learning and, further, to consider how the classroom context is understood by both the teachers and students to whom I have talked. To pose such a question has many precedents, not least in my own experience of teaching.

Getting Out of the Classroom

Back in the Summer Term of 1975, I worked with several Afro-Caribbean students to produce a black school magazine. Much of this work was undertaken off-site, at the teachers' resource base for the West Indian Supplementary Service. The process of writing and producing the magazine, for a real audience, involved some significant movement beyond the positions available to us within the more regulated domain of the school. It was, both in terms of the social process of the magazine's production and in the completion of a readable product, a satisfying if isolated educational event.

In subsequent years, the events surrounding teachers' strikes were also productive of important educational moments: students learnt that teachers were also workers and had more complicated lives than those made apparent within the constraints of classroom relationships. Strikes provided opportunities to open up discourses around teaching and being a teacher which, on the whole, were otherwise not spoken within the frame of lessons. In an important sense, the scope of teachers' identities was extended by the need to explain actions disruptive of the routine of teacher–student relations.

A different experience, and one which has related but also more ambivalent implications for the organization of learning, arose out of teaching Media Studies in the early eighties. At Archway School in North London, for example, I taught what I experienced as an extraordinarily difficult group of 22 boys, very few of whom had opted for the 'option' of Media Studies. To the contrary, they were there in Media Studies largely because other teachers, of English Literature for example, did not want to teach them. I had no sustained success with the class at all. At the end of five terms, only four or five remained to complete the course. However, one particular set of events had a lingering significance just because, in another context, all that was so utterly frustrating in classrooms seemed, miraculously, to dissolve out of the class and my relationship with them. The occasions when this happened were rare: visits to the Inner London Education Authority's television studio, presided over by a teacher–producer, provided a context which was seemingly understood to be 'not school' and thus to effect a marked change in the relation of these 'laddish' boys to learning. The provision of a technologically complex setting into which they were introduced not as observers but as active hands-on participants was an unanticipated, in fact a truly surprising, break in the routine of their positioning within the social relations of classrooms.

At the same time there is scope to be somewhat wary of this, for they clearly found some confirmation of a particular version of masculinity in this setting, aspects of which, back in school, were so counter-productive. To some extent, the studio, as a kind of workplace, provided an opportunity for them to reposition themselves outside the social relationships of school; but equally, they were enthusiastic because the positions they were expected to occupy were those of workers with circumscribed tasks to do and in the accomplishment of which they could swear and smoke and be what the school disallowed. In the studio, they were not required to be reflective subjects or to have ideas and purposes of their own; to the extent that any such expectation became apparent, their enthusiasm diminished. I recalled this in a paper written late in 1985, reflecting on what was then a much more recent experience:

> where people are being taught more or less compulsorily or have a strong instrumental understanding of education, the orientation is likely to be one which *defines boundaries* between what is personal and what is a matter of public skill or competence . . . 'Being taught' may be something in which people acquiesce or concede almost *on condition* that it does not undermine or weaken or challenge the boundaries between 'private' and 'public' regions of subjectivity (Richards, 1986).

The implications of these recollections are by no means straightforward. Indeed, to argue for a more practical base for learning of this kind could be seen as just giving in to the existing cultural dispositions of an inflexible and defensive minority. In some circumstances, merely pragmatic tactics can involve acquiescing in practices which are, at the very least, culturally conservative (cf. Willis, 1977). This is a risk which should qualify any easy movement from particular cases to the level of general conclusions. Indeed, I particularly want to underline the need to resist attempts to construct a vocationalism for the 'vocationally limited' and, rather, to emphasize the importance of those strategies which seek to integrate the forms of 'academic' and 'vocational' knowledge.[7]

An aspect of the studio experience from which I feel more inclined to draw broader conclusions lay in the studio-based teacher's working practice. It was important that the teacher–producer could do things that teachers could not – his identity was not contained by the students' expectations of teachers and the knowledge they could offer. But again, I want to both acknowledge the effective working relationship established with students and, simultaneously, recall how ill-at-ease I felt with a practice which seemed circumscribed by technical priorities; it was, contrary to my own priorities, too much as if they were being trained *to be good at* the skills of production.

Whatever my misgivings, the proof of active competence in practices which are not just internal to education itself (like making television programmes) may be a difference which has significance for the future formation of teacher identities. Teachers need to be more than 'experts' in educationally framed knowledge, skilled in the internal discourses of the school and its subjects. After all, many teachers, like myself, complete the route to becoming a teacher in little more than six years, between 16 and 22, from the General Certificate of Secondary Education to the Post-Graduate Certificate of Education. Typically, the combination of three A levels, a degree and a PGCE, returns the student as teacher to classrooms often unable to be other than competent within a narrowly defined range of educational practices. In the training studio, the presence of someone who was more than a teacher suggested, by contrast, the limits conferred by such hyper-specialization. Certainly my own mostly literary formation, like that of most English teachers, seemed a severely restricted cultural resource both in the context of Media Studies and in relation to my students' rather more diverse interests. A narrowly specialized training in particular academic disciplines must be regarded as, at best, a necessary but never sufficient cultural orientation for teachers working in schools, whatever their composition. David, as a Head of English, recorded similar doubts in the interview I discuss below and it is through these doubts that I want to pursue an argument for an expanded conception of 'being a teacher'.

Stephen, an Afro-Caribbean student, was perhaps the most explicit of any of those involved in my research when he drew attention to the limits of the classroom as a context for studying popular music and suggested, if tentatively, that a 'studio' might be a more useful place in which to learn. 'If you took us to the studio where they like . . . and showed us what they do there, maybe that would help us more understand some more things or something . . .'

Though I want to refuse the devaluation of teachers' classroom practice, and of their more academic knowledge, I also want to derive from Stephen's comment a further argument for the provision of settings in which students can be more than 'pupils' – with less of the subordination the latter term implies. Workplaces appear attractive because they offer work-identities and thus a greater degree of power than that allowed to children. The educational experiences which are possible within school classrooms tend to confine children to being 'pupils' but, without denying them their right to such a position, it is necessary to explore arrangements in which, still as students, learning can be achieved through forms of production. This should imply a repositioning of students as more than the risky and irresponsible 'adolescents' which, at 14, 15 and 16, schools expect them to be. If media education can contribute to a reconstruction of class inflected age-relations within schools, it has to do so with rather more than a classroom-based practice allows.

Remaking Classroom Space

However, this may not always entail a literal removal from the classroom setting for, clearly, the actual space of a classroom can be, partially and temporarily, both physically and discursively reconstructed. For example, in Edmonton, the Head of Media Studies, Pete Fraser, had contrived an arrangement which made it possible to redefine a classroom space in terms of a working studio. The physical and technical organization of the space made possible the effort to enact, and improvise around, positions in working relationships which, concomitantly, demanded of everyone some degree of relocation within a discourse otherwise unspoken in the classroom context. The production of a short television news programme, for example, can enable considerable discursive shifts in self-positioning to take place. The construction of an improvised studio in a large classroom made available positions such as news-reader, camera-person, vision-mixer and so forth. Equally, this also allowed a broadening of the knowledge–identity which might be attributed to the teacher by the students.

Forms of production involving the selection and representation of recorded music would provide a similar basis for a discursive reconstruction of the classroom context. To rearrange a classroom as an actively transmitting radio station may be illegal, but to provide the means to prerecord music programmes would facilitate, however artificially contained, aspects of a productive cultural practice. In themselves, these are slight examples, and not exclusive to media education, but they are suggestive of the scope for activities which might produce change in teachers' and students' understanding of what classrooms can become. The further implication is that processes of learning, often regarded as peculiarly dependent on the contexts provided by formal education, might be more fully recognized as also occurring in, and through, other contexts and the working relationships they allow.

Of course, the context referred to here was that of a selective Sixth Form and not that of compulsory schooling in a comprehensive school. In drawing attention, once again, to such a social and institutional difference I want also to suggest a strategy which explores another inflection of this chapter's title – 'Beyond Classroom Culture'. It would be very valuable, for example, to make the social location and composition of one classroom a matter for more conscious reflection. To achieve this may depend, above all, on the use of networks between teachers to facilitate the exchange and circulation of their students' media productions. My own specific example is that of writing, in which students represent their current, and past, experiences of popular music. Such writing could well be used to open up questions around the social differentiation of tastes and of music audiences by presenting it to students elsewhere. In this sense, the culture of one school, of one classroom, can be represented to others. In such a process, studying the social differentiation of audiences would be given a more concrete and exploratory turn.

This practice might also further the effort to enable students to under-stand how their own self-accounts are constructed, in part, through the dis-courses of the self which teenage magazines and popular music make available. Learning about the social forms in which subjectivity is articulated could thus be seen as the possible outcome of a reciprocal working practice in which teachers could exchange students' productions rather than only ever return them to the producers themselves, within the constraints of a single classroom.

I would expect, nevertheless, that these proposals may seem more plausi-ble to teachers in more middle-class schools like that in Edmonton. There are serious questions to pose about how reciprocal such exchanges might be and where the evidence of significant learning would be judged to have occurred. My research has tended to confirm that the initiatives I have suggested are always compromised by the larger context of age and class relations as they are condensed within the institutional forms of schooling. Opening up work in popular culture, devising less exclusively classroom-centred practices and seeking to develop a self-reflective understanding of students' tactical negotia-tions of their relation to childhood, on the one hand, and adulthood on the other, are all valuable means to make schools a little less 'schooling'. But the broader issues of children's rights, and of age-relations burdened also by the regulatory emphasis of working-class schools, are not thus eliminated. It is helpful, therefore, to turn to the comments made by the Hackney teachers, themselves continuing to negotiate the positions in which their school places them.

Hackney: Dialogues with Teachers

I want to begin with two comments from one teacher, Alison, because they offer an immediate contrast with the Edmonton school outlined above. For her the reality of classroom-based work is inadequate to the larger intentions of Media Studies:

> Well, if it was easier to do more practical work then I think practical work would be a good way in, y'know if it was easier to use videos and to use tape-recorders and so on. I mean our groups are very large and there's no technical help with equipment and so it's really, you've got to really psyche yourself up and be feeling very energetic and on top of things and you've got no space either side of the lessons to get anything ready. So you don't do as much practical work as you could, given the sort of conditions you're working in . . . it's easier to do the cutting and pasting . . . I mean at the moment we haven't really got the stuff that we need in terms of good paper and colouring stuff . . .

An earlier comment on the conditions for working with music is also worth citing:

> Well, I don't know, I mean for one thing technology is more difficult now because the technology has improved so much and people are really used to listening to a high standard of stereo in their own homes now . . . having a tape-recorder like that [pointing to my very basic cassette recorder] in your classroom and trying to play a tape of music on it is just crap – nobody wants to hear music like that including myself. So I mean in the old days there would be a Dansette record player in the school and you'd bring your LPs in, you'd bring it on the record player and everybody would gather 'round and listen and it wasn't that, that much worse than what you had at home. But now everybody's used to . . . even in your car you've got a decent, a decent . . . y'know everybody's perception of what sounds reasonable is much, much more advanced. So as there is such crap listening facilities in school, that's probably why I don't play much music . . . if I had better facilities to play it then . . . a stereo system somewhere, even in a bookable room, I would use it far more. But you can't hear the words with these – things . . . so there are reasons why I don't use it.

These may seem no more than mundane complaints but they do hint at different ways of organizing learning and thus suggest something of the potential for rethinking what student identities could be in a better resourced, more flexible and less classroom-dominated form of education. In dialogue with both of the Hackney teachers, it is possible to underscore some of the students' perceptions of the limits of their classroom location and to outline the potential of teaching which becomes defined across a greater diversity of practices – those of media production and of research, amongst others. In fact, it is often the case that teachers and students *share* their frustrations and can have similar perceptions of what kinds of change, what new arrangements and what new practices might make a difference.

David, whose Media Studies class I worked with, offered retrospective comments on both the particular group and the more general issues raised by the study of popular music. Within the frame of my own involvement with his class, the purpose and the orientation of my activities was, for me, to conduct research. I wanted to hear about their involvement with music and, on the whole, I was not primarily concerned to teach them; nevertheless, I expected to find out more by engaging the students in a process within which some learning might take place. Of course such learning, given my stance, was likely to be mainly a reflection on what they already knew. David's comments on this are perhaps double-edged, addressed both to a notional other and to myself as a researcher. He begins with an implicit self-positioning as an English teacher:

I had more anxiety actually about do- the practical side of things . . . setting the practical tasks up and getting them done, the pacing of them and the erm . . . I mean I'm not terribly clever with my hands myself and I'm not that brilliant with cameras and things so I was more anxious about that, erm, but that's perhaps a reflection of the nature of the course that there isn't that much up-front teaching of say views of news you know, what news is and things of the media that sort of kind of more theoretical input which perhaps there ought to be . . . I think, you know, this has come up before in the discussions, conversation, that in a way you're just picking up what they know and that's an important aspect of it but sometimes what are the sources of their own knowledge and so on and you're sort of taking that as a kind of something given and almost y'know with a sort of reverential attitude. But just as with everything else that they know, it's a mixture of real insight, their own development, their own purposes, as well as received wisdom and prejudice and all sorts of things. And I think you do actually have to have a better, a clearer theoretical stance and be, be more upfront about times when you need to be a bit more didactic and make an input, I think . . .

There are elements in this of a Gramscian perspective: the students' knowledge is represented as uneven, mixing together 'good sense' with more limited, and limiting, beliefs and (mis)conceptions. Teaching, in relation to such knowledge, is necessarily also a mix: of validation and recognition but with a more distinctly authoritative voice, both telling and challenging. In the more distant past, as a teacher, I probably understood my own practice in these terms and, positioned as a teacher, would undoubtedly do so again. However, as a researcher, I adopted a less interventionist classroom presence. Elsewhere,[8] I have suggested that doubt, including reflective self-doubt, is more central to the practice and subjectivity of researchers than it can be for teachers. For teachers, the immediate task tends to be that of reclassifying the existing knowledge of students in relation to more educationally legitimate forms. In that process, teachers tend to understand themselves to be at the point of achieved formation to which they wish their students would aspire. In the everyday work of teaching, they encounter, again and again, the accomplished fact of their own knowledge and skill relative to the lack, the naivety and the error of those they teach; the classroom and the purpose of the meeting between teacher and taught defines the terms in which such a familiar perception is constituted. In many important ways this perception is accurate enough but it can be, at the same time, also a feature of what can become a rigidity in teachers' professional identities. There is the possibility that such identities become too immune to doubt and the change that might follow from it.

Even here, in David's response to my questions, there is evidence which indicates that from the vantage point of a teacher, some questions make little sense in terms of the insistent priorities of everyday practice. I asked, for example, 'I mean in a way you're talking I suppose mainly about what they as students need to learn but I mean what do we as teachers need to know more about?' In the school context, knowledge is that which teachers have, and students do not. Those discourses which make it possible to say what it is that students may know and which teachers might learn more about are not widely spoken within the culture of teachers. Though this question was not answered directly, David did offer a variety of reflections on the problem which the question poses. His reflections are of two kinds – those which represent the value of a concern with student knowledge in terms of the classroom interactions it allows and those which dwell more on his own formation as a teacher and the difficulties this presents:

> they really did enjoy drawing on their own . . . it wasn't something which, where the knowledge lay with me and they had to kind of get it out of me, it lay with them . . . and that was very positive, that sense of ownership and of making their own contribution . . . I think it was really good.

> but I think what's, I think it's most valuable as a way of working precisely because it's drawing, as I said earlier, because it's drawing on something they know so it's a good – what was that word you used – paradigm for the kind of interactions which are possible . . . I think that is good.

and here, more self-reflectively:

> I think what fascinated me was the sources of their knowledge, I mean there's one aspect, I mean we think that there's something they should know more about, the history for example and so on, but it's actually where they got their knowledge of it from and I find all that very strange . . . I mean they, there were some things you would hear at raves so called or that, just from the radio or buying things and it didn't, it seemed to reflect different types of music as well, that you would listen to certain types of music on the radio whereas you would buy or borrow, you know, other kinds of music from your friends . . . I find all that very interesting and the, the sort of, I think I said jokingly too that I kept wanting to go to Vortex but hadn't been, this jazz club . . . I wasn't quite sure what to wear and that was a facetious remark and . . . but that seemed actually to be (laughter) connected for them . . . that these were particular roles you took on and so on . . . I mean I do feel slightly odd as a kind of, whether I like to admit it or not, a kind of middle-aged man who in some ways has interests which kind of go outside my stereotyped education and age and so on . . . I do feel slightly at sea culturally y'know because it's,

I'm allowing myself to proceed into something which is fundamentally for younger people and I'm interested in all that sort of thing and how actually . . . my brothers seem, I've always been very poor personally at learning and being able to kind of talk in a fluent and coherent manner about things which I have learnt impressionistically and from my own experience, I think I have got an academic mind, not in terms of cleverness, but in terms of my approach . . . I find it much easier to absorb something if I read a book and read about it from preface to index than actually kind of absorb it from living it and I'm fascinated that these children are able to do it so well and one of my brothers is very good at that . . . he can kind of give you a history of, you know, rock 'n' roll or something, which I'm completely unable to do, simply because he's listened to records not because he's read books about it, whereas I would be able to if I read about it, I think that . . . a dry and dusty way of experiencing the world . . . (laughter).

Here the difficulty of coming to know more, to know what the students know, is explained as a consequence of a particular formation, as an educated, bookish, kind of person. This was confirmation of my own sense of the difficulty in speaking to the students initially: having read books about popular music there was a degree of awkwardness and rigidity in my use of academic categories to apply to the constantly evolving field in which they participate. For both of us, despite our different purposes, attempting to teach a unit on popular music extended our own reflections on the limits conferred in our formation as teachers of English.

David also emphasized the different ways in which knowledge is constituted by social actors in particular settings and drew attention to the self-identifications evident in particular knowledge-practices. Slightly later in the conversation, he developed the point further with reference to one girl, Margaret:

I think much more interesting than the actual content is the process of learning and of making sense of it and indeed of, I mean from a kind of, even from your more academic point of view, of actually what constitutes a field of knowledge because in a way we were artificially saying it was music because they were, it had to do with dress styles, it had to do with language, the words they use to speak about it and it, I mean Margaret, for example, is basically a speaker of standard English but she would then sort of switch into a slightly self-conscious, well not self-conscious, a kind of deliberate use of non-standard forms in talking about music, you know, so there was the dress, there was the sense of cultural identity, the alternativeness of the culture, the references to booze and drugs and so on and I think that would be interesting if you could actually look at how you might recategorize things and what it, this vague process of how you make sense of something constituting it as a kind of distinct domain to be thought about . . .

Here, it is argued that the discourse which we employed recomposed the forms of lived cultural experience as organized knowledge, and thus the object of classroom discourse. The key issue is that of what social interests, and what purposes, are achieved in such work upon the everyday lives of the young people involved. Between myself, positioned as a researcher and not a teacher, and the two Hackney teachers, I was very much aware that we did not arrive at any very explicitly articulated statement of what our common purposes might be. In addition to the division between academic and teacher, the difference between my own location within media education and the teachers' main affiliation to English made our discussions more tentative than those which took place in Edmonton.

Historical and Institutional Knowledge

A little later David made suggestions for a further development of work on music, developments also advocated by Alison. The case they made implies that the students do lack an adequate knowledge of the history of popular music and that their knowledge is selectively skewed by omissions in the popular representation of that history:

> there are sort of historical aspects of it, for example there's the sort of equal opportunities bit . . . the, the contribution that black musicians have made y'know which is often not, they don't know about and so on, I think some of that might be interesting, a kind of straightforward historical kind of input . . . yes, but it was . . . not least because I know bugger all about popular modern music . . . I felt very alien somehow.

and,

> I think I'd want to address the, the idea of the sort of . . . a selective history of what, of what gets left out of account . . . and figures as contributors to popular music, popular culture and so on. I mean it's interesting that a current advert's . . . a lot of people, my little son who's nine, for Christmas wanted tapes of, wanted a Beethoven tape, blues and jazz tapes and this seems to have been because, is it Budweiser? have been using, is it John Lee Hooker? and the Heineken one . . . his little friend has picked this up because his dad is into it, so it's actually become a recognized category for him and the two of them had exactly the same independently made up, the

two had the same Christmas shopping lists and y'know we then bought him a, a ghetto blaster which he wasn't expecting at all and he actually does sit there listening to jazz or y'know Muddy Waters and he really seems to enjoy it . . . which absolutely left me gobsmacked y'know but he really seems to like it . . .

The concern here is partly that the reappropriation of black music by the media, and particularly by advertising, is compromised in that it does successfully create some awareness and enthusiasm for the music but does so without, of course, acknowledging the larger context of the production of such music or the longevity of the musical traditions from which such tiny fragments are taken.[9] There is also, perhaps, an implicit anxiety that if these fragments are the sources of new identifications for young people then such identities might be as circumscribed and as disembodied as the material on which they draw. Again, the importance of David's perspective here is that it has a constructive intent, pointing to the development and learning of larger contexts, both historical and institutional, for the fragmented and somewhat disparate knowledge of the students. The elements of passivity and of relativism lingering in my own quasi-ethnographic self-positioning are effectively highlighted – I could say shown-up – by contrast with this more pro-active pedagogic interest.

Alison, interviewed on an earlier occasion, suggested similar concerns. Certainly a wish to circumvent the artifice of selves seemingly made through engagement with the media does emerge in Alison's account of her own teaching:

the other thing is that kids feel uncomfortable about being construed as audiences so when you're sort of teaching genre and marketing and 'how is this music reaching its audience' and you know 'you have been told . . . sucker, come and spend your money on this because you're black or because you're female or whatever', they feel very uncomfortable about that and they sort of say 'no, that's not true I buy it because I like it, it's nothing to do with that' and yet how come you've got your black kids who're only into some kind of sub-sub-culture of American black music that is not distributed by any mainstream, which you would not be able to hear about or even know about unless you knew a black person who could actually tell you about it and where to get it and stuff because it's so sort of minority that it's under underground and yet they're saying 'well y'know 'cause I like it, I'm not targeted', you know, it's . . . how do you teach that sort of thing?

Alison explains the case for teaching about music in Media Studies in perhaps appropriately defensive terms. At the same time, and despite a seeming conviction in her use of a discourse which represents every choice in popular music as manipulated and determined, there is also, elsewhere in her comments, an equally vehement articulation of that discourse in which music is understood to acquire a personal and enduring importance in people's lives, locating and affirming particular identities in the moments of their formation. There is a struggle to achieve several purposes simultaneously: to defend the teaching of popular music, to theorize the field of popular music as an industry, to acknowledge students' feelings about music and to find some way of reasserting the agency of young people in popular culture.

Earlier in this chapter, I argued that working-class students claim a degree of agency through self-positioning in discourses of work and of sexuality. However, such self-positioning, though unsurprising in their social and institutional circumstances, is not unequivocally worthy of affirmation. I have noted the conservative features of working-class boys' fantasies of themselves as workers and, elsewhere,[10] that girls' claims to sexuality are similarly problematic – tactically satisfying in the school context but likely to be reproductive of subordination in terms of their social and sexual futures. Nevertheless, I do still want to argue for a form of media education which works with these assertive self-positionings by encouraging forms of production; there should be a commitment to ways of extending what young people can do with popular media forms now and in the future.

Yet without succumbing to gloomy warnings of manipulation by the media industries or arguments for excessively retrospective histories, it is also essential to recognize that the forms of knowledge which both David and Alison invoke are equally fundamental to media education. Such forms are clearly crucial to the development of the students' social self-understanding as potential producers, and continuing consumers, in the fields of popular music and the media. In particular, the history and institutional form of the popular music industries should be a continuing concern of media education. Of course, as I have argued, we need to acknowledge that there are continuing tensions here. For myself, even more than for Alison and David, the continuing difficulty is that of laying claim to the superiority of knowledge of this kind in a context where, otherwise, teachers trail behind the more mobile and expansive knowledge of their students.

Unsettling English

As with much of what is most productive in Media Studies teaching, getting into popular music is a disconcerting step, one which upsets the firm division between teacher and taught, between school and home and between supposedly distinct age phases. It opens a space for many of the more submerged limits and assumptions of teaching and learning in a secondary school classroom to be made more visible, more an object of criticism and of contest. Its difficulty, and the uncertainties it magnifies, might provoke a retreat to what feels more secure and more bounded by a 'discipline'. Indeed, I can remember well enough the feeling of relief in moving from a Media Studies to an English lesson during my years at Archway School; English was, relatively, a more stable curricular space within which being taught was often a little less insistently contested. Nevertheless, my own response then, and that of both the teachers interviewed here, though from different vantage points, has been to pursue further this more awkward practice. Disciplines, substantially reasserted in the formulation of the Conservative National Curriculum, do have a coherence and a validity but such things are provisional and, repeatedly, are challenged by the interconnectedness of the worlds they claim to explain. The pace of changes in practices, particularly those driven by the meshing together of social, economic and technological imperatives, places disciplines – such as English – under an enormous pressure to reconfigure their priorities and their relations with other, supposedly separate and discrete, domains.

David, provoked both by events internal to the school and by broader debates, offered this series of observations:

> I think what would be interesting is, would be to see the extent to which all these kind of reorganizations of departments and schools and so on, which is prompted by a greater emphasis on tightness of management, is actually going to lead to reconceptualizing the curriculum, I mean 'cause the original HMI [Her Majesty's Inspectorate] thing would talk about clusters, won't they, they'll talk about areas of experience or something, aesthetic and moral and so on, and this has been the problem with the National Curriculum, that it's actually basically stuck with these ten subjects, kind of, however many they are, and, and, for example, we had a draft standard staffing structure announced yesterday which said English and Drama and left Media Studies off, y'know, when Alison spoke to them . . . I think it's the bottom . . . but we now have to make a case why we should talk about English and Media and Drama, and Drama used to be with Music as Performing Arts but has been shunted over to us and so on and so forth and, I mean . . . you keep seeing these, erm, it's particularly American, who call themselves cultural critics, you know . . . I don't know what their training has been but, sort of, it's probably sociologist and lit. crit. kind of mixture and that doesn't seem to correspond to the way we see ourselves as teachers you know, that you're basically an English teacher, I mean . . . our Head of Music, could presumably, in an ideal world, have a slot in Media Studies couldn't he? And approach it or vice versa and, and, that would be an interesting development wouldn't it? 'Cause I think a lot of the, there's a sense of frustration and artifice about this whole business of . . . sealed in separate categories . . . we've been thinking about what to call ourselves for example because the Head sort of came and wrote some . . . papers which nobody knew about and said, well, 'the Heads of Faculty' and everybody sort of blinked and ques-

tion marks popped up and he said, 'Well, I mean by Faculty those like Humanities which covers Geography and History, and English which covers Media and Drama' and so on and so we've been saying should we call ourselves the Faculty of English, Media and Drama and mention those areas or should we say English and it means everything – which is more advantageous? And I'm not quite sure we've got the right answers 'cause there is a sense in which if we say just call ourselves English, then you broaden your, you don't need to specify each time you want to, say for the sake of argument, you want to bring in a bit of music . . . you wouldn't have to call yourself English, Music, Drama and Media . . . and Gunther Kress is talking about, that seemed to be his angle in the *Times Ed.* that if you ask Cox and company to start a new description of English now, it'd be entirely different from what had been there so why try and rescue it, just tick over for the next five years and really have a proper twenty-first century information technology incorporated, blah, blah, blah, thing but I mean that kind of debate is a million miles away from here, that's what's artificial about it.

The reference to Gunther Kress's argument in the *Times Educational Supplement* (Kress, 1993) alludes to the following perspective:

> A curriculum is a design for the future. It predicts, and shapes the future of a society and of its citizens . . . Despite the present fury, a curriculum is never a document for now, even though it works in the present to make the future . . . Perhaps this is the time for the reinvention of that forgotten genre, the utopia . . . (1993:18).

By contrast, David's argument is located much more firmly in the particular circumstances of his school and, though I find Kress' future-oriented perspective helpful, it is crucial here to place the main emphasis on the practical realities of current teaching. The turning over of questions of teacher identity in this lengthy quotation is particularly helpful at this point. In its hesitations, shifts of focus and thoughtful uncertainty, much of what I wish to stress can be observed. That supposedly stable identity – an 'English teacher' – is every-where in education suffering, but also sometimes thriving upon, a protracted crisis in which it is difficult to reclaim singular or predefined identities. There is, rather, a process of restless redefinition in which judgments of advantage are difficult to settle. The strength of English is as an umbrella beneath which, almost traditionally, innovations have been made; its weakness is that it thus makes no secure public claim to a newly constituted field and is thus vulner-able to external reassertions of its proper concerns. From the vantage point of this Head of English, the debate has its most immediate reality within the internal politics of staffing and of cross-departmental liaison. The attainment of a more mobile teacher identity, more alert to the scope for collaboration, and secure in that less subject-bounded form, seems impeded by a necessarily defensive tactic – an unwillingness to risk that curricular space which is within the English department's control. At this level of institutional negotiation, the debates which may be regarded by academics as larger and more significant appear, to the contrary, equally marked by *their* institutional location in the domain of higher education.

Conclusions

A broad conclusion to be drawn from my wider research is that the social interests of the students are fundamental to their understanding of popular culture and to their forms of engagement with the school curriculum. This, in itself, is hardly new or surprising. However, the specific evidence provided by my case studies suggests how gendered differences in relation to popular music are negotiated within the school context and in terms of students' social and discursive positioning as adolescents. Thus, popular discourses of sexuality figured in the discursive tactics adopted by many of these students. Allusions to the overtly sexualized imagery of Madonna or Prince or, in some cases, gestures towards the machismo of ragga and rap can become, in the context of classroom assignments, a means to reinflect the attribution of school identities and thus to impede one's positioning as only a 'pupil' or a student.

Against the view that these are the natural expressions of adolescent development, I have argued that they are, on the contrary, highly over-determined modes of self-identification in a cultural and institutional context where age-relations are organized through a division between childhood, adolescence and adulthood and the power relations they entail. The conclusions which I want to draw from this are that schools are fully implicated in the formation of the identities they seek to proscribe and that, for both teachers and students, considerable effort should be applied to identifying many of the routine assumptions about social and sexual identity made in that institutional context. To amplify the point, the attraction of 'work' and 'sexuality', as discursive resources, is that they provide a repertoire for the assertion of non-child identities and thus, in effect, ways of claiming a degree of social power denied to students by their location as 'adolescents in school'. In themselves, such claims to social power cannot be simply endorsed as expressive of youthful agency. It is essential therefore that teachers rethink their customary understanding of 'adolescence' and review those aspects of their own practice which may contribute to the enactment of those attitudes and behaviour they experience as awkward and intractable.

It is a part of my argument to suggest that media education, or Media Studies, provides one curricular space in which some of the work of analyzing the contradictory and intensely naturalized assumptions which inform life in school can be developed. I have given only outline suggestions, rather than the detail, of a pedagogy appropriate to the work of developing a social self-understanding. However, as I have suggested, the practice I advocate should engage with an enlarged discourse of education as change and innovation within which teachers might more readily place themselves along with their students, rather than always and only as the agency of change in others. In the discussions which took place in Edmonton, with first year Advanced Level students, there was already significant evidence of this engagement. In my own experience of teaching in working-class schools, it was perhaps the strikes and other crises which, more precariously, made this possible. As I suggested earlier, unusual circumstances sometimes produced dialogues with students in which the limitations of teacher–student positions were surpassed. Tentatively, it became more possible to identify and discuss the social purposes of education and to confront, rather than be confronted by, the need to explain, and sometimes change, the terms on which being taught took place.

It is here that the importance of media education, in this case for English teachers, can be given more substantial recognition. The practice of media education moves teachers into a more radically unsettled curricular space than that provided by most English teaching. The tensions and conflicts between popular discourses and between discourses arising from media education itself are productive of an uncertain and uneven, but also potentially innovative, struggle. The struggle is to conceive of a more flexible practice, attentive to the forms and the detail of the emergent and disparate cultures in which school students locate themselves. The effort of teaching, and of sustaining the discursive coherence and credibility of media education, involves teachers in some work upon themselves, drawing on experiences of change and possibility in the past, but also necessarily rethinking the more settled features of their own formation as teachers of English. To some extent, new forms of teacher identity are achieved in this process. Ken Jones (1994), in a discussion of the 1993 boycott of National Curriculum testing, has argued that those events, in which the teachers interviewed here also participated, can be interpreted in terms of a 'social movement' in which new kinds of teacher identity were created. My own view is that, within the larger political context of English teaching, media education has continued to suggest other kinds of practice, both potential and actual. Media education has been a discursive resource upon which teachers have drawn in redefining what they might be and might achieve. Of course, this has not just been a peculiarity of the recent past but, as Jones argues:

> the categories employed by a collective agent are not all provided for it by the central struggle in which it is involved: agents are formed by their participation – usually, over a number of years – in a multi-discursive, multi-conflictual context. It is this many-sided engagement which supplies agents with the material from which to construct complex and effective discourses (1994:101).

Both of the teachers represented here have histories which confirm this observation. Like myself, they were in their early forties at the time of the research, and thus shared, biographically, 'adolescence' in the sixties and entry into teaching in the seventies. However, I do not intend to imply that the present circumstances were simply read from within fixed symbolic moulds formed in earlier decades of educational politics. Of course, such politics informed the broader concerns of these teachers. But the effort has been to sustain the social purposes of education within contexts shaped by both the unfamiliar cultural worlds of the students and, less welcome, by the disorganization of Conservative educational policy in the early nineties. It is important to stress that, even in the midst of the more urgent conduct of the boycott, the *effort* of making media education more attentive to the forms of popular culture it has tended to neglect – pop music in this case – was also a kind of struggle against the strictures of Conservative educational policy.

In conclusion, my argument is for the enlargement, rather than the reduction, of the cultural meanings which can be engaged within the school curriculum. But it is also for some movement beyond the more bounded forms of identity within the professional domain of teaching. This chapter, to the extent that it may be read by teachers, is intended to continue a debate in which we might consider what kind of teachers to be and what kinds of knowledge to recognize and develop in our dialogues with students.

[An earlier version of this chapter was presented at the European Conference on Educational Research, University of Bath, September 1995].

Notes

1 The research referred to in this chapter was conducted in two north London schools over a period of three years (1992–95). It focused on the study of popular music with General Certificate of Secondary Education, and some Advanced Level, Media Studies students. For a full account, see Richards (forthcoming).
2 See Richards (1995).
3 See Richards (1992).
4 See Richards (1994).
5 See Frith (1983); Hewitt (1986); Hollands (1990); Jones (1988); Willis (1978); Willis (1990); Richards (forthcoming).
6 See Richards (1992).
7 See the work of Michael Young and his colleagues: The Learning for the Future Project, Post 16 Education Centre, Institute of Education, University of London.
8 See Richards (1996).
9 It is worth noting that *David* (a pseudonym) is of Ghanaian origin.
10 See Richards (forthcoming).

Chris Richards

References

EDUCATION GROUP II (Department of Cultural Studies, Birmingham University) (1991) *Education Limited*, London: Unwin Hyman.

FRITH, S. (1983) *Sound Effects*, London: Constable.

HEWITT, R. (1986) *White Talk, Black Talk*, Cambridge: Cambridge University Press.

HOLLANDS, R. G. (1990) *The Long Transition*, London: Macmillan.

JOHNSON, R. (1990) A new road to serfdom? A critical history of the 1988 Act, in CCCS EDUCATION GROUP II, *Education Limited*, London: Unwin Hyman.

JONES, K. (1994) A new kind of cultural politics? The 1993 boycott of testing, *Changing English*, **2** (1), 84–110.

JONES, S. (1988) *Black Culture, White Youth*, London: Macmillan.

KRESS, G. (1993) No time for nostalgia, *Times Educational Supplement*, 12 February 1993, 18.

RICHARDS, C. (1986) Anti-racist initiatives, *Screen*, **27** (5), 74–85.

RICHARDS, C. (1992) Teaching popular culture, in JONES, K. (Ed.) *English and the National Curriculum: Cox's Revolution?*, London: Kogan Page.

RICHARDS, C. (1994) The English curriculum: What's music got to do with it?, in *Changing English*, **1** (2), 66–82.

RICHARDS, C. (1995) Popular music and media education, in *Discourse: Studies in the Cultural Politics of Education*, **16**, 3 Carfax/University of Queensland Australia.

RICHARDS, C. (1996) From a privileged position: Teachers, research and popular culture, in DENZIN, N. K. (Ed.) *Cultural Studies – A Research Annual*, Greenwich: JAI Press.

RICHARDS, C. (forthcoming) *Teen Spirits: Music and Identity in Media Education*, London: UCL Press.

WILLIS, P. (1977) *Learning to Labour*, Farnborough: Saxon House.

WILLIS, P. (1978) *Profane Culture*, London: RKP.

WILLIS, P. (1990) *Common Culture*, Buckingham: Open University.

Chapter 8

Tricks of the Trade: On Teaching Arts and 'Race' in the Classroom

Phil Cohen

An intelligible field of historical study is not to be found within a
national framework; we must expand our historical horizon to think
of an entire civilisation. But this wider framework is still too narrow,
for civilisations, like nations, are plural, not singular (Arnold
Toynbee, 1962).

When my son started secondary school he had to do a project about
a famous artist and he came home and said all they tell me about is
Michelangelo and Leonardo and people like that. Aren't there any
black artists? So I had to show him some of the work by Caribbean
artists today. They don't have a proper multicultural curriculum in
art so that all children can grow up with respect for a diversity of
different cultural traditions (Calvin Karbella).

Starting Points

The challenge issued by the eminently Victorian philosopher of civilizations
and reiterated half a century later by a well-known black community activist
might, at first sight, seem to be a cause for both optimism and alarm. It would
seem to be a sign of hope that people coming from two such different vantage
points nevertheless converge on the notion of the primacy of multiculturalism,
and share at least some elements of a common stance against blinkered, one-
dimensional versions of Western society.[1]

At the same time, it must be a cause for grave concern that despite the
gigantic labours of scholars, educationalists and cultural practitioners from
many backgrounds over the past two decades in the effort to deconstruct the
'civilizing mission' of the West, so little of the spirit and substance of that work
seems to have filtered through to inform what is taught as art to young people
in our schools.[2]

There is, of course, an explanation ready to hand for this. The persistence
of Eurocentric standpoints in teaching visual arts and cultural history, and the
absence of alternative, critical, non-European perspectives, can be attributed

to an act of wilful ignorance and/or censorship on the part of educational and political authorities. Seen as such, it is simply a function of prevailing relations of knowledge and power in the wider white society, mediated through the cultural bias built into the formation of the teaching profession, and reinforced by chauvinistic political ideologies.[3]

This kind of multidimensional conspiracy theory continues to be popular in some areas of black cultural politics, as well as amongst many anti-racist teachers. It has the virtue of simplicity, of allowing the finger of blame to be pointed at identifiable political targets, and it addresses the very real issue of how far advances towards a more multicultural curriculum made under some progressive local education authorities in the early 1980s have been reversed by the onward march of the New Right philosophy of education over the last 15 years.[4]

The argument also yields a secret consolation prize for those whose more generous vision of art education has lost out in the scramble to reach academic attainment targets and come out top of the exam league. For along with the monolithic model of a national curriculum ruthlessly squeezing out anything which does not conform to its normative vision of cultural relevance goes the notion that there already exists, waiting in the wings, marginalized but nevertheless in place, a powerful antidote – a counter-hegemonic answer. This body of alternative knowledge, this bag of cultural tricks and teaching strategies, once properly installed in the curriculum, will help to overcome student alienation, transform the learning experience into a process of self-empowerment, and provide a framework within which racial antagonisms can be worked through and at least partially resolved.

As someone who has spent the past five years working with a team of artists, educationalists and cultural historians to produce, pilot and evaluate just such an alternative curriculum, this is a story line in which I would very much like to believe. Indeed, unless we had thought that it held at least some germ of truth, I doubt very much whether we would have persisted in the face of so much official indifference and structured neglect. But as a result of this experience I have also come to the conclusion that the problem is much more complicated than substituting a multi- for a mono-cultural perspective in art history, or replacing racist image/texts with anti-racist ones. Indeed as I will try to show, those who practice such 'conversions' are as responsible for creating false principles of hope and unnecessary despair around the enterprise of cultural decolonization as their traditional adversaries who set their face against any departure from the established canons of western art.

To break out of this deadlock, I think two moves are necessary. First, we have to grasp the contradictory nature of the popular multicultures which currently exist, in music, fashion, and the vernacular idioms of 'youth'; at least then we stand a chance of avoiding the twin pitfalls of a populism which uncritically celebrates local styles of engagement with 'difference', or an intellectualism which ignores them altogether in the name of some higher, more global principle of 'differance'.[5] Second, we have to critically interrogate not only the dominant educational discourses but also the hidden curriculum and invisible pedagogies of multiculturalism and anti-racism themselves, to see how far they have in fact broken with long established assumptions and rationales about race and representation. In the two case studies which follow I look at different aspects of these deeper and more hidden problematics of change.

Goya and the Dream of Reason

In Goya's famous etching from the Los Caprichos series, the artist is depicted slumped across a desk, head cradled in arms, surrounded by the spectral shapes of ferocious creatures from his imagination. The etching is captioned 'el sueno de la razon produce monstros'. Usually this is translated 'The sleep of reason produces monsters' and as such it has become a founding image/text of the western enlightenment project. However on closer inspection the message yields a more complex and interesting reading.

The caption invites us to assume that the figure is asleep, rather than in the throes of agonized introspection. But *sueno* can mean dream, as well as sleep, and, as Walter Benjamin reminds us, there are many forms of waking dream to be observed in western culture, including the dream of Reason itself.[6] It follows that monsters may not be created by the simple absence of critical reflexivity, but by the return of what a certain kind of closed rationality has repressed, in the form of unconscious desires expressed not only in dreams or daydreams but in all manner of ideological practices.

Translated into the context that concerns us here, we might say that it is the dream of racism to turn other human beings into monsters, and sometimes this can make their lives into waking nightmares; and it these same dreams, once embedded in social institutions and practices, which generate a system of secondary rationalization in which the reality principles of racial violence and discrimination remain dormant, but nevertheless active.

This reading can be supplemented by an alternative version of the caption given to a later edition of the print in which Goya seeks to clarify his message. This now reads 'Fantasy, deserted by Reason, produces Monsters, and united with it, is the mother of the arts'. In other words, monsters are produced by the splitting apart of reason and feeling, mind and body, conscious and unconscious, into self-contained systems; the re-integration of these split-off elements of experience is what the work of art is all about.

The Enlightenment, as we know, drew the line between civilized and primitive, in the terms of these very binaries, and made the social institution of this divide central to its project of modernity.[7] What is specific to the enterprise of racism, and what makes it simultaneously for and against the rationalism of modernity is the perverse way it both constitutes *and* magically dissolves that split. Racist discourse, whether it uses biological or cultural terms, refers to an ideal of harmonious integration, an aesthetics of reason and refinement asso-

Figure 8.1 *Goya: The Dream of Reason*

ciated with the artistic canons and conventions of the 'master race', and simultaneously, to its negation by a monstrous miscegenation of forms associated with 'lesser breeds without the Law'. Fantasy is here reunited with Reason in a way which creates, rather than dispels, Monsters.[8]

One of the main problems with anti-racist education, at least in the way it has approached issues of visual representation in the arts, is that on the whole it does not grasp the subtle dialectic of reason and fantasy at work in cultures of racism. It remains tied to a rationalist pedagogy whose roots remain within the Enlightenment tradition.[9]

The Enlightenment saw education as essentially a civilizing process designed to transform children from little monsters or wild beasts into useful, and if possible cultured, members of society. Its programme was originally formulated in the eighteenth century in the following terms:

> Receive them and with tender care
> For reasons use their minds prepare
> Shew them in words their thoughts to dress
> To think and what they think express
> Their manners form, their conduct plan
> And civilise them into man (cited in Elias, 1994).

It has been easy for black radicals and socialists to expose the ethnocentric and class bias built into this perspective, but much more difficult for them to see similar assumptions built into their own models of learning. For example, presenting the true historical facts about Empire, explaining the different structural causes of unemployment and immigration, demonstrating the processes of unequal exchange between European countries and the Third World, all this is supposed to enable students to break with racist common sense and adopt more enlightened and tolerant positions.

In some schools the methods and styles of instruction which are used to convey this message are often imaginative and suitably 'non-academic', but sugaring the pill in this way does not always make it any easier for children to swallow. Some students do not believe in this particular story line because they see it for what it is, a piece of political wishful thinking. But others, reading through its pedagogic form, resist it because it is complicit with another, much more familiar version of their reality.

The common sense of many of the more conservative elements in the teaching profession is that racism is a form of irrational prejudice, a product of ignorance or superstition, and as such, a defining characteristic of the more backward or deprived members of society. From a different starting point many Left anti-racists reached a rather similar conclusion, except that they talked about 'false consciousness' rather than ignorance. If white working-class children were so prejudiced, it was because they were simply echoing their parents' beliefs, which were in turn a reiteration of what they got from the mass media. Underpinning both accounts is the assumption that reason and progressive values are the prerogative of the educated classes, and that unreason is the lot of everyone else. Underneath the radical rhetorics one can often detect the same elitism, the same middle-class 'racism of the intellect', as can be found more openly expressed in neo-conservative ideologies of culture and education.

Anti-racism is therefore all too easily recruited to the traditional remit of the civilizing mission of education. This can lead to a kind of blindness about how young people themselves make sense of the anti-racist message, how its hidden curriculum is read and reworked through young people's own cultural understandings. It is as if what was taught was entirely transparent, and simply presented an alternative, better and more enlightened view of the world. But if the hidden curriculum of anti-racism works behind the back of the teacher, it is often in full view of the students, because it is realized in a particular pedagogic form, a particular model of learning, an implicit epistemology of race.

Beyond Positive Thinking?

In the early triumphalist phase of anti-racist education, the search for images, words or whole texts which might be thought offensive, their removal and/or replacement by material which promotes a 'positive image' of ethnic minorities, was an important activity. It is here that the discourse of political correctness articulated its own theory and practice of representation.[10]

There is, of course, no question about the need to challenge the hegemony of viewpoints and image repertoires which marginalize or misrepresent ethnic minorities in the mass media, popular culture and the arts, and to do so by providing platforms for alternative perspectives.[11] But what perhaps does need to be looked at are the strategies which are employed for this purpose.

The underlying premise of many anti-racist initiatives in this field is the notion that the meaning of an image can be fixed by its 'objective' social relation to its referent, and that this in turn determines its effect on the viewer. So, for example, a photograph which showed a group of black youth standing in threatening attitudes on a street corner would be a racist image because it confirmed the negative association between black people and street crime. Alternatively a photograph which showed a well-known black academic entrepreneur opening a new Afro-Caribbean cultural centre would be a positive image, because it showed someone from an ethnic minority in a position of power and influence performing a civic duty.

One of the achievements of semiological analysis has been to demolish this kind of essentialist reading of images, which reduces them to a fixed relation between signifier and signified.[12] Images are by definition polysemic; their meaning is always provisional, being decided by their anchorage in specific texts and contexts. The black youth may be a group of famous rappers, posing for their next album cover. The photograph of a black VIP may be placed within a story about how he is being accused of mistreating his wife or misappropriating public funds. So now the first photograph seems to have become a positive image, signifying the vibrancy of black popular culture, and the second a racist slur on the black community, suggesting that one of its leading representatives is a hypocrite, and that public virtue is being used to hide private vice. But even that may not be the end of the story: there may be black leaders who object strongly to this particular group of rappers, because their sexist and violent language is bringing the community into disrepute; it may be argued that they should be denied media coverage, and certainly their photographs should not be published in any community newspaper. These same leaders may, however, approve the publication of the photograph of their colleague, as a warning that those who betray the trust of their community by their unseemly behaviour must expect to be publicly exposed.

No representation can sum up its subject so that there is nothing else left to say. There is always and already, *pace* Derrida, another supplementary reading. However, under the sign of PC, every image tends to be judged in isolation, as if it were the last word, a statement which grasps the essence or totality of what it represents. The possibility of any more complicated kind of image which plays on contradictory aspects of its subject matter is not allowed for in this model.

The reason for the last word rule is precisely to permit a final judgment to be made – this image is positive, that one is negative. Yet the significance of any image, including the most blatantly racist ones, always remains open to multiple interpretations. There is no ideal viewer, there is no unitary spectatorship, and there is no necessarily correct view. But starting with socialist realism, there has been no shortage of attempts to legislate as if there was. To project a positive image of the proletariat, and to expose the negative characteristics of the bourgeoisie, was supposed to be the first duty of the artist under socialism. Today socialist realism is dead, but ironically a version of its aesthetics is still alive within some sections of the anti-racist movement – not among black artists who long ago abandoned such one-dimensional practices, but amongst those whose job is to instruct the public and especially the youth.

There is a good reason for this. In this educational setting, a positive image is whatever serves as a point of identification and motivates young people to succeed by giving them a sense of pride in the achievements of their people or 'race'. Equally a negative image is whatever undermines their confidence in their own abilities. In other words, the meaning of the image is defined by its function as an agency of socialization. Images furnish role models. Implicit in this approach is a particular paradigm of learning and identity. It is a model in which unitary subjects learn about their true origins and destinies through certain strategic images which narcissistically mirror back to them their own preferred selves. Positive role models represent certain essential defining characteristics of Blackness, Jewishness, Africanicity or Islamism. It is no longer a question of whether a particular image conveys an accurate reflection of *how things really are* but whether it represents some normative ideal of *how they should be*.

But norms have to be policed, as well as stated. In order to discriminate between positive and negative, to decide whether this or that photograph could be exploited by racists or reinforce stereotypes, the image police have to continually look at the world through racist eyes. This keeps them quite busy, since there is literally no image which could not be invested with a racist connotation by someone with a mind to it. Images of Jewish achievement in the arts or sciences can always be given an anti-Semitic reading, as confirming conspiracy theories about the all-pervasive power of 'cosmopolitan' intelligentsias; pictures of African American astronauts can always be read to convey the message that now the blacks are taking over the moon!

This instability (or over-determination) of meanings is such a massive feature of everyday cultural experience in the post/modern world that it cannot be altogether evaded even by the most blinkered exponents of political correctness. How then to justify a standpoint epistemology, which enables solidarity positions to be taken up against racism?

One approach, which conserves a tactical essentialism while conceding polysemy, is to argue that the validity of images, their empirical verification or normative strength, rests on their degree of cultural authenticity. An image is valid provided that it is endorsed by authoritative insiders as expressing something 'true' about the culture, irrespective of how it might be interpreted by others. We have arrived at the central language game of multiculturalism.[13]

The appeal to authenticity privileges the role of gatekeepers, and there is a strong (though not inevitable) tendency for these positions to be filled by people who have the most static and conservative models of race, culture and identity. Only work by those who are themselves cultural insiders, and/or who follow a prescribed aesthetic is then likely to be given the stamp of approval. Priority is often given to artists who work from a 'black perspective', who are also more acceptable to the white liberal arts establishment, because their work can be more easily placed as representing their community within the framework of arts patronage.[14]

Nevertheless once the stakes are raised and the players multiply, *authenticity* becomes a hotly contested property. In my first example, I look at how knowledge and power games around the negotiation of race and ethnicity may be further complicated in this way.

Multiculturalism Rules OK?

For this purpose I want to look at a conversation between a white teacher who was head of art at a large comprehensive school in a multiracial – and multiracist – area of London's East End, and a 14-year-old Bangladeshi girl. They were working on a project which involved students making a multi-layered image/text, using a range of public and private media to map the places which they associated with their life journeys and their sense of home. This was part of a wider cross-curricular project for secondary schools which was applying ideas and methods from the field of postcolonial cultural studies to tackling issues of race and identity through the arts.[15] However, the teacher defined the project in terms of conventional multiculturalism. For him it was to do with learning about other cultures and dissolving stereotypes of prejudice *en route*.

Zeeshan produced a complex and visually sophisticated picture focused on a specific historical moment in the struggle for independence in Bangla-

Figure 8.2 *Zeeshan's Map*

desh. Written on the map is an account which gives the context of the work:

> It was a long time ago, in 1971, I think. Many Bengali students died fighting in front of the Medical College. They were fighting because of their language, Bengali. Bangladesh was called East Pakistan at the time and no-one could speak their own language. Because of that they fought and died. So they built a memorial to them which I show here, and every 21 February they go there with flowers. The soldier in the picture is to remind us of what the military did. They went to knock down the memorial again and again, and again and again we rebuilt it until they had to give up and we were free.

In amongst the wreaths and the pictures of different scenes from life in Bangladesh, she places a photograph of herself aged 5, the age at which she left home. The inscriptions in Bengali refer us both to the actual events she describes and to the issues of language and representation which were their focus. These issues clearly do not just belong to the past or to the origins of Bangladesh as a nation. They are very much alive in her own personal struggle for independence as a Bengali girl growing up in the East End today.

This dual articulation is also picked up on the other side of the picture where she explores signifiers of Englishness: the archaic English script, with echoes of Bengali, country houses, her school, a Christmas scene, a jar of coins, stamps and various conventional symbols of modernity. The cross-referencing is deliberate – she compares Bengali and Christian rituals, and picks up the colour of the Christmas tree in the area around the Memorial. The two sides of the story are held in tension, and literally stitched together, with this suture placed along the exhaust trail left by the plane which has carried her from Bangladesh to England.

The teacher decided to interview Zeeshan about the work; he asked her to give him a guided tour of the map, discussing the personal and political meaning of the different images.

> *Teacher*: Tell me about this side of the picture, which is something you know about and I know absolutely nothing about. Where did you get the pictures from and what do they represent?
>
> *Zeeshan*: This cart is being driven by an ox, people travel round in them from one village to another. They carry their clothes and food in them.
>
> *T*: What exactly is going on in this one, just tell me, it looks like some kind of agriculture but I can't work it out. Are they rice planting?
>
> *Z*: No, I dunno, they're digging the land with something.
>
> *T*: It's very obviously irrigated because there is a helluva lot of water around. It's a very fertile looking area.
>
> *Z*: um.
>
> *T*: You're not clear on that one by the sound of things.
>
> *Z*: No.
>
> *T*: What about that one?
>
> *Z*: It's a mosque. It's in the capital city and it's very famous. I think it's the largest one.
>
> *T*: So it's a tourist attraction. What about this one, where did it come from?
>
> *Z*: It's from a booklet I found in a restaurant, about old calendars and cards.
>
> *T*: Could you tell me a bit about that one, it's a very peaceful scene, everyone looks very quiet and relaxed.
>
> *Z*: They are all washing clothes and there is a man over here, I think he's selling something.
>
> *T*: Is this village typical of what you'd see or is it prettified?
>
> *Z*: That's quite typical. Most of the villagers are farmers and they have cows like the ones shown here. This is the picture of a big forest . . .
>
> *T*: Would that be in Silhet, in the north?
>
> *Z*: No it's in the south.
>
> *T*: So it's in the delta where there was that terrible flooding.

Z: That one there's from Silhet where they have tea plantations. The women and children pick the leaves . . .

T: Which is backbreaking work, I imagine. This looks like a special kind of tree.

Z: It's a banana tree, which you get mostly in South-east Asia.

T: Is it an export commodity, something Bangladesh sells to the rest of the world, or is it mostly for home consumption?

Z: I don't really know.

T: What about this lady, she's all dressed up looking very smart. What is she up to?

Z: I dunno (giggles) but that's one of these carriages driven by cows.

T: But she's not dressed for work, this woman is going somewhere special, any ideas? She's rich by the look of things. I wondered whether she might be a bride going to a wedding, a princess even?

Z: She could be. Maybe she's just going somewhere.

T: Now I've never seen that in my life before. Tell me about that.

Z: There are festivals, and the women decorate their hands with jewellery or um . . .

T: Henna? I've seen them draw the patterns. And what about the hands? Are they in prayer?

Z: In India it's a form of greeting.

T: Yes, that's right. That's lovely, it's like a greeting card. What festival might it be? Is it Diwali because of all the light?

Z: Could be Diwali or it could be Eet.

T: Ok, they are the only two I *do* know so it has to be one or the other! Now tell me about this one. This is a monument to Bangladesh. It's not the same as this other one though, is it?

Z: No that one was built earlier . . .

T: This is more famous, I've seen this one more.

Z: 'Cos a lot of people fought to get rid of the dictators who didn't come from the country but took out all the riches.

T: Sheik Mujib was the leader of the Bangladeshi side, wasn't he? That was the period. So back to the village life, there is that cart again. Right this looks like a fortress. What the hell is it?

Z: It's the parliament building.

T: Oh.

Z: And there's a park round there. And there's a mosque nearby, there's a very famous poet buried there and there's an art college nearby. And this monument, the big one, is near the medical college. This is a peacock, it also symbolizes the country, because there used to be a lot of those around.

T: You've taught me something there, because I knew about the tiger, but I had no idea about the peacock. There is an awful lot of traditional stuff on this. Does this represent in your view a rather romanticized view of the country, rather a tourist view of the country?

Z: Yes.

T: Yeah.

Z: I used to go there every year with my grandparents and my cousin lives in a place like that with hills, so um (sighs).

The teacher starts by making a profession of his ignorance. True to the multicultural formula, he is here learning about other cultures. The roles and even the power relations are supposedly being reversed. The student is supposed to be one who knows, the cultural insider with the authentic voice of truth, while the teacher sits back and takes notes. However, in practice nothing of the kind takes place. The teacher reads the picture, continually offering interpretations which are signalled as displays of his intimate knowledge of Bangladeshi history and culture. Zeeshan is put in the position of simply confirming the teacher's superior power of understanding over her own culture. At several points she is made to profess ignorance. In many cases when she starts to offer her own reading, the teacher interrupts to foreclose her interpretation with one of his own. Despite all this she still manages at several points to assert the validity of her own locally situated knowledge, based on visits to her family in Bangladesh. For the rest of the time she can only resist teacherly imposition by keeping silent or playing dumb.

One way of reading this encounter is to see it as a mirror image or action replay of the colonial relationship between the European anthropologist and the native informant.[16] The Bangladeshi girl produces the 'raw material' in the form of artefacts (in this case the picture map) which is then transformed by the white man into a finished product of knowledge. This process has little or nothing to do with local understandings, and everything to do with a certain form of scientific rationality imposed upon them as a condition of their intelligibility. The invisible pedagogy of this teacher silently communicates this pattern: even as it claims to be overturning the colonial forms of knowledge/ power at another level it is reproducing them.

This teacher was an imaginative, dedicated and caring member of his profession, apparently sensitive to issues of race and ethnicity in the school; he was completely unaware of the inhibitory effect of his approach, and was genuinely distressed when we pointed this out to him. He was in fact trapped in a particular language game which had the effect of closing down any potential space of negotiation over meanings. His irritable reaching after fact, the desire to fix and pin down the multiple associations, was all in aid of demonstrating to his own satisfaction the authenticity of Zeeshan's work as an expression of her culture and her history; it is that 'authentic provenance' which makes her work a suitable object lesson for rational pedagogic exposition. But in the process the very space of representation which it was the purpose of the project to create was effectively destroyed.

Technologies of Self

How then are young people, many of whom are so vulnerably preoccupied with their self-image, to find their way through this maze of conflicting strategies of representation and arrive at a viable frame of reference?

We have already discussed a number of possible 'technologies of self' which can be adopted to counter or challenge dominant images of otherness, and criticized them for their lack of theoretical sophistication.[17] But the real test is whether they are appropriate or relevant to young people who are struggling with an already heavy burden of representation, in everyday contexts where issues of social impression management are often highly racialized. Unless teachers understand where students are coming from at this most intimate and passionately held level of cultural politics, they are unlikely to be able to devise programmes or curricula which are as serviceable to individual needs as they are to collective aspirations.

So let us briefly summarize the practical payoffs or disadvantages with each strategy:

Positive Images

A strategy of self-imagineering, focusing on qualities which are generally admired – enterprise, courage, resourcefulness, ambition, achievement, success and so on. This may challenge the negative racial underclass imagery associated with poverty, urban deprivation, violence, drugs and crime and to that extent promote both a public re-evaluation of particular communities, and enhance the self-esteem of their members. This approach tends to be associated with the creation of a new 'ethnic' middle class; it may also be linked to the notion of a *model minority* (i.e., those who have supposedly espoused traditional British values and/or integrated themselves into the wider society). Consequently it may serve to draw a familiar, racialized line between sheep and goats – between those who assimilate and/or are upwardly mobile and those who are left behind or remain marginalized. A final objection is that this strategy tends to produce one-dimensional stereotypes and hence offers an impoverished resource for constructing complex identities.

In Your Face – or Niggers With Attitude

This involves taking the negative image and giving it an affirmative spin. Yes, we are everything you say we are and more. We are dangerous, angry, sexy, wild and out of our heads, but at least we are not dead white middle-class family men! The strategy of positively celebrating images of deviance which

Figure 8.3 *Positive Images*

you find in queerness, and also certain kinds of black cultural politics, can be liberatory in so far as it neutralizes certain terms of abuse and opens up spaces of representation which have otherwise been closed off; it also yields a fun, feel good factor for those directly concerned. But by definition it reinforces marginality and, far from challenging dominant images of otherness, depends on their existence to produce its special rhetorical effect.

Roots Radicalism

This ignores the dominant images and discourses – these are outsider stories which have no bearing on our real lives. To pay attention to them is to give them power over us which they do not deserve. Instead our sense of identity derives from an insider story, a story about roots to which only we have access and which others cannot properly penetrate or understand. So the struggle is to protect this inside from contamination or corruption by external influence. The quest for a positive self-identity based upon authenticity of origins can thus lead to various kinds of separatist or fundamentalist cultural politics. This may provide young people with strong sense of where they have come from and are going to in a way which helps them over the worst angsts of adolescence, but it is open to many of the objections raised against the previous two approaches.

All three strategies share some common assumptions: 1) that it is possible to own and control one's collective self-image; 2) that it is possible to do this without reference to the Other; 3) that such re-inventions provide an internally self-regulating system of representation which does not depend on any external influences; and 4) that this is a means for creating cultural capital out of one's oppression and legitimating claims over resource and amenity.

Poststructuralism has done much to challenge these assumptions. It has argued that the Other is always present in our self-images, and that this is a key factor in considering the more intimate and intrusive strategies of racial domination or resistance;[18] and indeed that these images are constructed with a certain other, a certain audience, in mind. For example, we learn how to pose for the camera at an early age and those poses often stay will us all our adult lives, becoming part of our second nature; and in that sense we perform our identity for and by means of the Other. At the same time, the Other can also function as that part of our selves which has become foreign to us, but which is nevertheless present in our dreams, our phantasies and indeed in much of our waking life as the subject we secretly hope to become, or once believed we were.

The argument may be taken a step further, to suggest that this internal other/hidden self may be taken over by quite destructive feelings of hatred or envy, stirred up by external attacks, namely racial abuse; but in order to effectively counter these attacks it is important to distinguish clearly between these two kinds of othering, internal and external, as well as to recognize the kinds of anxiety and ambivalence to which their articulation may give rise.[19]

This model points towards two further, rather different strategies of self-positioning:

Masquerade

This involves the ironic deconstruction of dominant images, through parody, mimicry, playful juxtaposition, the interjection of elements which break up commonsense flows of meaning – a preferred technique of performance artists, video artists and photographers, of course, and which you might think is not so readily available to young people who don't go to art school. In fact, at least one way of reading contemporary youth cultures is to see them as a popular aesthetic which is playing with and subverting essentialized identities of every kind.

Complex Narrative

The creation of multidimensional image/texts which explore the tensions and contradictions between different kinds of identification, without imposing any single authorized story line on them. This certainly provides a very open-ended framework of representation, and one which I personally have found useful in doing image-based work around issues of race with young people. But some people have argued that it is likely to reinforce the sense of fragmentation which many young people feel; others object that it underwrites a moral relativism which fails to give them a firm sense of value and purpose which they need to deal with the oppressive circumstances of their everyday lives. Against this it could be argued that it is precisely those young people who are on the front lines of struggles against racism and social injustice, who are rejecting the traditional political or religious ideologies in favour of more complex and fragmentary narratives.

These last two approaches break with the whole enterprise of self-imagineering and social impression management. They do not depend on role models, stereotypes or public relations exercises. Indeed they tend to challenge the collective narcissism which characterizes the cultural politics of the big battalions. But what then do they have to offer those young people who are growing up 'on the wrong side of the tracks', and who so desperately want to make it out into a better life?

The Making of the Indian Cowgirl Warrior

We are faced with an apparent paradox. Young people who belong to communities which are marginalized may be especially attracted to cultural forms and practices which conjure up omnipotent selves lording it over others in grandiose landscapes of aspiration; but by the same token, they are the ones who can least afford the luxury of such self-delusion, if they are in reality to move on and out from where they have been made to start from. It is only by confronting the ambivalences of their situation that they can survive its oppressions, with their own images to draw, their own tales to tell.

Our task as teachers must be to create a framework which makes that possible in the classroom. For this purpose we need to construct a potential space in which children are free and able to negotiate over the meanings which they produce, yet one which is structured enough to hold and work through the conflicts and anxieties which are released in the process.[20] In what follows I describe an attempt to do just this with a small group of 7- and 8-year-old girls. Amanda was Vietnamese Chinese, Sharon was from a local Irish family, Rachel's mother was a local white East Ender, and Yolande's family were from Kurdistan. And they were all growing up together in the poor working-class neighbourhood of London's Docklands.[21]

We wanted to devise a cooperative activity which would encourage the children to explore more directly the imaginings which could be mobilized in constructing a multi- rather than mono-cultural image/text. Collage techniques are obviously useful in generating such composite images, but they remain at the level of a more or less mechanical sifting and shuffling of different cultural bits and pieces, a process in which the deeper reaches of feeling and imagination remain essentially disengaged. So instead we drew a large outline figure and invited the girls to work together to create a character by filling in the features as they wished. What happened next was to be an object lesson in what can sometimes be released by such simple means.

There was very little preliminary discussion. Each of the girls took a different part of the body and started drawing with their coloured felt tip pens. But as they drew they talked: this took the form of a running commentary on the whole character they imagined they were constructing from the parts they were immediately working on, and these discussions in turn affected what they drew. Out of these negotiations what came to be known as the Indian Cowgirl Warrior gradually took shape.

As the children worked they wove an intricate web of phantasies around this figure, yet in a way which integrated all its elements into an considered

Figure 8.4 *Indian Cowgirl Warrior*

aesthetic whole. This was no Frankenstein's monster, but a creature given life through a shared impulse to narrate (rather than dominate) the process of its creation. So where does 'it' come from? The figure bears some resemblance to the character in Chinese mythology described by Maxine Hong Kingston at the beginning of her autobiography. This is not a case of direct cultural influence, I think, but because the *warrior* plays a similar function in articulating these girls' dreams of a different, and non-traditional, feminine role. Nevertheless, as we will see, the way this role is envisaged and deliberated about contains its own highly localized set of histories.

The first problem in giving birth to this collective brain child was to give her a name, and after that to define her essential mission in life:

> She's called Sandy . . . No Jo . . . Sandy Jo . . . she fights and bangs people's heads together but only the baddies . . . she's a warrior . . . she's a bad warrior . . . no a good warrior . . . 'cos if people beat up their best friends she helps them out . . . sometimes she's mad . . . she's mad about the baddies shooting people dead . . . she chases after them and bangs their heads together, saying 'pack it in' . . .

An issue which in a boys group might have triggered bitter dispute is here quickly resolved by the intervention of Sharon: she combines the two suggestions into a single composite name in which all the 'parents' can feel they have an equal stake. Such cooperative, compromise solutions characterized most of these discussions, and again this may be considered a strongly gendered pattern.

The role of gender is also foregrounded in the way moral characteristics are debated. The girls want to portray female assertiveness in a positive light, but this causes some problems. Yolande felt it was always bad or mad to fight. But Rachel and Sharon argue that it's OK if you are on the side of the goodies, and do it to rescue people from trouble and help friends out! So the militant superego can take on a feminine form. But in the process the Warrior is somewhat domesticated, cast in the role of a mother or teacher banging naughty children's heads together and telling them to pack it in .

In the next sequence, the *mise-en-scene* shifts and the Warrior finds herself suddenly transported to the Wild West. But this relocation in turn sparks off a debate about her ontological status – is she real or imaginary?

> She's a cowgirl . . . a cowgirl warrior . . . I saw one in a film, she had boots on and these prickly things on behind [i.e., spurs] . . . I like Supergirls . . . so do I . . . the cowgirl lives in heaven . . . No Way . . . No Way . . . she lives in a desert. Every morning she gets up, she cleans everything up, and she goes to work . . . she does something very important . . . she's not real, is she, 'cos she's just in a film . . . she cleans everything up then she goes to the man making the film and says, 'can I have a cup of tea first 'cos I've come a long way to get here' . . .

Again we see how quickly a new element is integrated into the story line, but this 'syncretic' impulse also begins to undermine the realism of the whole enterprise, especially with the entry of Supergirl. We are in the ethereal world of movie and TV heroines, where 'anything is possible' (even heavenly choirs of cowgirls!).

But Sharon will have none of this. She brings the discussion down to earth with a bump by grounding Supergirl in the realities of women's work. Her cowgirl is a working-class girl who lives in a desert (it is certainly no heaven), who is involved in both domestic and waged labour, but is nevertheless positively valued; her work is very important to the community. At this point Yolande gets confused and more than a little anxious about the sudden switch from Hollywood to the kitchen sink. She can't handle the contradiction if it is real, though it wouldn't matter if it was 'just a movie'. But Sharon is more able to integrate aspects of social rationality and phantasy into a single construction, without confusing them. She does this by drawing a pen portrait of someone who first cleans up the film set and then stars in the picture being made. At one level this startling juxtaposition of charlady and film star represents an extreme, polarized version of women's dual roles as drudge and idol. Sharon mimics the daydream of the housewife she might yet become: to escape the confining realities of the domestic round by having one's true talents discovered at last. But in daydreams the promise of transcendence is contained and neutralized within the structures of its own negation – in this case by the sexual double standard which precisely destroys the imaginative link by splitting its terms into an either/or. Sharon does not take this path. She is not writing a script for the Hollywood dream factory. Quite the reverse. She is trying to reconcile her positive sense of working-class realities with her wider social aspirations as a girl. And she does it precisely by debunking the mythology of instant stardom. Her movie actress is a working cowgirl, someone who goes to the director and says, 'Can I have a cup of tea because I've come a long way to get here?' She wants her aspirations recognized in material as well as symbolic terms. It is the man's turn to make the tea, while she puts her feet up and has a well-earned rest!

The class status of the cowgirl warrior having been resolved, the debate now moves onto another terrain of confusion: her ethnic origins. Rachel is doing her face and announces, 'I'm going to do the colour of the skin.' Thereupon Amanda speaks for the first time, 'Do it yellow.' But Rachel refuses, 'No, I'm going to do it brown . . . I know let's make her an Indian . . . an Indian cowgirl.' And this suggestion is greeted with a chorus of Yeses from Yolande and Sharon, but not from Amanda, who looks hurt. Yolande then turns to Amanda and says in a comforting tone of voice, 'You're an Indian.' But this is immediately contradicted by Sharon, 'No's she's not,' at which Rachel and Sharon break out into giggles.

Care has to be taken in interpreting this exchange. The effect on Amanda is crushing and echoes other contexts of social exclusion she experienced in the school. But there is also another, more complex, process of negotiation going on. Amanda makes a bold move to claim the cowgirl as her own. Rachel, however, knows that cowgirls are not usually Chinese, although warriors most definitely are. However at this point it is the cowgirl not the warrior who is uppermost in their minds. In saying she is 'going to do it brown', Rachel is denying Amanda exclusive ownership of the image by giving it a skin colour which belongs to *no-one* in the group. However this also means that the cowgirl is magically metamorphosed into an Indian. When Yolande turns to Amanda and offers her honorary membership of an Indian tribe, she seems to be denying her real ethnicity. But at another level she is expressing a shared kinship between a Turkish and a Chinese girl, as members of ethnic minorities who face racial discrimination. But that act of solidarity is immediately attacked by the two white girls, who must feel threatened: if they giggle, it is partly perhaps out of the sense of dissonance aroused by the thought of a Chinese Indian; but it is also partly out of anxiety lest their own ethnic credentials should be put on the line. It is exactly at this point that colouring the face brown ceases to be an act of identification with black people, or a means of preventing the figure being monopolized by any one member of the group; it becomes instead part of a strategy to divide and rule ethnic minorities on the basis of skin difference.

Yet this device did not, in fact, resolve the issue; it only compounded the confusion. For there is an ambiguity about the term *Indian* in this context. Are they referring to American Indians, or the inhabitants of India? At this point I intervened for the first time to ask them what they knew about 'Indians', where did they come from? Rachel suggested Africa; Yolande, loyal to Amanda, suggested Hong Kong, while Rachel said simply, 'the desert'. Their answers revealed a personal geography of identification with the figure which had little or nothing to do with the real world. Yet this also made their own creation wholly 'Other'. How then could they then reclaim it as the product of a shared enterprise?

For this purpose it was necessary to construct a new myth of origins. And now it became clear to which *mise-en-scene* this Indian belonged:

> First there were cowboys ... no, the Indians ... then the cowboys came along ... they were looking for treasure ... a great big block of gold ... they fight a lot ... they fight about money ... and princesses ... the Indians come along ... they're warriors ... they bang the baddies' heads together and tell them to stop.

In this dialogue Amanda for the first time fully participated. She could bring her gift for story-telling to bear in reclaiming the figure for everyone. Sharon starts by stating the traditional colonial mythology of the American frontier. But this is quickly contradicted by Rachel, who knows better – the Indians were there first. Amanda now suggests one of the real motives behind the settlement of the American West – they were looking for gold. This appeals to Sharon's material imagination – there were a lot of fights about money. She would no doubt have appreciated *The Treasure of the Sierra Madre* and Von Stroheim's *Greed*! But for Amanda gold and buried treasure clearly have a more mythological significance and she persists in adding a fairy tale theme about princesses. When the Indians make their entry it is implicitly to avenge this pillage and rape. Naturally they are warriors, and in a reprise of the opening motif, they are invested with a legislative and peacekeeping role. They bang the cowboys' heads together and tell them to stop.

But now it is perhaps becoming clear just who or what these cowboys represent: they are the boys in the playground whose racist and sexist taunts were, I later discovered, making their lives a misery. In lieu of any effective intervention by adults, these girls can only look to themselves, to their own power of social combination, here symbolized in the hybrid character they have jointly created, to step in and stop the racism going on around them.

In this way, through a process of indirection, the whole group comes finally to recognize the issue of racial injustice. This vantage point is reached through their own internal negotiations and it necessarily follows a tortuous path. For *en route* they have to grapple with a whole series of contradictions related to gender, ethnicity and class. Members of the group are continually shifting their positions *vis à vis* each other and the issues under debate. In the process they are setting their own agenda and staking out areas for further work. My job was to support what might emerge in this potential space of representation, rather than foreclose it through any irritable reaching after fact or interpretive intervention.

Finally, we should not forget that what held the group, and their collective creation, together was not just talk, but the act of drawing. In looking at the final picture it is hard to believe that it was made by so many hands. The process of figuring out always has to be iconic as well as discursive. It is about redrawing the inner landscape of thought and feeling around a significant image. This is something that can never be forced upon children by the imprimaturs of 'correct thought'; it resists prescriptive 'insights' and the rhetorics of 'positive imagery'. Instead we are directed towards a more complex theory of subjectivity and meaning, one which focuses on the unconscious process of representation. It was because the Indian Cowgirl warrior worked at this level that its making authorized Amanda to speak out and thus helped her to begin to find her own distinctive voice, as a Chinese girl, within the group. And in doing so, she made space for other stories to be told, including this one.

Notes

1 In *A Study of History* (1962), Toynbee's main work, he sets out his general theory of world civilizations. Written against the rise of fascism during a period of seemingly chronic crisis for western capitalism, Toynbee's work is preoccupied with the question of how far the descent into 'barbarism'

might be arrested from within, and in that sense prove an exception to the historical rule. More recent historical overviews have challenged this exceptionalism, and the implicit Eurocentrism of Toynbee's comparative methodology: see for example Fernandez-Arnesto (1995).

2 In this respect it is salutary to compare Karbella's remarks, which were made in the late 1980s after a decade of 'multicultural education', with the very similar comments made in the CRE report *Art Education in a Multicultural Society* published in 1981.

3 See for example the account given by Owusu (1988).

4 On the development of New Right policies in education see the contributions to Levitas (1986) and Education Group II (1991).

5 The work of Les Back on urban youth multicultures is exemplary in avoiding the extremes of populism and postmodernism. See Back (1995).

6 See Benjamin (1979).

7 See for example Hulme and Jordanova (1990) and Bauman (1991).

8 This point is developed further by Zygmunt Bauman (1989), who stresses that the Holocaust was not an outburst of atavistic irrationality, but a precise organization of racial myths and phantasies through a modern technology of government. For a discussion of the role of the monster in popular cultures of racism see Cohen (1988).

9 The link between rationalism, racism and anti-racism is developed by Goldberg (1993). On the rationalism of anti-racist pedagogy see the contributions by Rattansi and Cohen in Donald and Rattansi (1992).

10 For a general discussion of the debate on political correctness see the contributions to Dunant (1994) and Williams (1995). In Britain this debate was preceded and in some senses pre-empted by the development of a purely internal critique of anti-racism in the 1980s, focusing on the negative effect of its more moralistic, symbolic and doctrinaire forms. See for example Macdonald (1990) and Cohen (1988).

11 Much of the research in this area has focused on questions of stereotyping and the construction of racialized scenarios of social conflict in the mainstream media. See for example Van Dijk (1991) and Campbell (1995). Husband's survey of ethnic minority media (1994) provides a useful view of issues of race and representation from the other side of the tracks.

12 The analysis of visual ideologies of race remains dominated by the cognitivist model of the stereotype, which from a strictly semiological point of view begs several important questions, for example concerning the rhetorics of the image and its structures of addiction. The semiotics of race is a largely neglected field, but see the useful discussion by Amossy (1991) and Gilman (1985).

13 For a discussion of the philosophical foundations of multiculturalism see Taylor (1992). The classical statement of pedagogic principles is to be found in Craft (1984); and for a discussion of their application see Lynch, Modgil and Modgil (1992). The implication of cultural authenticity in the construction of 'ethnic arts' and the discourse of primitivism is well illus-

trated in the work of Beyreuth (1988) and Barnard (1991). A critique of this position is developed by Gilroy (1993).

14 See, for example, the Arts Council Report by Constanzo and Alexander (1986) and also Pankratz (1993). For a general discussion of race and the politics of representation in the arts in Britain see Lucie-Smith (1993).

15 The Tricks of the Trade project is a collaboration between art educators and cultural researchers based at the Centre for New Ethnicities Research, University of East London. The project has been funded by the London Arts Board, the Paul Hamlyn Foundation, the Arts Council of Great Britain, and a number of other trusts. A video and teaching materials from the project are available from CNER.

16 For a general discussion of the colonial power relations which operate through the ethnographic contract see the contributions to Asad (1973).

17 The term is Foucault's (1988), but may be taken to refer to any strategy which positions the subject in relation to the other via specialized techniques of imagineering or impression management.

18 See Niranjan (1992) for a discussion of the relation between poststructuralism and the postcolonial subject, and also Pieterse (1992) on the epistemology of emancipation in the era of globalization.

19 Recent theoretical research influenced by psychoanalysis has tended to focus on racism as structure of desire/discourse of the Other. See, for example, Bauman (1991), Bhabha (1994) and Kristeva (1991).

20 The linked concepts of potential space and negative capability are discussed in a psychoanalytic context by Marion Milner (1986) and in their political implication by Unger (1984). Their relevance to a postmodern pedagogy is discussed in Cohen (1996).

21 This work is discussed in greater detail in Cohen (1995).

References

AMOSSY, R. (1991) *Idees Recues: Semiologie des Stereotypes*, Paris: Le Seuil.

ASAD, T. (Ed.) (1973) *Anthropology and the Colonial Encounter*, London: Ithaca.

BACK, L. (1995) *New Ethnicities and Urban Youth Cultures*, London: UCL Press.

BARNARD, N. (1991) *Living with Folk Art*, London: Thames and Hudson.

BAUMAN, Z. (1989) *Modernity and the Holocaust*, Cambridge: Polity.

BAUMAN, Z. (1991) *Modernity and Ambivalence*, Cambridge: Polity.

BENJAMIN, W. (1979) *One Way Street*, London: Verso.

BEYREUTH, C. (1988) *Towards African Authenticity*, Berlin: Chicago University Press.

BHABHA, H. (1994) *The Location of Culture*, London: Routledge.

CAMPBELL, C. (1995) *Race, Myth and the News*, London: Routledge.

COHEN, P. (1988) The perversions of inheritance, in COHEN, P. and BAINS, H. (Eds) *MultiRacist Britain*, London: Macmillan, 9–118.

COHEN, P. (1995) *Verbotene Spiele*, Berlin: Das Argument.

COHEN, P. (1996) *Rethinking the Youth Question*, London: Macmillan.

COMMISSION FOR RACIAL EQUALITY (1981) *Art Education in a Multicultural Society*, London: CRE.

CONSTANZO, J. and ALEXANDER, P. (1986) *Art in a Multicultural Society*, London: Arts Council.

CRAFT, M. (1984) *Education and Cultural Pluralism*, Lewes: Falmer Press.

DIJK, T. VAN (1991) *Race and the Press*, London; Routledge.

DONALD, J. and RATTANSI, A. (Eds) (1992) *Race, Culture and Difference*, London: Sage.

DUNANT, S. (Ed.) (1994) *The War of Words*, London: Virago.

EDUCATION GROUP II (Department of Cultural Studies, Birmingham University) (1991) *Education Limited*, London: Unwin Hyman.

ELIAS, N. (1994) *The Civilizing Process*, Oxford: Blackwell.

FERNANDEZ-ARNESTO, F. (1995) *Millennium*, London: Methuen.

FOUCAULT, M. (1988) *Technologies of the Self*, London: Tavistock.

GILMAN, S. (1985) *Difference and Pathology*, Ithaca, NY: Cornell.

GILROY, P. (1993) *The Black Atlantic*, London: Verso.

GOLDBERG, D. (1993) *Racist Culture, Philosophy and the Politics of Meaning*, Oxford: Blackwell.

HULME, P. and JORDANOVA, L. (1990) *The Enlightenment and its Shadows*, Manchester: Manchester University Press.

KRISTEVA, J. (1991) *Strangers to Ourselves*, London: Harvester.

LEVITAS, R. (Ed.) (1986) *The Ideology of the New Right*, Cambridge: Polity.

LUCIE-SMITH, E. (1993) *The Rise of Minority Cultures*, London: Thames and Hudson.

LYNCH, J., MODGIL, C. and MODGIL, S. (Eds) (1992) *Cultural Diversity and the Schools* (4 volumes), London: Falmer Press.

MACDONALD, I. (1990) *Murder in the Playground: The Burnage Report*, London: Longsight.

MILNER, M. (1986) *Eternity's Sunrise*, London: Virago.

NIRANJAN, T. (1992) *Siting Translation*, Oxford: Blackwell.

OWUSU, K. (1988) *Storms of the Heart: An Anthology of Black Arts and Culture*, London: Camden.

PANKRANTZ, D. (1993) *Multiculturalism and Public Arts Policy*, London: Routledge.

PIETERSE, J. (1992) *Emancipation, Modern and Postmodern*, London: Pluto.

TAYLOR, C. (1992) *Multiculturalism and the Politics of Recognition*, Princeton, NJ: Princeton University Press.

TOYNBEE, A. (1962) *The Study of History*, Oxford: Oxford University Press.

UNGER, R. (1984) *Passion*, London: Routledge.

WILLIAMS, J. (Ed.) (1995) *PC Wars*, London: Routledge.

Chapter 9

Teaching for Difference: Learning Theory and Post-critical Pedagogy

Bill Green

What are the prospects now, in this last decade of the twentieth century, for 'radical pedagogy', as a key movement in postmodern, socially-critical educational practice? What new imaginings and other cultural and technical resources are now available? What risks and possibilities? What dangerous memories and subjugated knowledges need to be revived and mobilized, in order to move into a future marked as always by both fear and hope, but now arguably even more ambivalent and complex than ever before? Indeed, what *does* it mean to talk of radical pedagogy today?

Questions such as these have been engaged and explored elsewhere in this volume. In this chapter, I want to draw on work in, and across, the fields of English teaching, media education, cultural studies and critical pedagogy to address issues more specifically of *teaching* and *learning*, curriculum and pedagogy. My interest is in bringing together the disjunctive worlds of British and American academic–intellectual work in education studies, along with those of educational theory and classroom practice. Further work is needed if radical pedagogy is ever to be realized as educational praxis, and hence my focus here is firstly on *pedagogy*, as a concept in itself, and also on *learning*, as arguably the most inadequately theorized issue in this whole debate. I seek to bring together initiatives and arguments in 'critical pedagogy' with what I shall simply designate here as a distinctive 'London' tradition of curriculum and cultural work.

Reconceptualizing Learning

My particular concern is with exploring the concept of *learning*, and with initiating a reconceptualized account of learning in and for the semiotic society. Such work has clear implications for the re-evaluation of the critical pedagogy project. In a recent account of critical writing pedagogy and school geography, Lee (1996:20) points to the need for socially-critical educators to engage questions such as 'what might count as learning, how it might be constituted and how it might be traced'. She indicates the significance of attending more directly and deliberately to notions of discourse, desire and difference, as well as to what she calls 'student productions', not just 'what students *get* – the materials of the curriculum – but what different students *make* of what they get'. She cites Alan Luke to this effect:

> While neomarxist educational theory has developed a range of theories of knowledge transmission and, even more recently, accounts of human agency via resistance and contestation, it has failed to address the need for a theory of learning (1989:61).

And as Luke further observes:

> While theories of transmission can account for the coding of a dominant ideology, any theory of cultural hegemony must also account for the cognitive processes by which the individual (non-coercively) acquires knowledge. It also follows that such a theory would be a prerequisite for any positive thesis for emancipatory education (cited Lee, 1996:20).

The importance of this line of argument is indicated in Buckingham's (1992) account of media education and critical pedagogy. As he writes, what is urgently needed in such work, and what currently constrains and limits them both, is 'an adequate theory of learning' (Buckingham, 1992:300). He identifies two contrasting positions in British media education, one based on a commitment to radical theory and knowledge as 'content', the other on popular culture and resistance, and sees them both as falling short of their programmatic aims of social transformation and educational change, essentially because neither offers or works with an adequate learning theory. The consequence is, in effect, a binary trap: 'Either learning is something that "just happens" through a process of osmosis, or it is something which follows inevitably as a result of teaching' (Buckingham, 1992:300). The emphasis in one view is thus on 'teaching' and 'transmission', while in the other it is on 'learning' and 'interpretation'. To escape this unhelpful binary, we need a view that links the two organically – as 'teaching–learning' – a new curriculum logic of *both* teaching- *and* learning-centredness. This is what has been described as a distinctive *negotiation* paradigm, understood not so much in its liberal connotation as in critical-semiotic terms (Boomer *et al.*, 1992). To date, however, the formulation of the paradigm has remained on the level of descriptive theory. Work is now urgently needed on its 'scientific' elaboration.

Although Buckingham (1992:300) suggests that this might be usefully engaged through a critical reappropriation of Vygotskian psychology, it can also be addressed through poststructuralist accounts of discourse and subjectivity. At issue here is partly what Buckingham calls '*conceptual learning*', by which he means (following Vygotsky) the dynamic interanimation of 'scientific' and 'spontaneous' conceptualization.[1] Following James Gee (1990), this means taking into account the relationship between primary and secondary Discourses, as cultural frames for action and meaning. Within a post-structuralist framework, conceptual learning involves working to take up positions in available discourses, or specific discursive–disciplinary fields. Importantly, 'discourses' and 'disciplines' are to be understood both as formal and informal in nature and orientation, and hence as reaching across the domains of schooling, family life and popular culture. This makes for a view of discursive–disciplinary fields as necessarily complex and contradictory, dynamic and always shifting, or in process and movement. Learning is therefore seen as a particular relationship between discourse and subjectivity – as a matter of taking up and working with particular subject-positions as these are made available in and through discursive practice and struggle. The point to stress is that these positions are always multiple and often conflicting and contradictory.

Rethinking learning along these lines means, then, developing more adequate, grounded views and understandings of *pedagogy*, as itself a specific concept. As commentators such as Gore (1993), Lusted (1986) and Simon (1992) have observed, with direct reference to discourses of critical pedagogy, the term itself needs to be carefully delineated and defined. Working more specifically within what I have called the London tradition, Levine (1992) argues that pedagogy is to be understood as a key 'concept-framing word' indicating how teaching is to be grasped as a complex activity, in terms of 'an extensive understanding of educational theory interrelated, in practice, with a wide range of classroom management skills' (Levine, 1992:197). Pedagogy brings together theory and practice, art and science, conventionally and commonly understood as separate and distinct. This is a position well established within the tradition of language and literacy education, English teaching, and the language and learning movement; and, as I have indicated, it is usefully paralleled with certain lines of development and argument in British cultural studies. At its best, it involves the integration of 'radical' and 'progressive' impulses in pedagogic practice, and stresses the dynamic interplay and interanimation of 'inside–outside', 'text–context' and 'micro–macro' relations.

With this in mind, it is possible to argue that pedagogy is best understood as referring to the structured relationship between teaching and learning, as forms of social–discursive practice. That is, pedagogy refers specifically to teaching *and* learning, as dynamically interrelated although necessarily not identical or isomorphic activities. Moreover, it is best conceived as 'teaching *for* learning', with teaching understood not as the *cause* of learning but rather as its *context*. The work of teaching is thus directed towards and oriented around learning, which can be understood as a system-environment, or eco-systemic, relation (Lemke, 1984). This view of teaching as contextual rather than causative with regard to learning leads to a semiotic view of pedagogy and curriculum, rather than one that is mechanistic in nature. Moreover, theories of learning and theories of subjectivity are brought together in such a view, with learning understood expressly in terms of subject-positioning and subject-production. Teaching is thus understood as directed towards the positioning and production of learning-identities – as addressed to the discursive production of subjects of knowledge. Importantly, however, 'teaching for learning' needs itself to be understood as 'teaching for difference', in the sense that schooling and curriculum work is best conceived as always and necessarily future-oriented (Kress, 1995:9). Learning, that is, is to be conceived in terms of the engagement and production of difference.

More specifically for my purposes here, what increasingly needs to be taken into account is the need to work with difference in terms of both study objects (texts) and study subjects (students, learners) – what is taught, and to whom it is taught. On the one hand, an important shift is underway from canonic forms and orders of knowledge, culture and textuality to what can be called the realm of the techno-popular. In terms of English teaching, this means shifting from literature to media, and hence from literary culture to popular culture as the focus for curriculum practice (Green, 1995). On the other hand, new and different formations of subjectivity are arguably emerging among young people, the constituency of schooling and the subject-citizens of the future, as they are characteristically immersed in new intensities of media culture, the flow of images and information, and their associated forms of life (Green and Bigum, 1993). Taken together, these aspects of difference represent significant challenges for educational theory and practice.

Work such as that of Levine and Buckingham represents different perspectives on, and elaborations of, the work of the London tradition, as a distinctive historical and institutional position in educational theory and practice. As I shall indicate later, that tradition can usefully be articulated with work in the North American critical pedagogy movement, which offers a more explicit engagement with *theory*, both in terms of poststructuralism and postmodernism and in terms of post-reproductionist critical educational studies. Taken together, these perspectives have specific implications for developing a theoretical account of critical pedagogy, media education and postmodern culture. What is still needed, however, in seeking to further this project, is a more nuanced and complex understanding of the modernism–postmodernism debate (Green, 1993). It is in this sense that it becomes appropriate to refer to *post-critical pedagogy* – that is, the form that critical pedagogy takes in postmodern contexts, or more simply the relationship between postmodernism, as a distinctive theoretical genre as well as a new form of life, and a reconfigured, transformed 'critical pedagogy'. In Lather's (1992:132) sense, this involves 'struggl[ing] to use postmodernism to both problematise and advance emancipatory pedagogy'. She expressly draws upon deconstruction as a resource for reconceptualizing and renewing the project of critical pedagogy, which elsewhere I have described as a distinctive attitude towards textuality, knowledge and politics (Green, 1996). In this context, accounting thus for learning and pedagogy is consistent with the project first eloquently articulated by Gregory Ulmer (1985) – that is, 'how to achieve a postmodernised pedagogy' – in describing and evoking a new alliance between the postmodern and the pedagogic, as organizing principles for understanding and intervening in cultural and educational politics in the Age of Information.

Pedagogy and Transformation

How are we to envisage the relationship between learning and social change? How are we to understand learning as a social practice, inextricable from and organic to the practice of the Social more generally? Giroux (1996) cites Raymond Williams on the political significance of the notion of 'permanent education', observing 'the centrality of teaching and education to his notion of cultural politics' (Giroux, 1996:20). For Williams: 'the deepest impulse [informing cultural studies] was *the desire to make learning part of the process of social change*' (cited Giroux, 1996:20; my emphasis). In considering how learning is understood in critical pedagogy, we should recall Gore's (1993:5) point that 'instruction and social vision are analytical components of pedagogy', and hence 'insofar as the concept implies both, each requires attention'.

A key word in this regard is the notion of *transformation*. Luke observes, not altogether sympathetically, that for critical pedagogy 'the transformative task is for teachers to enable students to name and give voice to their experience (their subject positions) and then transform and give meaning to those experiences by critically examining the discourses that give meaning to those experiences' (1992:35). Something of the complexity and ambiguity of the concept can be readily detected here, I suggest. What is the relationship between *levels*, *kinds*, *orders* and *scales* of transformation? What is the operative view of the relationship between power and pedagogy, and how are these terms themselves to be understood? As Gore (1992:4) notes, the tendency in 'radical pedagogy' is to work with a 'macro' orientation, *within* which there is 'an attempt to connect the macro and the micro'. She rightly observes that these terms are themselves unsatisfactory, none the less this kind of formulation, appropriately problematized, does have value. This is because the work in question (including that of its critics, once again) characteristically operates within the terms of a binary logic, with a privileged status afforded in effect to the 'global' and the 'contextual' over the 'local' and the 'textual'. This manifests itself in various ways: for instance, in a disciplinary division between sociology and psychology, as well as in the attention directed, respectively, to 'outer' and 'inner' dimensions of social life and human existence.

By contrast, I want to argue against this binary logic, and the privileging of broader social visions which it often seems to entail. In this respect, I want to draw upon poststructuralist understandings of social subjectivity. As Henriques *et al.* (1984) suggest:

> From the point of view of a politics of change, a theory which com-
> bines this set of relations between power, knowledge and desire
> within the same theoretical framework would combine two often
> unfortunately separate struggles: the changing of subjects and the
> changing of circumstances (Henriques *et al.*, 1984:226).

In such a view, transformation is to be understood both in the realm of
subjectivity (including identity formation) and in that of *social relations*, the
two necessarily seen together and as thoroughly implicated in each other.

From this perspective, even 'critical' teaching might be best understood
not primarily as a means of bringing about 'macro' social or political change,
but as a means of provoking *learning*, wherever that occurs and is situated.
This enables a humbler, more realistic view of pedagogy, and due recognition
of its limits. But it also means concentration of energy in what can realistically
be done in specific *educational* sites, of whatever scale. Consistent with a
Foucauldian perspective, this means working with and through the specific and
local power relations of pedagogic practice, and on this basis, seeking various
forms of articulation and affinity with other sites and practices. Moreover, this
is best conceived within a conceptual framework that is sensitive to the need to
attend to global structures and dynamics, and works with an active sense of
local–global relations (Hayles, 1990) – a version, that is, of 'thinking globally,
acting locally'. In this context, learning is to be grasped as transformative
practice, and as the production of difference – more particularly, the generation of 'a difference that makes a difference'.

Critical Pedagogy, Knowledge and Learning

In beginning to reassess the project of critical pedagogy in this way, it would be
useful to return to some of its exemplary accounts of learning. Two figures
seem particularly significant in this regard. Interestingly enough, the work of
both is distinguished by a focus on classrooms as sites of educational practice,
at whatever level, and also on learning as a form of social-semiotic practice.
Even more pertinently, both stress the importance of media practices and
cultural pedagogies. These are, respectively, Roger Simon and David Lusted,
key reference-points in the discourse of critical pedagogy, and of its critics, and
it is useful therefore to review their work here.

David Lusted's 1986 paper 'Why pedagogy?' has become an almost ob-
ligatory or 'canonic' reference in subsequent accounts of radical pedagogy and
socially-critical curriculum work. Published in the British journal *Screen*, it was
the Introduction to a special issue on pedagogy in media education, continuing
a consistent line of engagement with media pedagogics, teaching, and broader
educational issues and debates in British cultural and media studies. A central
theme is that of transformative practice: 'What pedagogy addresses is the
process of production and exchange in [the cycle of 'theory' and 'practice'], the

transformation of consciousness that takes place in the interaction of three agencies – the teacher, the learner, and the knowledge they together produce' (Lusted, 1986:3). The 'Why pedagogy?' paper is understandably much-quoted and -discussed; however, what is less well known is that Lusted was one of the first to publicly use the term *critical pedagogy* some years previously. His 1977/78 paper 'What would constitute a critical pedagogy?' is therefore usefully reread in this context. Immediately noticeable here is the neo-marxist framing for the account that Lusted provides, with reference specifically to work in what was then the New Sociology of Education. He presents this in terms of an explicit link between the concept of 'critical pedagogy' and what he describes as a 'materialist perspective' (Lusted, 1977/78:16) – as he puts it, a view of 'materialist pedagogy' in media education and more broadly that does more than simply 'radicalising the curriculum' (Lusted, 1977/78:18). A theme resumed in the latter paper, he emphasizes the importance of 'process' as well as 'content', and points to 'the tendency in the [screen] education movement to take pedagogy and the learning process for granted' (Lusted, 1977/78:18).

What is particularly interesting in this context is the account Lusted offers of learning. He cites Douglas Holly to the effect that 'systematic learning in schools . . . is what education is about', glossing this as 'socially organised learning, the planned development of consciousness' (cited Lusted, 1977/78:23). Drawing explicitly on Marx and Freire, he makes connections with the 'language and learning' movement of the London School and also what he calls 'child cognition', which he presents in terms of 'an alternative notion of cognition, a notion of learning as social' (Lusted, 1977/78:23). He stresses, further, that what is needed is an adequate social account of 'cognition', one which 'assumes that language is critical'. As he writes:

> An absolutely central concept for developing a materialist pedagogy . . . is that of teacher mediation of knowledge. A second central concept must be that of learning as consciousness-changing, understood in relation to materially-specific teaching situations (Lusted, 1977/78:26).

The latter he glosses as 'a social act of consciousness-changing', and the very 'basis' of 'a materialist pedagogy' (Lusted, 1977/78:27). Certain aspects of this account fall away in the later paper; for instance, the explicit reference to theories of cognition and learning, and to the London tradition itself. However, the links are important as historical traces, I suggest, and provide further evidence of the intimate connections between socially-critical forms of English teaching, media education, cultural studies, and the critical pedagogy project (Green, 1995; see also Lusted, 1987).

The 'Why pedagogy?' paper is notable, first, for the continued emphasis on 'consciousness-changing', within a focus on 'the *process* through which knowledge is produced' (Lusted, 1986:2), and second, for its refusal of traditional 'transmission' accounts of teaching, learning and knowledge. *Theory* and *pedagogy* are explicitly linked, as different but related forms of knowledge *production*. The following is worth presenting at length:

> To insist on the pedagogy of theory, as with the pedagogy of teaching, is to recognise a more transactional model whereby knowledge is produced not just at the researcher's desk nor at the lectern, but in the *consciousness*, through the process of thought, discussion, writing, debate, exchange; in the social and internal, collective and isolated struggle for control of understanding; from engagement of the unfamiliar idea, the difficult formulation pressed at the limit of comprehension or energy; in the meeting of the deeply held with the casually dismissed; in the dramatic moment of realisation that a scarcely regarded concern, an unarticulated desire, the barely assimilated, can come alive, make for a new sense of self, change commitments and activity ... [T]hese are also *transformations* which take place across all agencies in an educational process, regardless of their title as academic, critic, teacher or learner (Lusted, 1986:4).

This is an extraordinary passage, powerfully evoking the very character of learning, particularly so when set in the larger context of his strong affirmation of the importance of the concept of *pedagogy* and alongside the call for 'attention to open-ended and specific pedagogies, sensitive to context and difference, addressed to the social position of any learning group and the positions of individuals within it' (Lusted, 1986:10). It is all the more crucial, then, that it is itself subjected to a careful critical reading, along with the overall argument and account that Lusted presents here. This is especially so since it would appear that this paper functions as a kind of magical icon in the discourse of critical pedagogy, often cited and quoted but rarely interrogated. The question that must be asked, given its curious status, is, then: what discursive work does the paper do within that larger, historically situated project?

The first thing to note is that, notwithstanding its materialist ambitions and antecedents, there is a persistent *idealism* here. This is evident in the initial location of 'the transformation of consciousness' in the thoroughly dematerialized 'interaction of three agencies – the teacher, the students, and the knowledge they together produce' (Lusted, 1986:3). This is later presented in terms of the need for 'an effective pedagogy that precisely work[s] on *changing* the consciousness of the students' (Lusted, 1986:9). Bodies and classrooms seem curiously far removed from such an account, as lived forms of materiality. This sense is further evident in the view taken of *knowledge*:

> Knowledge is not produced in the intentions of those who believe they hold it, whether in the pen or in the voice. It is produced in the

process of interaction, between writer and reader in the moment of reading, and between teacher and learner in the moment of class-room engagement. Knowledge is not the matter that is offered so much as the matter that is understood (Lusted, 1986:4).

There is no room here for a view of knowledge as accumulated, as *embodied*, subject to storage, reorganisation and commodification. Instead, a simple bi-nary is enacted whereby, to draw on an influential 'London' account (Barnes, 1976), *transmission* is opposed to and supplanted by *interpretation* as a primary organizing curriculum principle. History is effectively denied in such a view – specifically, the history of the institutionalized and practical relation between 'lived' and 'commodified' forms of knowledge, culture and learning. This makes the use here of notions of 'consciousness' and 'transformation' prob-lematical, to say the least.

Yet there are other, more useful ways of understanding these notions, and of recuperating the argument as a whole. Indeed, the text is sufficiently rich and contradictory to push itself against the edges of the problematic that it stages. In the lengthy passage cited previously, for instance, 'consciousness' is arguably recontextualized as *semiotic practices*, operating moreover across the realms of 'inside' and 'outside' ('through the process of thought, discussion, writing, debate, exchange'). More importantly and intriguingly, for my pur-poses here, is the depiction of learning ('social and internal . . . collective and isolated') as 'struggle', as fraught with 'difficulty', as traumatic and dynamic, as emphatically about desire, a radical engagement with and experience of 'lim-its', interruption and change. Elsewhere, what is emphasized is exchange, relationality, difference, 'context', transformation, and 'process'. Learning is foregrounded: 'How one teaches is therefore of central interest but, though the prism of pedagogy, it becomes inseparable from what is being taught and, critically, *how one learns*' (Lusted, 1986:2–3; my emphasis). Priority is given to 'the nature of the relations' in pedagogy. Moreover, such a view

> refuses any tendency to instrumentalise the relations, to discon-nect their interactivity or to give value to one agency over another . . . Instead, it foregrounds exchange between and over the categories, it recognises the productivity of the relations, and it renders the parties within them as active, changing and changeable agencies (Lusted, 1986:3).

What emerges very clearly therefore is a *semiotic* understanding of pedagogy – an emphasis on 'difference', 'context', 'process', on the priority of 'relations' and 'exchange', on 'transformation'. Importantly this is a matter of referring equally to the three 'agencies' of 'teacher', 'learner' and 'knowledge'. All are subject to transformation; all undergo 'crisis' and 'change' as a direct result of their interaction; all are rendered *different* accordingly.

This is still, however, a relatively (en)closed pedagogic space, curiously de-institutionalized, de-materialized. What needs to be brought more explicitly into calculation therefore is, first, the *plurality* of learners making up any classroom; second, their *heterogeneity*, as well as their location within larger social contexts, practices and structures; and third, their situated *embodiment* in time and space. This complicates the picture enormously, but it also arguably does more justice to the necessary complexity of a properly social account of learning.

Critical Pedagogy, Meaning and Power

Roger Simon's work on pedagogy is similarly a key reference point for any account of critical pedagogy. As he indicates, the term entered into more or less common (albeit always strategic) usage for him and his colleagues in the latter part of the 1970s. That it was expressly conceived as a 'legitimation exercise' for work that was deliberately and avowedly socially-critical in orientation ('teaching and research rooted in specific commitments to enhancing the degree of justice and compassion present in our community', p. xv) he makes very clear. At the same time, Simon is clearly attentive to the dangers of reifying the term *critical pedagogy*, and thereby of creating an orthodoxy:

> For me critical pedagogy is a useful term only to the extent it helps bring together people who share enough in the way of political commitments and educational perspectives to be able to learn together, refine our vision, and support our diverse efforts as educators. The utility of the term 'critical pedagogy' is its reference to an ongoing project and certainly not a prescriptive set of practices. When it no longer performs this function, it would be better abandoned (Simon, 1992:xvi).

With that in mind, his contribution is of particular interest and importance here.

Central to Simon's work is the relationship between politics, pedagogy and practice, and within this, an understanding of politics and pedagogy alike as forms of practice. He notes 'the importance of a turn toward pedagogy as a vital mode of engaging in the task of social transformation' (Simon, 1992:35), which indicates the extent to which he is committed to the elaboration of a social and political vision. At the same time, he is keenly aware of the complementary importance of what might be called 'method', the technical, pragmatic dimension of everyday educational practice in often inhospitable conditions. Hence: '[T]alk about pedagogy is simultaneously talk about the details of what students and teachers might do together *and* the cultural politics such practices support' (Simon, 1992:57).[2]

What makes Simon's work particularly pertinent and generative is his account of meaning and power, within a view of education as a specific form of cultural politics. Along with the notion of 'productive power', drawn from Foucault, he emphasizes the importance of the notion of 'semiotic production', or 'meaning making'. As he writes: 'In introducing the term *semiotic production*, I am attempting to signal the centrality of those practices implicated in the formation and regulation of meaning and imagination' (Simon, 1992:37). It is in this regard that he sees the work of critical pedagogy as addressed to the construction of a new *educational* imaginary – a project of possibility, that is, which brings together practice and politics in and through the specificity of pedagogic work. Importantly he sees teaching as cultural work, itself addressed specifically to the practical interrelation of meaning and power:

> As educators, our work is explicitly located within the realm of semiotic production. Our attempts to engage students are constructed within specific modes that we hope will provoke particular forms of communication, comprehension and interest. How we provoke this engagement, within which productive regimes and with what corresponding strategies and questions, defines much of our pedagogical practice (Simon, 1992:38).

In short, he brings together themes of 'consciousness' and 'transformation', much as Lusted does, but within a more explicit *semiotic* framework that enables a stronger sense of the relationship between education and cultural politics.

Of particular interest here is his view of pedagogy as 'a provocation of semiosis' (Simon, 1992:56), by which I understand him as pointing to learning itself as a form of *semiotic practice*. Moreover, this is understood explicitly in terms of struggle, contestation, contradiction and conflict: as a production of *difference*, both in the sense that 'difference' is what is produced and in the sense that it is itself produced out of 'difference'. Teaching is about the 'provocation' of learning conceived explicitly as meaning making and hence as 'semiosis', itself always risky and indeterminate. As he writes:

> While the image of learning within a critical pedagogy may be characterized as occurring within a structured provocation and challenge, it must remain open and indeterminate. Required is practice rooted in an ethical–political vision that attempts to take people *beyond the world they already know but in a way that does not insist on a fixed set of altered meanings* (Simon, 1992:47; my emphasis).

What I want to take from Simon's account of pedagogy and learning is a way of grasping specific understandings of 'transformation' and 'change' as fundamental to the issue at hand here. Pedagogy is described as 'a practice within which one acts with the intent of provoking experience that will simultaneously organize and disorganize a variety of understandings of our natural and social world' (Simon, 1992:56). It is therefore a *practice*, a mode of working on and with aspects of material existence, on the part of a teacher, in interaction with a learner or a community of learners, that simultaneously seeks to order *and* disorder the latter's experience, as one moment within a larger social and cultural movement of (re)production, renewal, change, and transformation.

It is this simultaneous, dialectical process of 'order' and 'disorder', 'organization' and 'disorganization' that I want to emphasize at this point. This is usefully understood in terms of the dynamics of identity and difference, and yet always within a non-foundational(ist), properly semiotic view of the priority of difference over identity. This would be to emphasize the value of 'disorganizing' practices and effects over those that are 'organizing', in terms of learning, without dismissing the value of the latter. Rather, the formation of learning 'identities' is to be seen as necessary but provisional, unstable and dynamic, and always already subject to crisis and change, challenge and revision. The first order of things is complexity, process, change, whether that be observed in knowledge and understandings, in the world or in ourselves, as subjects in formation. Hence, Simon's observation of graduate students in education studies, and what he describes as the entirely understandable 'fear of theory', can be readily extended to take in the characteristic challenges and 'disruptive potential' of socially-critical curriculum work:

> To the extent that our pedagogy demands that students take the [knowledge] we offer seriously, it implies the potential negation of aspects of one's personal and professional identity and the corresponding investments one has in retaining those identity positions (Simon, 1992:86).

Pedagogy thus entails a challenge to, and 'potential negation' of, one's life and identity investments: 'What is on offer is access to a discourse and, through this discourse, the possibility of engaging the social world differently' (Simon, 1992:91), in such a way as to generate what might well be appropriately called an existential *crisis*. The point is that this is always, at least potentially, a significant and serious challenge to the sense of self that learners bring to educational encounters, as subjected subjects within an always-already compromised social world. Moreover, it is only in bringing learners to a sense of crisis in this way that the possibility exists for change, across the social field linking subjectivity to social practice more generally. Learning, in this fashion, *is* linked to social change, although the connections are certainly complex and clearly mediated in all sorts of ways.

At issue here is a social-semiotic view of learning that brings together notions of the productivity of power, the practice of meaning, and the generation of difference. Moreover, this needs to be grasped and theorized within an explicit, socially-critical, postmodern frame, one which is properly sensitive to the challenges, opportunities and dilemmas associated with poststructuralist frameworks and postmodernist problematics, such as the new understandings of discourse and subjectivity, the 'crisis' in representation, networked forms of power, culture and capital, and new complexities of technocultural change. It is in this sense that one can begin to work usefully and reasonably with the concept of 'post-critical pedagogy'.

Beyond Critical Pedagogy: Critiques and Alternatives

Criticism of the critical pedagogy project has ranged across feminist, Marxist and liberal persuasions and orientations. Perhaps the most telling critiques have been those from an explicitly feminist perspective (Luke and Gore, 1992), discussed elsewhere in this volume. While the broader political and theoretical issues raised here are obviously pertinent to my account, much of the critique has remained at a distance from the concrete realities of classrooms – and particularly classrooms in schools. By contrast, I would argue that more useful and appropriate accounts are available in the work of what I have called the London tradition, addressed as it is characteristically to the practices, institutions and discourses of mainstream schooling, more specifically at the compulsory primary and secondary levels.

In referring to this latter work, I have in mind a larger, more complex and heterogeneous formation than that of the so-called 'London School' in curriculum research and English teaching (Green, 1993, 1995). Rather, I am referring more generally to work across the fields of English teaching and media education, and related curriculum areas and concerns, with reference points in institutions and forums such as the London Institute of Education, the Birmingham Centre for Contemporary Cultural Studies, the Open University, and journals such as *Teaching London Kids* and *Screen Education*, and the particular challenges associated with urban classrooms, multicultural diversity, and the 'crisis' in state-sponsored schooling. Although not unproblematically so, this work has been characterized by a long-term commitment to socially-critical curriculum and schooling, on the one hand, and the significance and centrality of student learning, on the other. Further, importantly, it has increasingly sought to reckon into account the need to extend its terms of reference to include and embrace media culture and new information and communication technologies, increasingly drawing what Collins (1995) terms 'techno-textualities' within its pedagogic ambit of concern. In this regard, critical interventions such as that of Kress (1995), and others, represent both a continuation of the London tradition, understood as outlined here, *and* its necessary critique and renewal.

Yet it is also crucial not to lose sight of the range and specificity of existing and ongoing work in that tradition, nor of the importance of its practical and empirical investigations in teacher education, classroom practice, critical literacy, and 'cultural making' (Hardcastle, 1985). Writing of work extending across the latter part of the 1970s into the early 1980s, McLeod (1986) notes that although there was due recognition and acknowledgement of the congruence between then emerging American initiatives in 'critical literacy' and 'critical pedagogy' and London action–research studies in 'classroom writing and critical inquiry', there was also a sense that the American work was 'difficult to define precisely' or to operationalize, either in research or in teaching. Referring specifically to figures such as Paulo Freire and Henry Giroux, he stressed the importance and significance of the London focus on classroom studies, in presenting brief accounts of literacy and learning in practice. As he puts it: '[w]e do not normally think of classrooms as locations for conscious practical action which can transform the world', yet '[c]lassrooms where serious extended discussion [and engagement] of complex issues . . . are constantly taking place, where students' writing extends and deepens that discourse, are making a first move towards the transformations' called for in critical pedagogy work (McLeod, 1986:40). Hence, with reference to institutionalizing such a view of education: 'We do not claim to have achieved it, by any means, but we are concerned to establish that we have gone beyond the stage of having a good theory and wishing it could be tried' (McLeod, 1986:41). In a similar vein, work such as that of John Hardcastle and Tony Burgess, separately and jointly, indicates very clearly the manner in which notions such as discourse and difference, classroom practices and cultural production, and an appropriately complex sense of the always negotiated relationship between teaching and learning, are fundamental to the work of the London tradition (Burgess, 1984, 1988; Burgess and Hardcastle, 1989; Hardcastle, 1985).

Of particular interest here is the manner in which difference is theorized and researched within the actual sites of classroom praxis, and the view of learning that is associated with such work. Burgess (1988:160) points to the need to focus on 'difference in language, languages and culture', tracing the emerging recognition that matters of culture and history are inextricable from language and power, and that together these are crucial to 'a social theory of language and development' in education and English teaching (Burgess, 1988:167). Importantly, work such as this highlights the significance of difference as a *resource* for pedagogy. Attending to learners and learning and to the situated specificity and heterogeneity of classroom processes and exchange becomes a first principle, and due account is made accordingly of complexity and contradiction. Praxis thus understood is inherently risky. Teaching for learning becomes a matter of probing into the unknown, of constructing futures that can only ever provisionally be planned in advance of practice, in all its undecidability and productive power. Hence learning by definition is a matter of difference and danger, always *excessive* with regard to curriculum and institutional protocols and frames, and the formal logics of timetabling and disciplinarity. Teaching must proceed in the face of the impossibility of mastering difference and fixing meaning, except provisionally and strategically, in actively attending to otherness. A sophisticated, situated view of peda-gogy emerges, as teaching *for* learning:

> First, the learner not the teacher is at the centre of the process. Teaching expectations drawn from experience have to be re-interpreted in the light of learners' particular strategies and histories. If learning is not without its benchmarks and recurring patterns, nor is it in any simple sense predictable. Secondly, learning which takes place in classrooms may be shaped and patterned by evolving expec-tations, pupil relations and longer term processes in the classroom history (Burgess and Hardcastle, 1989:3).

Importantly this is always a matter of *teaching–learning*, understood as inextricable although never identical. It is certainly not to be seen simply, and simplistically, as 'learner-centredness'. Classrooms in such a view are therefore to be grasped as 'sites for the production of culture and not just of its reproduction' (Burgess and Hardcastle, 1989:10), as crucial sites for local politics and the exercise of (re)productive power and educational agency. Learning is, in these terms, always a local, grounded achievement, 'accomplished by the learner, against the background of the teacher's in-structions and support but not directly attributable to action on the teacher's part. *Learning emerges in classrooms in ways which are not always predictable even if they are not wholly unexpected*' (Burgess and Hardcastle, 1989:2; my emphasis). Given this, there can clearly be no guarantees in and for critical pedagogy, notwithstanding its overt political interests and intentions – which means that it must, of necessity, become sensitive to and aware of the limits of its own (im)possibility, and accordingly more patient and modest in attending to the complexity of the educational enterprise and (r)evolutionary politics.

Towards Post-critical Pedagogy

What are the prospects for post-critical pedagogy in the context of the 'semi-otic society'? (Wexler, 1990). What once might have been seen as simply futuristic considerations and speculations shade here into the forms, textures and imperatives of the present. Increasingly teaching for difference is inextri-cable from the larger project of schooling the future.

The need to take into account the emergence of media culture as a key and decisive reference point for education is crucial. In neo-Althusserian terms, this involves a shift from the School to the Media as the dominant educational apparatus. It also involves due acknowledgement of the historical significance of the communications revolution, and the emergence of informa-tion and the image as new principles of social life (Hinkson, 1991). Among other things, this has meant engaging and constructing new formations of curriculum and literacy, in accordance with profound technocultural innovations and transformations, and the effective decoupling of both curriculum and literacy from schooling. Like cultural practice and identity formation, both knowledge (re)production and textual practice are increasingly disengaged from schooling as the principal and privileged site of social learning and skills development. In attempting to respond to these changes, schools are thrown into their own measure of crisis. They are compelled to adapt to new conditions and change accordingly, which is a matter both of *de*-schooling and *re*-schooling. As I have argued elsewhere, in relation to the emergence of television and other media as new sources of information and learning, social integration and identity-formation, this does 'not necessarily mean the end of schooling but rather, its *transmutation*, with a new emphasis on notions such as "on-line education" and the "virtual classroom"' (Green, 1993:208–9; emphasis added). Other ideas that might well be emphasized include 'open and flexible learning', hypertextuality, electronic cognition, and 'metamedia literacy' (Lemke, 1996/in press).

Such change can be best understood as a shift in dominance from the print apparatus to the digital-electronic apparatus, as the defining cultural–technological complex of postmodernity. Ulmer (1989) utilizes the concept of the 'apparatus' to bring together technologies, institutional practices, and forms of subjectivity within a single historico–discursive formation. His argument suggests that shifting from the print complex to digital-electronic culture represents new opportunities and formats for culture and communication, subjectivity and social practice. He evokes a distinctive digital 'ecology' or electronic 'environment', which he describes as 'the new discursive and conceptual ecology interrelating orality, literacy and videocy' (Ulmer, 1989:vii). Elsewhere, he points to the particular significance and cultural value of 'the convergence of video and the computer in hypermedia', noting 'the eventual need for a grammatology of virtual reality' and the emergence of new forms of multimedia composition, bringing together all 'the resources of pictures, words and sound' (Ulmer, 1994:17). Kress (1995) also points to the significance of new realizations of curriculum and literacy, and their associated educational and social challenges. As he writes:

> New technologies are having effects on the potentials of communication which are as yet incalculable, but seem already at least as far-reaching in their potential effects as the shift from orality to literacy, or the newer shift from literacy to 'visuality' (Kress, 1995:22).

These are 'deep effects', and they are already noticeable across a range of sites and fields. Kress notes them, for instance, in terms of 'unmaking and remaking social relations', in their impact on 'the basis of the rule-system of language', and in interrupting and reconstructing notions of writing and reading, text and context, authorship and readership, and more generally, in their implication for 'the place of language in the landscape of communication, in the semiotic landscape overall' (Kress, 1995:22). Work such as this is usefully linked to the 'London' tradition of 'language and learning' that I have drawn attention to here. However, it also brings to that work new theoretical resources in linguistics, semiotics, discourse analysis, and poststructuralist theory, and hence opens up new possibilities for textual and cultural practice.

Writing almost a decade ago now, one commentator pointed to 'language [as] a main area where cultural studies and English teaching might come together but which both recurrently neglect' (M. Green, 1987:6). A more appropriate focus, as in work by Lemke and Kress himself, draws on a larger field of semiosis, through a focus on semiotics and poststructuralism, while continuing to exploit the possibilities of Hallidayan linguistics. But further work is still needed to develop better understandings of semiotic practice and what Simon calls 'semiotic production', particularly given the shift in emphasis not only towards culture generally but also towards 'multimodality' in cultural forms and expression. This means going beyond an exclusive orientation to and emphasis on the print apparatus and 'the verbal sign [with] its associated forms of abstract rationality and decontextualization'. It means embracing and engaging the semiotic possibilities of electronic media and the (postmodern) body, and thus allowing for an expanded, regenerated sense of language and semiosis (Green, 1995:398). Morgan (1993) argues that this involves problematizing the concept–metaphor of *text* and (at the very least) putting emphasis on discursive practices and contexts and on relationalities and articulations between and across fields of knowledge and identity, culture and power. A much richer sense of semiosis emerges from work such as this, significantly extending the project of 'language and learning'.

But what is still underdeveloped is the second part of this formulation: the reference to and emphasis on *learning*. It is not that the work referred to doesn't have implications for a view of learning, since it manifestly does. Rather, 'learning' as such tends to be held steady while the other term ('language') is increasingly problematized and interrogated. Once again, Morgan's (1993) critique of the corresponding concept–metaphor of *meaning* is extremely important in this regard: 'Hothouse versions of meaning are undercut by electronic space and the embodied practices of an expansive popular culture' (Morgan, 1993:34). Given a long-standing view of learning as 'meaning making', it is clear that arguments of this kind imply a reassessment of existing accounts of learning, linked as they are to humanist perspectives on cognition and subjectivity. His concern with 'relay effects' (as distinct from 'reality effects') is not only an important contribution to a semiotic, poststructuralist account of learning but is a clear register of 'the manner in which we now live within and between hybrid cultural technologies' (Morgan, 1993:35). As he puts it:

In speaking of semiotic relays, syncretic cultural practices and strategic articulations of unstable configurations of meaning, I am interested in escaping from arbitrary pedagogical distinctions between textuality, visuality and oracy (Morgan, 1993:35).

The implications and possibilities in such arguments for rethinking learning in and for the semiotic society are important considerations for us now. The history outlined here, in all its contradiction and its possibility, remains a crucial resource, but it needs to be carefully and critically reworked *and* retheorized; among other things, it is too logocentric and print-bound. In this task of rereading, Ulmer's account of the new forms of cognition and learning associated with the digital-electronic apparatus becomes particularly intriguing and immediately suggestive (Ulmer, 1985, 1989, 1994). With regard to the significance of 'the electronic paradigm' for educational–institutional practices, he observes that the transformative effects of informationalizing and technologizing language in this context are such that, as he puts it, 'something "happens" . . . that alters the whole ecology of learning' (Ulmer, 1985:301). This is inextricable from broader semiotic transformations in an increasingly media-saturated lifeworld. He draws attention to 'the possibility that cognition itself might be changing in a civilization switching to electronics' (Ulmer, 1985:2). He explores these speculations with reference to the integration and convergence of television and computing, which he sees as impacting both on schooling ('the role of the school in preparing individuals to live in the electronic machine': Ulmer, 1992:160) and on the semiotic environment more generally, as well as the relationship between them. His emphasis is therefore increasingly on new forms of 'mixed-mode learning' – what he describes as 'the new order of learning', formed out of and bringing together 'oral, literate and video conduct in our society', and involving 'a cognitive style articulating these three orders of discourse' (Ulmer, 1989:xi).

Herein lies our challenge, then: how to work with the emerging and different forms of learning and cognition characteristic of the semiotic society. How to teach the new subjects, in all their difference and their danger. Indeed, the question becomes how to teach *for* difference, and also *with* difference.

Notes

1 See also Buckingham (1990). The relationship between Vygotsky's notion of 'spontaneous conceptualisation' and media learning clearly warrants further investigation. A deconstructionist reading of Vygotsky might well question formulations such as 'mature thought' and his emphasis on 'depth understandings'. Further lines of relevant work with regard to media learning, 'electronic cognition' and 'post-formal thinking' are indicated in Kincheloe and Sternberg (1993), Taylor and Saarinsen (1994), and Ulmer (1989).

2 See also Simon (1987). A matter for further investigation is indicated in Simon (1995), where he seeks to extend the focus of education studies

beyond schooling; such work points to the urgent need for a reassessment of learning in the contexts of everyday life, as a form of *practical cognition*.

References

BARNES, D. (1976) *From Communication to Curriculum*, Harmondsworth: Penguin.

BOOMER, G., LESTER, N., ONORE, C. and COOK, J. (Eds) (1992) *Negotiating the Curriculum: Educating for the Twenty-first Century*, London: Falmer Press.

BUCKINGHAM, D. (1990) Making it explicit: Towards a theory of media learning, in BUCKINGHAM, D. (Ed.) *Watching Media Learning: Making Sense of Media Education*, London: Falmer Press, 215–26.

BUCKINGHAM, D. (1992) Media education: The limits of a discourse, *Journal of Curriculum Studies*, **24** (4), 297–313.

BURGESS, T. (1984) Diverse melodies: A first-year class in a secondary school, in MILLER, J. (Ed.) *Eccentric Propositions: Essays on Literature and the Curriculum*, London: Routledge & Kegan Paul, 56–69.

BURGESS, T. (1988) On difference: Cultural and linguistic diversity and English teaching, in LIGHTFOOT, M. and MARTIN, N. (Eds) *The Word for Teaching is Learning: Essays for James Britton*, London: Heinemann and NATE.

BURGESS, T. and HARDCASTLE, J. (1989) A tale of three learners: The cultural dimensions of classroom language learning, [mimeo], Institute of Education, University of London.

COLLINS, J. (1995) *Architectures of Excess: Cultural Life in the Information Age*, New York: Routledge.

GEE, J. P. (1990) *Social Linguistics and Literacies: Ideology in Discourses*, London: Falmer Press.

GIROUX, H. A. (1996) *Fugitive Cultures: Race, Violence and Youth*, New York: Routledge.

GORE, J. M. (1992) *The Struggle for Pedagogies: Critical and Feminist Discourses as Regimes of Truth*, New York: Routledge.

GREEN, B. (1993) Literacy studies and curriculum theorizing; Or, the insistence of the letter, in GREEN, B. (Ed.) *The Insistence of the Letter: Literacy Studies and Curriculum Theorizing*, London: Falmer Press, 195–225.

GREEN, B. (1995) Post-curriculum possibilities: English teaching, cultural politics, and the postmodern turn, *Journal of Curriculum Studies*, **27** (4), 391–409.

GREEN, B. (1996) Reading with an attitude; Or, deconstructing 'critical literacies', in FREEBODY, P., MUSPRATT, S. and LUKE, A. (Eds) *Constructing Critical Literacies: Teaching and Learning Textual Practices*, Cresskill, NJ: Hampton Press.

GREEN, B. and BIGUM, C. (1993) Aliens in the classroom, *Australian Journal of Education*, **37** (2), 119–41.

GREEN, M. (1987) Introduction: Points of departure – 'new' subjects and 'old', in GREEN, M. in association with HOGGART, R. (Eds) *English and Cultural Studies: Broadening the Context*, London: John Murray, 1–19.

HARDCASTLE, J. (1985) Classrooms as sites for cultural making, *English in Education*, **19** (3), 8–22.

HAYLES, N. K. (1990) *Chaos Bound: Orderly Disorder in Contemporary Literature and Science*, Ithaca, NY: Cornell University Press.

HENRIQUES, J., HOLLWAY, W., URWIN, C., VENN, C. and WALKERDINE, V. (Eds) *Changing the Subject: Psychology, Social Regulation and Subjectivity*, London: Methuen.

HINKSON, J. (1991) *Postmodernity: State and Education*, Geelong, Victoria: Deakin University.

KINCHELOE, J. L. and STERNBERG, N. R. (1993) Towards a tentative description of post-formal thinking: The critical confrontation with cognitive theory, *Harvard Educational Review*, **63** (3), 296–320.

KRESS, G. (1995) *Writing the Future: English and the Making of a Culture of Innovation*, Sheffield: National Association for the Teaching of English.

LATHER, P. (1992) Post-critical pedagogies: A feminist reading, in LUKE, C. and GORE, J. (Eds) *Feminisms and Critical Pedagogy*, New York: Routledge, 120–37.

LEE, A. (1996) *Gender, Literacy, Curriculum: Re-Writing School Geography*, London: Taylor & Francis.

LEMKE, J. L. (1984) *Semiotics and Education*, Toronto: Victoria College/Toronto Semiotic Circle Monographs.

LEMKE, J. L. (1995) *Textual Politics: Discourse and Social Dynamics*, London: Taylor & Francis.

LEMKE, J. L. (1996/in press) Meta media literacy: Transforming meanings and media, in REINKING, D. et al. (Eds) *Literacy for the 21st Century: Technological Transformation in a Post-typographic World*, Hillsdale, NJ: Erlbaum.

LEVINE, J. (1992) Pedagogy: The case of the missing concept, in KIMBERLEY, K., MEEK, M. and MILLER, J. (Eds) *New Readings: Contributions to an Understanding of Literacy*, London: A. & C. Black.

LUKE, A. (1989) Open and closed texts: The ideological/semantic analysis of textbook narratives, *Journal of Pragmatics*, **13**, 53–80.

LUKE, C. (1992) Feminist politics in radical pedagogy, in LUKE, C. and GORE, J. (Eds) *Feminisms and Critical Pedagogy*, New York: Routledge, 25–53.

LUKE, C. and GORE, J. (Eds) (1992) *Feminisms and Critical Pedagogy*, New York: Routledge.

LUSTED, D. (1977/78) What would constitute a critical pedagogy?, *Screen Education*, **25**, Winter, 16–36.

LUSTED, D. (1986) Why pedagogy?, *Screen*, **27** (5), 2–14.

LUSTED, D. (1987) English teaching and media education: Culture and the curriculum, in GREEN, M. in association with HOGGART, R. (Eds) *English and Cultural Studies: Broadening the Context,* London: John Murray, 118–28.

McLeod, A. (1986) Critical literacy: Taking control of our own lives, *Language Arts,* **63** (1), 37–50.

Morgan, R. (1993) Transitions from English to cultural studies, *New Education,* **15** (1), 21–48.

Simon, R. I. (1987) Empowerment as a pedagogy of possibility, *Language Arts,* **64** (4), 370–82.

Simon, R. I. (1992) *Teaching Against the Grain: Texts for a Pedagogy of Possibility,* New York: Bergin & Garvey.

Simon, R. I. (1995) Broadening the vision of university-base study of education: The contribution of cultural studies, *Education/Pedagogy/Cultural Studies,* **17** (1), 107–14.

Taylor, M. C. and Saarinsen, E. (1994) *Imagologies: Media Philosophy,* London: Routledge.

Ulmer, G. (1985) *Applied Grammatology: Post(e)-pedagogy from Jacques Derrida to Joseph Beuys,* Baltimore, MD: Johns Hopkins University Press.

Ulmer, G. (1989) *Teletheory: Grammatology in the Age of Video,* New York: Routledge.

Ulmer, G. L. (1992) Grammatology (in the stacks) of hypermedia, a simulation; Or, when does a pile become a heap?, in Tuman, M. C. (Ed.) *Literacy Online,* Pittsburgh, PA: University of Pittsburgh Press, 139–63.

Ulmer, G. L. (1994) *Heuretics: The Logic of Invention,* Baltimore, MD: The Johns Hopkins University Press.

Wexler, P. (1990) Citizenship in the semiotic society, in Turner, B. S. (Ed.) *Theories of Modernity and Postmodernity,* London: Sage, 164–75.

Notes on Contributors

DAVID BUCKINGHAM is a Reader in Education at the Institute of Education, London University, UK. His research and teaching have focused on classroom practice in media education and on children's interactions with electronic media. He has directed several research projects on these issues, and is the author, co-author or editor of nine books, including *Children Talking Television* (Falmer Press, 1993), *Cultural Studies Goes to School* (Taylor and Francis, 1994) and *Moving Images* (Manchester University Press, 1996). He is currently working on a major new project on entertainment and education in children's media culture.

PHIL COHEN is a Reader in Cultural Studies at the University of East London, UK, where he currently directs the Centre for New Ethnicities Research. He has researched and published widely on changing patterns of education, popular culture and identity in contemporary Britain. His most recent book is *Rethinking the Youth Question: Education, Labour and Cultural Studies* (Macmillan, 1996).

DONNA J. GRACE is an Instructor in the College of Education at the University of Hawaii at Manoa, where she teaches a range of courses including early childhood education, curriculum and instruction, language and literacy, and media literacy. She earned an MEd at the Ontario Institute for Studies in Education and an EdD at the University of Hawaii. She taught at primary level for nine years and has published on various aspects of early childhood education.

BILL GREEN is Senior Lecturer in the School of Social and Cultural Studies, Faculty of Education, Deakin University, Geelong, Victoria, Australia. His research and teaching interests are in English teaching and Cultural Studies, curriculum and literacy studies, media and educational politics, the 'modernism–postmodernism' debate, and the educational implications of new technologies. He has published widely in these areas, including the edited collections *The Insistence of the Letter: Literacy Studies and Curriculum Theorizing* (Falmer Press, 1993) and *Teaching the English Subjects: Essays on English Curriculum History and Australian Schooling* (Deakin University Press, 1996).

CARMEN LUKE is an Associate Professor in the Graduate School of Education at the University of Queensland, Australia. Her teaching and research interests are in feminist theory, Cultural Studies and the sociology of education. She has written several books on children and media, and on feminist pedagogy, including *TV and Your Child* (Sydney, Angus and Robertson, 1990; Toronto, Kagan and Woo, 1989), *Pedagogy, Printing and Protestantism* (Albany, NY, SUNY Press, 1989), *Constructing the Child Viewer* (Praeger, 1990), *Feminisms and Critical Pedagogy* (edited with Jennifer Gore, Routledge, 1992) and *Feminisms and Pedagogies of Everyday Life* (Albary, NY, SUNY Press, 1996).

ROBERT MORGAN is an Associate Professor in the Department of Curriculum at the Ontario Institute for Studies in Education, University of Toronto, Canada. His areas of research and teaching include media education, cultural theory and schooling, and critical histories of English studies. He has published articles in a number of journals including *College English, New Education, Discourse, Journal of Educational Thought* and *Continuum*.

CHRIS RICHARDS taught English and Media Studies in schools and in further education in London, England, for several years. He was subsequently a Lecturer in Education (Media Studies) at the University of London Institute of Education, and is currently a Senior Lecturer in Education at the University of North London. He has contributed to several books, including *Watching Media Learning* (Falmer Press, 1990), *Reading Audiences* (Manchester University Press, 1993) and *English and the National Curriculum: Cox's Revolution* (Kogan Page, 1992). His book *Teen Spirits: Music and Identity in Media Education* will be published by Taylor and Francis in 1997.

JOSEPH TOBIN is a Professor in the University of Hawaii's College of Education, where he teaches qualitative research and poststructural theory courses in addition to working in a field-based teacher preparation programme. His publications include *Preschool in Three Cultures: Japan, China and the United States* (Yale University Press, 1989) and *Making a Place for Pleasure in Early Childhood Education* (Yale, 1997).

SUE TURNBULL currently teaches Media Studies at La Trobe University in Australia, although she was born in England and taught English and Media Studies for ten years in high schools there and in the US. She has published widely on media education, media audiences and on soap operas, advertising and screen comedy in Australia. She is the co-editor with Kate Bowles of *Tomorrow Never Knows: Soap on Australian Television* (Australian Film Institute, 1995). She is currently working on a study of women in Australian television, and on an international study of crime fiction and its readership networks.

Index